LAWYERS' ETHICS
IN AN
ADVERSARY SYSTEM

LAWYERS' ETHICS
IN AN
ADVERSARY SYSTEM

By

MONROE H. FREEDMAN

Dean and Professor of Law
Hofstra University School of Law

THE BOBBS-MERRILL COMPANY, INC.
PUBLISHERS
INDIANAPOLIS • NEW YORK

For
Audrey
Alice and Gerald
Sarah, Caleb, and Judah

Preface

Professor Andrew Kaufman of Harvard Law School recently remarked that he and I had been classmates at law school and that, therefore, we had learned about legal ethics at the same time and place—that is, in practice, because we learned virtually nothing about legal ethics while in law school.

Behind that quip lies an extremely serious concern. Our profession has never given adequate attention to the hard issues of the professional responsibilities of lawyers in an adversary system. Rather, the most difficult issues have been ignored, or they have been avoided in two ways. The first is by simplistic generalization, as illustrated by the law school dean and leading member of the American Bar Association, who once remarked to me that all of legal ethics could be stated in a single precept: "A lawyer should never do anything that a gentleman would not do."

The other way of avoiding the difficult questions has been by issuing statements or codifications of rules of conduct in such a way as to give lip service to basic systemic values, while ignoring the fact that some of those values are fundamentally at odds with each other. For example, as discussed in Chapter 3 of this book, the criminal defense lawyer is required to know everything about the client's case, maintain that knowledge in the strictest confidence and, at the same time, be candid with the court. Obviously, one cannot do all three of those things, which is why Professor Anthony Amsterdam of Stanford Law School once observed that the Canons of Professional Ethics "are of as much use to the practicing attorney in the courtroom as a Valentine card would be to a heart surgeon in the operating room".

There are probably a number of reasons for the profession's persistent failure to face up to the nature of its own responsibilities. One reason, undoubtedly, is that the issues really seem to defy satisfactory resolution. Another, probably, is the assumption that practitioners will instinctively do the right thing or, if there are some who will not, that it is useless even to try to induce in those people an awareness of what the norms are or should be. Yet another reason for the lack of serious consideration of the difficult issues of lawyers' ethics is an attitude of intolerance within the profession toward public exposition of embarrassing intra-professional difficulties, or toward any suggested departure from assumed but unarticulated norms.

About fifteen years ago, I began engaging in serious discussions of legal ethics with a small number of other lawyers, most of whom were also doing criminal defense work. We found that we were all attempting to cope with some vexing ethical dilemmas, each in his or her own way, and that sharing our experiences and talking them out helped us considerably in attempting to resolve our difficulties, even though, in a number of respects, we continued to disagree.

Subsequently, in 1966, I was serving as Co-Director of the Criminal Trial Institute, which had been established to train practicing members of the Bar to handle the defense of criminal cases. As part of that training, I gave an opening lecture on legal ethics, in which I discussed what my colleagues and I had found to be the three hardest questions faced by the criminal defense lawyer. Those questions were: (1) Should you put a witness on the stand when you know the witness is going to commit perjury? (2) Should you cross-examine a prosecution witness whom you know to be accurate and truthful, in order to make the witness appear to be mistaken or lying? (3) Should you give your client advice about the law when you know the advice may induce the client to commit perjury? I concluded, with admitted uncertainty, that the adversary system, with its corollary, the confidential relationship between lawyer and client, often requires an affirmative answer to those questions.

A brief report of my lecture appeared in the *Washington Post* the next morning, producing two different but oddly similar reactions. First, a very liberal federal judge wrote to me, saying that I had done a disservice to the profession and to the rights of criminal defendants by publicly airing such issues. Second, several very conservative federal judges, led by Chief Justice Warren Burger (then a judge in the United States Court of Appeals for the District of Columbia Circuit), unsuccessfully attempted to have me disbarred and dismissed from my position as a Professor of Law at George Washington University. In fact, only one day after the *Washington Post* story appeared, I received a registered letter from the United States District Court Committee on Admissions and Grievances, informing me that disciplinary proceedings had been begun against me, on the complaint of several federal judges that I had "expressed opinions" in apparent disagreement with the Canons of Professional Ethics.*

---

* Prior to that episode, I had not intended to write about professional ethics. Indeed, my first article on the subject was induced in part by the extraordinary effort to use disciplinary proceedings to prevent discussion of the issues. I was therefore tempted for a time to dedicate this book "To the Chief Justice of the United States, but for whose efforts this book would never have been written."

Those reactions to my lecture emphasize the resistance within the profession to candid analysis of serious questions of legal ethics, and suggest why those issues have not been adequately explored. This book, in a sense, illustrates another reason, that is, the extraordinary difficulty, if not impossibility, of resolving the dilemmas presented by conflicting ethical values.

For example, what are the lawyer's practical choices when the ethical obligation to keep a promise of confidentiality is pitted against the ethical obligation to be truthful? In the course of their professional work, lawyers come to know, in the classic phrase, where the bodies are buried. The first chapter of this book, therefore, begins to explore the issue of how lawyers should respond when faced with a forced choice between violating the moral imperative to be truthful and the moral imperatives to keep promises and to respect confidences received in trust. There are no easy solutions to such ethical dilemmas, but it is possible, at least, to attempt conscientiously to suggest answers and, perhaps, to stimulate responsible discussion. That is the effort of this book.

March, 1975   *Monroe H. Freedman*

Acknowledgments

I am extremely grateful to the Ford Foundation for providing a grant that made it possible for me to write this book, and to do research for it in England, Scotland and Canada, as well as in the United States.

Dean Robert Kramer, of the George Washington University National Law Center, resisted considerable pressure from some judges and others who felt that I should not be permitted to teach law and to express controversial opinions about professional ethics at the same time. His firm defense of academic freedom was invaluable to me.

Apart from my wife, those who contributed most significantly to my thinking in this area are Anthony Amsterdam, Barbara Babcock, Addison Bowman, Sam Crutchfield, Sam Dash, Marvin E. Frankel, John Kaplan, Andrew Kaufman, Howard Rochestie, David E. Seidelson, Richard Uviller and Jonathan Weiss. Ralph Temple and Gary Bellow contributed most of all. I should note, however, that they all disagree with me on some of the issues, in greater or lesser degree.

Parts of this book have previously been published by the author in the Michigan Law Review, the Georgetown Law Journal, the Ohio State Law Journal, the University of Pennsylvania Law Review, the American University Law Review, the Journal of Legal Education, the Colorado Law Review, the Civil Liberties Review, the New York Law Journal, the ABA Litigator, Juris Doctor, the Criminal Law Bulletin, the New York State Bar Journal, The Brief, Trial, Hall & Kamisar, Modern Criminal Procedure, Kadish & Paulsen, The Criminal Law and Its Processes, Weckstein (ed.), Education in the Professional Responsibilities, and Nader (ed.), Verdicts on Lawyers.

Table of Contents

WHERE THE BODIES ARE BURIED: THE ADVERSARY SYSTEM AND THE OBLIGATION OF CONFIDENTIALITY

In a recent case in Lake Pleasant, New York, a defendant in a murder case told his lawyers about two other people he had killed and where their bodies had been hidden. The lawyers went there, observed the bodies, and took photographs of them. They did not, however, inform the authorities about the bodies until several months later, when their client had confessed to those crimes. In addition to withholding the information from police and prosecutors, one of the attorneys denied information to one of the victims' parents, who came to him in the course of seeking his missing daughter.

There were interesting reactions to that dramatic event. Members of the public were generally shocked at the apparent callousness on the part of the lawyers, whose conduct was considered typical of an unhealthy lack of concern by lawyers with the public interest and with simple decency. That attitude was encouraged by public statements by the local prosecutor, who sought to indict the lawyers for failing to reveal knowledge of a crime and for failing to see that dead bodies were properly buried. In addition, the reactions of lawyers and law professors who were questioned by the press were ambivalent and confused, indicating that few members of the legal profession had given serious thought to the fundamental questions of administration of justice and of professional responsibility that were raised by the case.*

One can certainly understand the sense of moral compulsion to assist the parents and to give the dignity of proper burial to the victims. What seems to be less readily understood—but which, to my mind, throws the moral balance in the other direction—is the

---

* Henry Rothblatt, who is the author of a book on criminal trial advocacy and writes a column on that subject for the *New York Law Journal*, suggested that the lawyers might have consulted others in the profession. From his comments, however, it appears that if the lawyers had consulted Mr. Rothblatt, they would have been advised that the issue is "touchy and interesting" and that it is "an unsettled area". N.Y.L.J., June 21, 1974, at 4. Similarly, Professor David Mellinkoff of UCLA Law School, who has written a book on legal ethics, gave an "on the one hand, . . . on the other hand" response, concluding that "the lawyers seemed to be under two conflicting obligations". N.Y. Times, June 20, 1974, at 26.

obligation of the lawyers to their client and, in a larger sense, to a system of administering justice which is itself essential to maintaining human dignity. In short, not only did the two lawyers behave properly, but they would have committed a serious breach of professional responsibility if they had divulged the information contrary to their client's interest. The explanation to that answer takes us to the very nature of our system of criminal justice and, indeed, to the fundamentals of our system of government.

Let us begin, by way of contrast, with an understanding of the role of a criminal defense attorney in a totalitarian state. As expressed by law professors at the University of Havana, "the first job of a revolutionary lawyer is not to argue that his client is innocent, but rather to determine if his client is guilty and, if so, to seek the sanction which will best rehabilitate him".[1]

Similarly, a Bulgarian attorney began his defense in a treason trial by noting that: "In a Socialist state there is no division of duty between the judge, prosecutor, and defense counsel. . . . The defense must assist the prosecution to find the objective truth in a case."[2] In that case, the defense attorney ridiculed his client's defense, and the client was convicted and executed. Sometime later the verdict was found to have been erroneous, and the defendant was "rehabilitated".

The emphasis in a free society is, of course, sharply different. Under our adversary system, the interests of the state are not absolute, or even paramount. The dignity of the individual is respected to the point that even when the citizen is known by the state to have committed a heinous offense, the individual is nevertheless accorded such rights as counsel, trial by jury, due process, and the privilege against self-incrimination.

A trial is, in part, a search for truth. Accordingly, those basic rights are most often characterized as procedural safeguards against error in the search for truth. Actually, however, a trial is far more than a search for truth, and the constitutional rights that are provided by our system of justice may well outweigh the truth-seeking value—a fact which is manifest when we consider that those rights and others guaranteed by the Constitution may well impede the search for truth rather than further it. What more effective way is there, for example, to expose a defendant's guilt than to require self-incrimination, at least to the extent of compelling the defendant to take the stand and respond to interrogation before the jury? The defendant, however, is presumed innocent; the burden is on the prosecution to prove guilt beyond a reasonable doubt, and even the guilty accused has an "absolute constitutional right" to remain silent and to put the government to its proof.[3]

Thus, the defense lawyer's professional obligation may well be to advise the client to withhold the truth. As Justice Jackson said: "Any lawyer worth his salt will tell the suspect in no uncertain terms to make no statement to police under any circumstances."[4] Similarly, the defense lawyer is obligated to prevent the introduction of evidence that may be wholly reliable, such as a murder weapon seized in violation of the Fourth Amendment, or a truthful but involuntary confession. Justice White has observed that although law enforcement officials must be dedicated to using only truthful evidence, "defense counsel has no comparable obligation to ascertain or present the truth. Our system assigns him a different mission. . . . [W]e . . . insist that he defend his client whether he is innocent or guilty."[5]

Such conduct by defense counsel does not constitute obstruction of justice. On the contrary, it is "part of the duty imposed on the most honorable defense counsel", from whom "we countenance or require conduct which in many instances has little, if any, relation to the search for truth".[6] The same observation has been made by Justice Harlan, who noted that "in fulfilling his professional responsibilities", the lawyer "of necessity may become an obstacle to truthfinding".[7] Chief Justice Warren, too, has recognized that when the criminal defense attorney successfully obstructs efforts by the government to elicit truthful evidence in ways that violate constitutional rights, the attorney is "merely exercising . . . good professional judgment", and "carrying out what he is sworn to do under his oath—to protect to the extent of his ability the rights of his client".[8] Chief Justice Warren concluded: "In fulfilling this responsibility the attorney plays a vital role in the administration of criminal justice under our Constitution."[9]

Obviously, such eminent jurists would not arrive lightly at the conclusion that an officer of the court has a professional obligation to place obstacles in the path of truth. Their reasons, again, go back to the nature of our system of criminal justice and to the fundamentals of our system of government. Before we will permit the state to deprive any person of life, liberty, or property, we require that certain processes be duly followed which ensure regard for the dignity of the individual, irrespective of the impact of those processes upon the determination of truth.

By emphasizing that the adversary process has its foundations in respect for human dignity, even at the expense of the search for truth, I do not mean to deprecate the search for truth or to suggest that the adversary system is not concerned with it. On the contrary, truth is a basic value, and the adversary system is one of the most efficient and fair methods designed for determining it.

That system proceeds on the assumption that the best way to ascertain the truth is to present to an impartial judge or jury a confrontation between the proponents of conflicting views, assigning to each the task of marshalling and presenting the evidence in as thorough and persuasive a way as possible. The truth-seeking techniques used by the advocates on each side include investigation, pretrial discovery, cross-examination of opposing witnesses, and a marshalling of the evidence in summation. Thus, the judge or jury is given the strongest possible view of each side, and is put in the best possible position to make an accurate and fair judgment. Nevertheless, the point that I now emphasize is that in a society that honors the dignity of the individual, the high value that we assign to truth-seeking is not an absolute, but may on occasion be subordinated to even higher values.*

The concept of a right to counsel is one of the most significant manifestations of our regard for the dignity of the individual. No person is required to stand alone against the awesome power of the People of New York or the Government of the United States of America. Rather, every criminal defendant is guaranteed an advocate—a "champion" against a "hostile world", the "single voice on which he must rely with confidence that his interests will be protected to the fullest extent consistent with the rules of procedure and the standards of professional conduct".[10] In addition, the attorney serves in significant part to assure equality before the law. Thus, the lawyer has been referred to as "the equalizer", who "places each litigant as nearly as possible on an equal footing under the substantive and procedural law under which he is tried".[11]

The lawyer can serve effectively as advocate, however, "only if he knows all that his client knows" concerning the facts of the case.[12] Nor is the client ordinarily competent to evaluate the relevance or significance of particular facts.[13] What may seem incriminating to the client, may actually be exculpatory. For example, one client was reluctant to tell her lawyer that her husband had attacked her with a knife, because it tended to confirm that she had in fact shot him (contrary to what she had at first maintained). Having been persuaded by her attorney's insistence upon

---

* AMERICAN BAR ASSOCIATION, STANDARDS RELATING TO THE PROSECUTION AND DEFENSE FUNCTION, GENERAL INTRODUCTION 5 (1971). *Cf.* Justice Stewart: ". . . The basic purpose of a trial is the determination of truth. . . . By contrast, the Fifth Amendment's privilege against self-incrimination is not an adjunct to the ascertainment of truth. That privilege, like the guarantees of the Fourth Amendment, stands as a protection of quite different constitutional values. . . . To recognize this is no more than to accord those values undiluted respect." Tehan v. United States *ex rel.* Shott, 382 U.S. 406, 416, 86 S. Ct. 459, 15 L. Ed. 2d 453, 460 (1966).

complete and candid disclosure, she finally "confessed all"—which permitted the lawyer to defend her properly and successfully on grounds of self-defense.

Obviously, however, the client cannot be expected to reveal to the lawyer all information that is potentially relevant, including that which may well be incriminating, unless the client can be assured that the lawyer will maintain all such information in the strictest confidence. "The purposes and necessities of the relation between a client and his attorney" require "the fullest and freest disclosures" of the client's "objects, motives and acts". If the attorney were permitted to reveal such disclosures, it would be "not only a gross violation of a sacred trust upon his part", but it would "utterly destroy and prevent the usefulness and benefits to be derived from professional assistance".[14] That "sacred trust" of confidentiality must "upon all occasions be inviolable", or else the client could not feel free "to repose [confidence] in the attorney to whom he resorts for legal advice and assistance".[15] Destroy that confidence, and "a man would not venture to consult any skillful person, or would only dare to tell his counselor half his case".[16] The result would be impairment of the "perfect freedom of consultation by client with attorney", which is "essential to the administration of justice".[17] Accordingly, the new Code of Professional Responsibility provides that a lawyer shall not knowingly reveal a confidence or secret of the client, nor use a confidence or secret to the disadvantage of the client, or to the advantage of a third person, without the client's consent.[18]

It must be obvious at this point that the adversary system, within which the lawyer functions, contemplates that the lawyer frequently will learn from the client information that is highly incriminating and may even learn, as in the Lake Pleasant case, that the client has in fact committed serious crimes. In such a case, if the attorney were required to divulge that information, the obligation of confidentiality would be destroyed, and with it, the adversary system itself. Even so, it is occasionally suggested that a lawyer who does not divulge a client's self-incriminatory information would be guilty of such crimes as obstruction of justice, misprision of a felony, or becoming an accomplice after the fact. Such statutes, however, cannot be understood as applying to lawyers who have learned incriminating information after the crime has already been committed. First, criminal statutes should be strictly construed to avoid applying them more broadly than the legislature intended or to those who may not have been adequately on notice that their conduct was unlawful. Second, a statute should be strictly construed to avoid unnecessarily raising constitutional issues, particularly when there is a likelihood that the statute would have to be found constitutionally invalid. Finally, to construe an ordinary obstruction-of-justice statute or other criminal law in a way that would destroy the traditional lawyer-client relationship would violate the constitutional rights to counsel, trial by jury, and due process, and the privilege against self-incrimination.

That is not to say, of course, that the attorney is privileged to go beyond the needs of confidentiality imposed by the adversary system, and actively participate in concealment of evidence or obstruction of justice. For example, in the *Ryder* case,[19] which arose in Virginia several years ago, the attorney removed from his client's safe deposit box a sawed-off shotgun and the money from a bank robbery and put them, for greater safety, into the lawyer's own safe deposit box. The attorney, quite properly, was suspended from practice for 18 months. (The penalty might well have been heavier, except for the fact that Ryder sought advice from senior members of the bench and bar, and apparently acted more in ignorance than in venality.) The important difference between the *Ryder* case and the one in Lake Pleasant lies in the active role played by the attorney in *Ryder* to conceal evidence. There is no indication, for example, that the attorneys in Lake Pleasant attempted to hide the bodies more effectively. If they had done so, they would have gone beyond maintaining confidentiality and into active participation in the concealment of evidence.

The distinction should also be noted between the attorney's knowledge of a past crime (which is what we have been discussing so far) and knowledge of a crime to be committed in the future. Thus, a major exception to the strict rule of confidentiality is the "intention of his client to commit a crime, and information necessary to prevent the crime".[20] Significantly, however, even in that exceptional circumstance, disclosure of the confidence is only permissible, not mandatory. Moreover, a footnote in the Code suggests that the exception is applicable only when the attorney knows "beyond a reasonable doubt" that a crime will be committed.[21] There is little guidance as to how the lawyer is to exercise the discretion to report future crimes. At one extreme, it seems clear that the lawyer should reveal information necessary to save a life. On the other hand, as will be discussed in considerable detail in the next chapter, the lawyer should not reveal the intention of a client in a criminal case to commit perjury in his or her own defense.

It has been suggested that the information regarding the two bodies in the Lake Pleasant case was not relevant to the crime for which the defendant was being prosecuted, and that, therefore, that knowledge was outside the scope of confidentiality. That point lacks merit for three reasons. First, an unsophisticated lay person should not be required to anticipate which disclosures might fall outside the scope of confidentiality because of insufficient legal relevance. Second, the information in question might well have been highly relevant to the defense of insanity. Third, a lawyer has an obligation to merge other, unrelated crimes into the bargained plea, if it is possible to do so.[22] Accordingly, the information about the other murders was clearly within the protection of confidentiality.

The suggestion has also been made with respect to the Lake Pleasant case that the obligation of confidentiality was destroyed because the defendant had authorized disclosure to the prosecutor insofar as it might be helpful in plea bargaining. Plea bargaining is, unfortunately, an integral part of the criminal justice system and, as noted above, the lawyers had an obligation to attempt to dispose of the other murder charges in the same plea. Therefore, a defendant would be deprived of important rights if disclosure could not be authorized for the limited but crucial purpose of plea bargaining, without forfeiting confidentiality in general. A significantly different situation was presented in the case of a lawyer representing a figure in the Watergate investigations. There the client had authorized the lawyer to sell the client's story to a newspaper columnist. Since the authorized disclosure in that case went beyond the needs of effective representation in the judicial proceeding, the client forfeited the right to confidentiality, and the attorney was properly directed to testify before a grand jury. Similarly, if the attorney in the Lake Pleasant case had been authorized to inform the victims' parents, confidentiality would have been jeopardized.

It has also been suggested that the attorneys in Lake Pleasant were not bound by confidentiality once they had undertaken to corroborate the client's information through their own investigation. It is the duty of the lawyer, however, to conduct a thorough investigation of all aspects of the case, and that duty "exists regardless of the accused's admissions or statements to the lawyer of facts constituting guilt. . . ."[23] For example, upon investigation, the attorneys in the Lake Pleasant case might have discovered that the client's belief that he had killed other people was false, which would have had important bearing on an insanity defense.*

---

* The suggestion has also been made that the attorneys might have revealed the information through an anonymous telephone call. I do not believe that the proposal merits serious discussion—that a breach of the client's trust can be legitimated by carrying out the breach in a surreptitious manner.

In summary, the Constitution has committed us to an adversary system for the administration of criminal justice. The essentially humanitarian reason for such a system is that it preserves the dignity of the individual, even though that may occasionally require significant frustration of the search for truth and the will of the state. An essential element of that system is the right to counsel, a right that would be meaningless if the defendant were not able to communicate freely and fully with the attorney.

In order to protect that communication—and, ultimately, the adversary system itself—we impose upon attorneys what has been called the "sacred trust" of confidentiality. It was pursuant to that high trust that the lawyers acted in Lake Pleasant, New York, when they refrained from divulging their knowledge of where the bodies were buried.

Footnotes

1 J. KAPLAN, CRIMINAL JUSTICE 265-66 (1973); Berman, *The Cuban Popular Tribunals,* 60 COLUM. L. REV. 1317, 1341 (1969).

2 J. KAPLAN, *supra* note 1, at 264-65.

3 Escobedo v. Illinois, 378 U.S. 478, 84 S. Ct. 1758, 12 L. Ed. 2d 977 *passim* (1964).

4 Watts v. Indiana, 338 U.S. 49, 59, 69 S. Ct. 1347, 93 L. Ed. 1801, 1809 (1949) (separate opinion).

5 United States v. Wade, 388 U.S. 218, 256-57, 87 S. Ct. 1926, 18 L. Ed. 2d 1149, 1174 (1967) (dissenting opinion), citing, *inter alia,* Freedman, *Professional Responsibility of the Criminal Defense Lawyer: The Three Hardest Questions,* 64 MICH. L. REV. 1469 (1966).

6 *United States v. Wade, supra* note 5, at 258, 18 L. Ed 2d at 1175.

7 Miranda v. Arizona, 384 U.S. 436, 514, 86 S. Ct. 1602, 16 L. Ed. 2d 694, 746, 10 A.L.R.3d 974 (1966) (dissenting opinion).

8 *Id.* at 480, 16 L. Ed. 2d at 727.

9 *Id.* at 481, 16 L. Ed. 2d at 727.

10 AMERICAN BAR ASSOCIATION, STANDARDS RELATING TO THE DEFENSE FUNCTION 145-46 (1971).

11 *Id.*

12 *Id.* at 147.

13 EC 4-1.

14 MEECHEM, AGENCY § 2297 (2d ed. 1914).

15 AMERICAN BAR ASSOCIATION, COMMITTEE ON PROFESSIONAL ETHICS AND GRIEVANCES, OPINION 150 (1936), quoting E. THORNTON, ATTORNEYS AT LAW § 94 (1914).

16 Greenough v. Gaskell, 1 Myl. & K. 98, 103, 39 Eng. Rep. 618, 621 (1833) (Lord Chancellor Brougham).

17 AMERICAN BAR ASSOCIATION, COMMITTEE ON PROFESSIONAL ETHICS AND GRIEVANCES, OPINION 91 (1933).

18 DR 4-101 (B).

19 *In re* Ryder, 263 F. Supp. 360 (E.D. Va. 1967).

20 DR 4-101 (C) (3).

21 Canon 4, n. 16, quoting from ABA, OPINION 314 (1965).

22 AMERICAN BAR ASSOCIATION, STANDARDS RELATING TO PLEAS OF GUILTY 18 *et seq.* (1968).

23 AMERICAN BAR ASSOCIATION, STANDARDS RELATING TO THE DEFENSE FUNCTION § 4.1.

Chapter 2

ZEALOUS ADVOCACY AND THE PUBLIC INTEREST

As was noted in the preceding chapter, the adversary system assumes that the most efficient and fair way of determining the truth is by presenting the strongest possible case for each side of the controversy before an impartial judge or jury. Each advocate, therefore, must give "entire devotion to the interest of the client, warm zeal in the maintenance and defense of his rights and the exertion of his utmost learning and ability".[1] The classic statement of that ideal is by Lord Brougham, in his representation of the Queen in *Queen Caroline's Case*. Threatening to defend his client on a ground that would, literally, have brought down the kingdom, Brougham stated:

> . . . An advocate, in the discharge of his duty, knows but one person in all the world, and that person is his client. To save that client by all means and expedients, and at all hazards and costs to other persons, and, amongst them, to himself, is his first and only duty; and in performing this duty he must not regard the alarm, the torments, the destruction which he may bring upon others. Separating the duty of a patriot from that of an advocate, he must go on reckless of the consequences, though it should be his unhappy fate to involve his country in confusion.[2]

Let justice be done—that is, for my client let justice be done—though the heavens fall. That is the kind of advocacy that I would want as a client and that I feel bound to provide as an advocate. The rest of the picture, however, should not be ignored. The adversary system ensures an advocate on the other side, and an impartial judge over both. Despite the advocate's argument, therefore, the heavens do not really have to fall—not unless justice requires that they do.

The attorney's obligation of entire devotion to the interests of the client, and warm zeal in the maintenance and defense of the client's rights, would seem to be beyond serious controversy. From time to time, however, a critic with a particular ideological commitment will insist that there are public interest limits on how zealous the advocate should strive to be in a particular case or area of law. For example, Chief Judge George Hart of the United

States District Court for the District of Columbia has complained that criminal defense lawyers, in their zealous defense of people accused of crimes, are forgetting the public interest in controlling crime. In a debate before a group of law students, Judge Hart castigated lawyers for filing "frivolous" motions on behalf of their clients—although, when questioned, he was compelled to admit that motions he had denied on the ground that they were frivolous had subsequently been upheld by the Court of Appeals.

Coming from a rather different ideological viewpoint, Ralph Nader some years ago led a group of law students in the picketing of a major Washington, D.C., law firm, Wilmer, Cutler & Pickering. Mr. Nader's complaint was that the law firm, in representing General Motors in a case in which the company had been charged with practices harmful to the environment, had negotiated with the Justice Department to obtain a consent decree on terms favorable to the company, and thereby avoided a lengthy hearing at which evidence damaging to the company might have been adduced by the government. Mr. Nader's view was that it was in the public interest to have the adverse information made public (and thereby available to private parties who might want to sue the company), and that the lawyers had therefore violated their professional responsibilities in negotiating the consent decree.* Yet another illustration is provided by the efforts of the State of Virginia to limit the effectiveness of the advocacy of NAACP lawyers in school desegregation cases, by charging that the solicitation of clients for those cases violated public interest restrictions on advertising by lawyers and therefore warranted disciplinary action.[3]

A more recent and dramatic instance in which it was suggested that there are public interest limits on effective representation is the criticism that was directed at James St. Clair in his representation of Richard Nixon. First, it was suggested that Mr. St. Clair, and Professor Charles Alan Wright before him, had acted improperly in representing Mr. Nixon at all. Certainly, an attorney is permitted to decline a client for a variety of reasons, including personal dislike.[4] Although it is occasionally suggested that the attorney has an obligation to take any client who requests legal services, nothing could be further from the truth or practice. There is no rule, and never has been, that the attorney must serve as a "hired gun", and cannot elect to serve only selected clients or causes. Indeed, the attorney has a professional responsibility to refuse a case if his or her feelings are so strongly adverse to the

---

* If there was a breakdown of the adversary system in the General Motors case, it was not through the fault of the lawyers representing the company, but of those representing the government.

client's interest that the attorney's effectiveness might be impaired.[5] Nevertheless, if lawyers were to be vilified for accepting unpopular clients or causes, then those individuals who are most in need of representation would find it difficult if not impossible to obtain counsel, and a fundamental rationale for the adversary system would be nullified.* An attorney, therefore, may refuse any case, but should be entirely free to accept any case that is within his or her professional competence.

A second critical view of Mr. St. Clair recognizes that it was entirely proper and desirable for him to undertake representation of Mr. Nixon, but criticizes him for doing too good a job of it and thereby exceeding limits set by the critics in the name of the public interest. Thus, in an article on the Op-Ed page of the *New York Times*,[6] columnist Anthony Lewis charged Mr. St. Clair with "dangerous arrogance" in the conduct of Mr. Nixon's defense. Not only were Mr. St. Clair's arguments "surely wrong", and "worse than misleading", according to Mr. Lewis, but they reduced Mr. St. Clair to the status of a "political mouthpiece" who may have crossed the line of ethical limits on advocacy, thereby threatening to damage the attorney's reputation. Because Mr. Lewis is a commentator of considerable intellect and sophistication about the law, his views deserve serious consideration. For the same reasons, Mr. Lewis' views are extremely dangerous.

Mr. Lewis' specific complaint is that Mr. St. Clair said that he represented not Mr. Nixon, but "the Office of the Presidency". That claim was "worse than misleading" and "dangerous arrogance", said Mr. Lewis, because "it commit[ted] James St. Clair's reputation" to the fallacy that the interests of the Presidency and Richard Nixon were the same. Overlook the non sequitur. Mr. Lewis' concern appears to have been in two parts. The first is that Mr. St. Clair was endangering his own reputation. The second was that Mr. St. Clair's arguments (*e.g.,* to limit the law applicable to impeachment, and to limit the evidence) threatened to "undermine the institution" of representative government.

The first concern is in substantial part dependent upon the second. Mr. St. Clair's reputation was properly threatened only if he had gone too far in his zealousness as an advocate. And calling him a "mouthpiece", political or otherwise, hardly makes the case. In fact, that kind of rhetoric seriously, and irresponsibly,

---

* The *Washington Post* political cartoonist, Herblock, several times caricatured Mr. St. Clair in the garb of a burglar, implying complicity in his client's crime. Assuredly, though, Herblock would have been outraged if attorneys representing Communists during the McCarthy era had been caricatured as bomb-throwing anarchists.

threatens the adversary system itself. Let us say it plainly: a lawyer *is* a mouthpiece in the sense that one of the lawyer's most important functions is to speak for the client's interest in the most persuasive way possible. If Mr. St. Clair were to have changed his tactics because of concern for his own reputation, then he would indeed have been in ethical difficulty, for "it is the client's interests, not the law's or the lawyer's personal long-range interests, which the advocate is pledged to protect".[7]

That quotation speaks to both of Mr. Lewis' concerns. The client's interests are not only paramount to those of the lawyer, but are superior to "the law's" long-range interests. In short, Mr. Lewis is wrong in asserting that there is some "concern for history and institutions" that a lawyer must take into account before advancing a claim on behalf of a client. Or, rather, he overlooks the fact that the institution that the lawyer serves by zealous devotion to the client is the adversary system—a system for the administration of justice which, as we have noted, is uniquely protective of the dignity and the fundamental rights of the individual.

The question nevertheless remains: Did Mr. St. Clair go too far in his contentions, past the "ethical limits on what he is supposed to do for the client", as Mr. Lewis suggested? The Code of Professional Responsibility indicates that he did not. The client is entitled to any lawful argument,[8] and the advocate may urge any construction of law favorable to the client "without regard to [the lawyer's] professional opinion as to the likelihood that the construction will ultimately prevail".[9] The only limitation is that the argument not be "frivolous".[10] That standard is capable of being met if the lawyer can make a "good faith argument" for a change in existing law, even though the lawyer knows that the position being advanced is "unwarranted" under existing law.[11] As expressed in one Supreme Court decision, it is the right of counsel to press a client's claim "even if it appears farfetched and untenable".[12] Moreover, the advocate's obligations have a constitutional dimension as well, entitling the client to the benefit of any contention that is not "wholly frivolous" and that "might arguably" support the client's case.[13]

It is difficult to imagine a more sweeping formulation of the proper scope of argument by the advocate. Only a rule that is that broad, however, will serve to protect the independence of lawyers, and thereby their clients' rights, against efforts by some judges to delimit the scope of the argument as it has been determined by counsel and client. A recent case is instructive. In attempting to invalidate a criminal conviction, Professor Alan Dershowitz of Harvard Law School argued that members of the prosecutor's office had deliberately withheld exculpatory evidence from the courts. Thereupon, United States District Judge Arnold Bauman several times threatened Professor Dershowitz in open court with disciplinary action if he failed to prove his allegation to the Judge's satisfaction. Judge Bauman, a former member of the same prosecutor's office, was undoubtedly acting in good faith in voicing his outrage at the charges that Professor Dershowitz had made. Indeed, expressing the central concern of this chapter, Judge Bauman indicated that he did not consider it to be consistent with the public interest that unsupported charges be made against the public prosecutor. The fact of the Judge's good faith serves, however, to underscore how effective advocacy would be threatened by restrictive professional standards or by the notion that "public policy" might circumscribe the scope of appropriate argument. At a hearing held by Judge Bauman, the Judge decided not to proceed against Professor Dershowitz, in view of the breadth of permissible argument and the absence of any disciplinary rule or authority that would justify imposing sanctions on an attorney for making an argument that ultimately was determined by the court to be unsubstantiated.

To return to Mr. Lewis' criticism of Mr. St. Clair: Was Mr. St. Clair representing "the Office of the Presidency"? Obviously, Mr. Lewis did not think so, nor did I. But there are people who, in good faith, did think so (apparently they included Professor Charles A. Wright). For those who believe in the need for a strong presidency, at any cost, Mr. St. Clair's assertion was certainly not frivolous. Nor was Mr. St. Clair's contention even an uncommon one. A lawyer seeking to exclude unlawfully seized evidence against a client in a narcotics prosecution, for example, would similarly stress that the true issue is not the guilt or innocence of the defendant, but the integrity of law enforcement under the Constitution—in short, that the lawyer is not representing a heinous criminal, but the Fourth Amendment.

One of the great ironies about the various suggestions that public interest limits should be imposed upon zealous advocacy is that few, if any, of the proponents of such limits in specific areas would agree with those making the same proposal with respect to other areas of the law. For example, I doubt that Mr. Lewis or Mr. Nader would approve of the efforts of the State of Virginia to restrict the effectiveness of the advocacy of the NAACP. Nor, of course, would Judge Hart have much sympathy with Mr. Nader's denunciation of General Motors' attorneys, or with Mr. Lewis' criticisms of Mr. Nixon's lawyer.

A distinguished attorney, who was then the chairman of the ethics committee of a major bar association, once told me that a close friend of his had been involved in an automobile accident and had come to him to ask for representation. Although the attorney did not ordinarily handle personal injury cases, he agreed to do so as an act of friendship. The following day, however, the attorney told his friend that it would be a disservice to both of them if he were to represent him because, he explained, he could not bring himself to employ some of the tactics commonly used by personal injury lawyers. The tactics the attorney had in mind, he told me, included such things as "keeping on tap a stable of tame doctors who could be counted upon to find serious, life-long consequences in every injury, and to testify accordingly". That lawyer's own practice relates to government regulation of business, and I asked him whether, in selecting economics experts, he closes his eyes and sticks a pin into a list containing the name of every economist within a ten-mile radius of his office. He had the good grace to laugh and reply: "Of course not. But you don't seem to understand." And he then launched into an explanation of how the adversary system functions in his area of specialization. That is, the government has its experts in economics, who have a particular professional viewpoint, and the private companies have their own experts, who have a different professional viewpoint. That clash of professional expertise is then presented through examination and cross-examination before the impartial fact finder, who is thereby placed in the best possible position to make an informed judgment.

The same thing is true, of course, of the presentation of the conflicting professional expertise of doctors who testify for injured plaintiffs and doctors who testify for insurance companies. The adversary system not only takes the fact of disagreement into account, but takes advantage of it to produce a judgment informed by contrasting points of view. In doing so, the adversary system serves the public interest in a unique way.

Unfortunately, attacks upon lawyers representing disfavored clients and causes have gone beyond verbal abuse. As stated in an article in the *Harvard Civil Rights-Civil Liberties Law Review*: "It has become both professionally and legally dangerous to be a lawyer representing the poor, minorities, and the politically unpopular."[14] The article refers to the increasing tendency during the latter 1960's (continued into the early 1970's) to institute disciplinary proceedings and criminal contempt charges against lawyers representing unpopular clients and causes. That tendency has been encouraged by Chief Justice Burger, who also has been concerned that zealous advocacy has gone beyond the bounds of the public interest as he sees it. Thus, the Chief Justice has charged that "all too often" overzealous advocates commit a variety of improprieties, ranging from disruption of proceedings to seeing "how loud [they] can shout" or how many people, "including the judges", they can insult. According to the Chief Justice: "At the drop of a hat—or less—we find adrenalin-fueled lawyers cry out that theirs is a 'political trial'," with the result that "rules of evidence, canons of ethics and codes of professional conduct—the necessity for civility—all become irrelevant."[15] In response to that alarming circumstance, the Chief Justice has called for severe measures—"strict regulation and public accountability" of lawyers in order to safeguard the public interest.

In the light of the actual facts, however, Chief Justice Burger's repeated attacks on "adrenalin-fueled lawyers", who must be strictly controlled lest the judicial system be overwhelmed by courtroom disruption, have an air of unreality. For example, in 1971, the *New York Times* conducted a survey and independent interviews with legal authorities around the country and reported that courtroom disorder was "not a serious or growing problem".[16] Similarly, in an extensive study conducted by the Association of the Bar of the City of New York, it was found that "there is no serious quantitative problem of disruption in American courts".[17] It is, of course, questionable whether it comports with civility to make sweeping and unsubstantiated charges against lawyers representing unpopular clients and causes. The real threat to the proper administration of justice is in the effort to restrict the advocacy of such lawyers, on whatever ground.

Since the most strident attacks have related to alleged misconduct in the courtroom, particularly with reference to disrespect to the bench, it might be useful to consider some excerpts from actual transcripts. The first comes from a case in which the judge remarked that a particular item of evidence was "extremely vulgar". Counsel retorted that he had no doubt that His Honor was a better judge of vulgarity than was counsel. The second trial incident involved the following exchange between court and counsel:

> JUDGE: . . . You know that is a most improper question to ask.
>
> ATTORNEY: I know when a person has his mind made up, it is not easy to change it.
>
> JUDGE: I do not want you to make a speech now.
>
> ATTORNEY: I am going to make a speech—that is what I am paid for.

In the third transcript excerpt, the dialogue between attorney and judge went this way:

> ATTORNEY: I stand here as an advocate for a brother citizen, and I desire that the [record in this case be complete and accurate].
>
> JUDGE: Sit down, Sir! Remember your duty or I shall be obliged to proceed in another manner [*i.e.,* referring to disciplinary proceedings].
>
> ATTORNEY: Your [Honor] may proceed in any manner you think fit. I know my duty as well as Your [Honor] knows yours. I shall not alter my conduct.

Those incidents are of particular interest for two reasons. First, neither involved a modern American lawyer; in each instance the attorney was a highly respected English barrister. Second, far from resulting in disciplinary proceedings against the lawyers, each of those episodes has been cited by eminent authorities in the most favorable terms.

The comment on the judge's expertise in vulgarity was made by Sir Marshall Hall, a noted barrister of the earlier part of this century, and has been quoted by his biographer as illustrative of Sir Marshall's courtroom wit. The second exchange also involved Marshall Hall, and his biographer relates that having insisted upon making a speech, Hall did so and "won the day".[18]

The lawyer in the third instance was no less a figure in English law than Lord Erskine. According to Lord Campbell, Erskine's defiance of the court was "a noble stand for the independence of the bar". Similarly, one of the most highly regarded of American jurists, Judge Roger Traynor of the California Supreme Court, has used Erskine's statement as illustrative of the attorney's duty to assert the client's rights in a forthright manner. And Professors Louisell and Hazard introduce the incident with the following comment: "So much emphasis is currently placed upon avoidance of improper argument that it seems amiss not to remind today's young lawyer of his duty of effective representation of his client in an adversary system."[19]

In view of the notoriety achieved by the Chicago Seven case, it is particularly interesting to compare some of Judge Julius Hoffman's specifications of contempt of court against the attorneys in that case, with the excerpts already quoted above.[20] For example, compare Erskine's "I will not alter my conduct", and Hall's "I am going to make a speech", with the following item of allegedly contemptuous conduct by Leonard Weinglass:

MR. WEINGLASS: If the Court please, there is a defendant in court, Mr. Bobby Seale, who is sitting here. He is entitled to counsel. As of now he does not have counsel.

THE COURT: That is not a fact, as appears in the record.

MR. WEINGLASS: Mr. Birnbaum and Mr. Bass have withdrawn from the case as trial counsel. Mr. Seale is not represented here in court.

THE COURT: Mr. Weinglass, I direct you to sit down.

MR. WEINGLASS: If the Court please, I would like to know—

THE COURT: I would like you to sit down or I will ask the marshal to escort you to your chair.

MR. WEINGLASS: I will sit down, but I do so under protest.

THE COURT: Then do so.[21]

Similarly, one might compare Sir Marshall Hall's "vulgarity" joke, at the expense of the court, with an exchange between William Kunstler and Judge Hoffman. It began when one of the prosecutors told one of the defendants to "go to the bathroom". In the colloquy that followed, some of the defendants laughed at a further reference to the bathroom, leading to the following exchange:

THE COURT: Let the record show that after I requested the marshal to keep Mr. Dellinger quiet he laughed right out loud.

MR. DELLINGER: And he is laughing now, too.

THE MARSHAL: And the Defendant Hayden, your Honor.

MR. KUNSTLER: Oh, your Honor, there is a certain amount of humor when talking about a bathroom—but people can't help it sometimes, your Honor. You have laughed yourself.

THE COURT: I really have come to believe you can't help yourself. I have come to believe it. I have never been in a case where I have seen such bad manners.

MR. KUNSTLER: I know, your Honor, but when you make a joke and the courtroom laughs, nobody is thrown out.[22]

As a result of that minor quip, Judge Hoffman sentenced Mr. Kunstler to three weeks in prison.

Most disciplinary proceedings against attorneys representing unpopular clients and causes do not relate to allegations of improper courtroom conduct. The case of Professor Florence Roisman of the Catholic University Law School provides an example of the extent to which grievance committees will extend themselves to harass attorneys who are more concerned with law reform than with serving as hired guns for fee-paying clients. At the time the disciplinary proceedings arose, Professor Roisman was an attorney with the Neighborhood Legal Services in the District of Columbia. When she had been only a few years out of law school, Professor Roisman was instrumental in revolutionizing the archaic and unfair rules of landlord-tenant law in Washington. As a result of Professor Roisman's service to the poor people of the District of Columbia, charges were brought against her before the Grievance Committee by Sidney J. Brown, one of the most notorious slumlords in the District. Brown's complaint included such absurd charges as that Professor Roisman had sued him rather than other landlords who also had violated the housing code, that she had filed a suit against him that, in Brown's judgment, was without merit, and that she had on one occasion filed a complaint against him and later amended it pursuant to the rules of the court.

It should be noted that the District of Columbia Committee on Grievances* has earned a reputation for failing to act in any except the most egregious cases of professional impropriety. Even local judges have charged that their own complaints to the Committee have been largely ignored—complaints against lawyers for being drunk in court, chronically unprepared, and failing adequately to represent their clients, and even a complaint that one obviously deranged member of the Bar had been engaging in such bizarre conduct as defecating in the courtroom stairwell. The fact that the Committee has acted so promptly and tenaciously on patently frivolous charges against attorneys like Professor Roisman, therefore, provides strong justification for an inference that the Committee's powers have been abused for repressive purposes. As in other similar situations, the Grievance Committee was so eager to proceed against Professor Roisman that it violated its own rules. For example, the Committee instituted and maintained the proceedings over objections that Brown, a law school graduate, would not notarize his complaint, as required by the rules of the Committee.

---

* The full title is the United States District Court for the District of Columbia Committee on Admissions and Grievances. Since the District of Columbia Bar was unified a few years ago, a new Disciplinary Board and procedures have been established, and the Grievance Committee of the District Court is of less importance. Nevertheless, that Committee as recently as 1974 initiated disciplinary action against Professor John Banzhaf, III, under circumstances that unquestionably would not have resulted in any action by the Committee if Professor Banzhaf were not noted for his representation of political and consumer causes. The proceedings were ultimately dropped, with an admission by the Committee that there had been no justification for instituting them.

Indeed, despite the obviously frivolous nature of the complaint, and despite demands that it be dismissed both for failure to comply with applicable rules and for lack of substance, the Committee had failed to dispose of the complaint, or even to schedule a meeting to consider it, fully eight months later. That illustrates yet another abusive practice of the Grievance Committee in dealing with disfavored attorneys, that is, dragging out the proceedings, literally, interminably. One such case was left pending for several years because the Committee had failed to act, presenting the lawyer with the dilemma of leaving the matter unresolved or insisting upon going forward and thereby courting a result that might destroy his career.

Professor Roisman, with full awareness of the risk she was taking, decided to meet the issue head on. A suit was filed on her behalf in the United States District Court naming the nine members of the Committee on Admissions and Grievances as defendants. Within a matter of days, the Committee dismissed the complaint against Professor Roisman, and the law suit was withdrawn on the Committee's written stipulation that there had been no justification for having instituted the proceedings against her in the first place.

A closely related problem is the effort of some judges and grievance committees to take abusive action against lawyers who take seriously the obligation to assist in bringing about law reform through criticism of maladministration of justice and of particular judges as public officials.[23] As noted in the new Code of Professional Responsibility: "By reason of education and experience, lawyers are especially qualified to recognize deficiencies in the legal system and to initiate corrective measures therein."[24] However, when a prominent Washington attorney, serving as Chairman of the District of Columbia Lawyers Committee, publicly urged the Justice Department to appoint a special prosecutor in a case involving the killing of a citizen by a police officer,[25] the Grievance Committee initiated proceedings against him. In another case, Assistant Dean Louis Barracato of Catholic University Law School was subjected to disciplinary proceedings when, as a Neighborhood Legal Services Attorney, he publicly criticized a judge who had improperly ordered him to represent a client in a clear case of conflict of interest. In New York, a leading Legal Aid attorney, Martin Erdmann, was charged with contempt of court for publicly criticizing the administration of criminal justice, and for referring to those judges who knowingly participated in the travesty as whores and madams. In another case in Washington, Philip Hirschkop was the subject of a strenuous effort by a federal district court judge to have him disbarred. Ultimately, a panel of three other judges decided that no sanction other than a mild censure would be appropriate. When asked by a newspaper reporter what the significance of the censure was, Hirschkop replied that it meant nothing, amounting simply to a face-saving gesture by his judicial colleagues to the judge, who had so vigorously sought to destroy Hirschkop professionally. On the basis of that exercise of his First Amendment rights, Hirschkop was subjected to further proceedings before the Grievance Committee. In a related matter, Ralph Temple, Legal Director for the American Civil Liberties Union affiliate in the District of Columbia, protested in a television interview the continuing harassment of Hirschkop. As a result, the Grievance Committee sought to obtain the video tape of that interview in order to consider bringing charges against Temple for denouncing the violation of Hirschkop's civil liberties.

In none of those cases was any disciplinary action ultimately taken against the attorney (except for the censure of Hirschkop, which was, indeed, a face-saving gesture for the judge). The shocking thing, however, is that the attorneys were compelled to expend the time and money and to undergo the humiliation of having to defend their professional integrity. In fact, the Committee had at first been inexcusably ignorant of the relevant cases. However, it had quickly been apprised of the authorities imposing an obligation upon attorneys to criticize maladministration of justice, and of the cases upholding the constitutional rights that lawyers, like other citizens, have to criticize government officials. For example, in *Konigsberg v. State Bar*,[26] an applicant for admission to the bar had been turned down in part because he had accused the members of the Supreme Court of having "[sold] out to the enemy", and of being "an integral part of the cold war machine directed against the American people". But the Court rose above those vituperative charges against itself, finding them to be "not unusually extreme" and holding that "fairly interpreted" they "only say that certain officials were performing their duties in a manner . . . injurious to the public".[27] The Court held further that: "Citizens have a right under our constitutional system to criticize government officials and agencies. Courts are not, and should not be, immune to such criticism."[28] The Supreme Court concluded that it is essential "both to society and the bar itself that lawyers be unintimidated—free to think, speak, and act as members of an Independent Bar".[29]

There is one further category of attorneys who, along with lawyers representing the poor, minorities, and the politically unpopular, should be added to the roster of those who are in legal and professional jeopardy. Oddly enough, they are the lawyers who represent clients in the securities industry. Elsewhere, I have set forth a catalog of serious abuses by the Securities and Exchange Commission of the rights of those subject to its jurisdiction.[30] Of even greater concern, however, is the fact that the SEC has succeeded in intimidating the attorneys who appear before it, with the result that zealous advocacy has been sharply curtailed in securities matters. As one highly experienced and highly regarded securities lawyer commented to me: "The professional training of the New York securities bar is to cave in." Another equally prominent authority said: "The securities bar has abdicated its responsibilities to its clients in deference to the Commission."[31]

The Commission starts with the best of motives. It has an important job to do in the public interest, and it has been provided with a "meager" staff with which to achieve its goals.[32] One way the Commission has sought to resolve its difficulties is by insisting that attorneys, in the public interest, owe a higher obligation to the SEC—a federal agency—than they do to their own clients. Inevitably, that notion (which Commissioner Sommer has characterized as "revolutionary")[33] is expressed euphemistically in terms of an asserted "public responsibility . . . to the investing public".[34] As the Commission has observed: "This Commission with its small staff, limited resources, and onerous tasks is peculiarly dependent on the probity and the diligence of the professionals who practice before it."[35] Accordingly, "members of this Commission have pointed out time and time again that the task of enforcing the securities law rests in overwhelming measure on the Bar's shoulders".[36] The SEC attorney has thus become, in the phrase of Commissioner A. A. Sommer, Jr., "another cop on the beat",[37] with the result that "all the verities and truisms about attorneys and their roles [are] in question and in jeopardy".[38] It was not an exaggeration, therefore, when the New York Times referred to the SEC's practices as constituting a "major assault" on the adversary system.[39]

The Commission has succeeded in destroying the independence of the securities bar, and in transferring the attorney's primary allegiance from the client to a federal agency, through the use of what SEC Chairman Ray Garrett, Jr., has confessed are "overly crude weapons".[40] Mr. Garrett has explained that the Commission "keep[s] the pressure on the professionals" to do the government's job through "suitable incentives". Those incentives include "rewards" as well as "punishments".[41]

The rewards consist of favored treatment of some lawyers in their appearances before the Commission. For example, a few attorneys do receive the opportunity, denied to others, to appear before the Commission at a critical stage of the proceedings against their clients.[42] That, of course, represents a conscious effort to encourage lawyers to trade off the rights of some clients in order to curry favor with the Commission and thereby advance the rights of other clients. It also amounts to a denial of the right to effective assistance of counsel and of equal protection of the laws to the clients of those lawyers who are not so favored.

The punishments are directed toward intimidating attorneys into foregoing zealous advocacy on behalf of their clients. One attorney, engaged in vigorous defense of his client's rights, was advised by a staff member that he should "take a look at the National Student Marketing complaint". In that case, members of one of the most prestigious law firms in the country were named as defendants in an action by the Commission, in part on the ground that they had not informed the Commission of possibly incriminating information that they had received about their client in the course of the lawyer-client relationship. Indeed, an attorney may appear before the Commission on behalf of a client, and receive no warning that the attorney is also a target of the investigation. In one case, a lawyer who was attending a meeting at the SEC to discuss a forthcoming investigation of his client was served with a personal subpoena within minutes after refusing to disclose the contents of conversations he had had with witnesses in connection with his client's case. In addition, the attorney was reminded that his "primary duty was to the Commission, not to the client".[43] The "climate of fear"[44] that has thereby been engendered within the securities bar has been heightened by the reminder that an entire law firm might be disbarred or suspended for a lapse on the part of a single firm member[45]—a sanction that is particularly vicious in view of the fact that disbarment or suspension may result from simple negligence without any showing of improper intent.[46]

One of the most revealing comments that I have heard, illustrating the unhealthy relationship between the SEC and the attorneys who practice before it, was provided in a speech to SEC practitioners by William L. Cary, a former Commission chairman and now a Professor at Columbia Law School. Professor Cary related that an irate attorney had once appeared at the Commission to protest that a staff attorney had been engaging in arbitrary conduct toward the attorney's client. With obvious approval and delight, Professor Cary quoted the staff attorney as saying: "Listen, if we weren't as arbitrary as we are, you wouldn't be as fat as you are." The high-minded moral that former Chairman Cary drew from that episode was: "So keep in mind that your practice depends upon what the Commission does." Professor Cary then went on to admonish the attorneys that they have a professional responsibility to "force" their own clients toward a "process of disclosure".

Perhaps the most dangerous power of the Securities and Exchange Commission is that of instituting its own disciplinary proceedings against attorneys whose conduct displeases members of its staff. There is an important distinction to be noted, of course, between disciplinary proceedings that are carried on by an impartial disciplinary board of the bar, and those conducted by one's adversary. When the SEC seeks to discipline an attorney, it acts not as a disinterested third party, but as a partisan. It is as if prosecutors had disciplinary powers over defense attorneys, or attorneys representing plaintiffs in personal injury cases had disciplinary powers over those representing insurance companies. We can hardly expect an advocate to give "entire devotion to the interest of the client [and] warm zeal in the maintenance and defense of his rights", when the attorney representing the other party has the power to suspend or disbar that advocate. Moreover, the situation is made far worse by the vagueness of the standards imposed by the Commission. For example, the SEC claims the power to discipline adversary attorneys on grounds that they are "lacking in character".[47] Nor is it fanciful to infer that such power will be abused. As Commissioner Sommer has conceded, young staff attorneys, "short on experience, long on desire", may "very often" find that the best way to counter skilled adversaries is through "strong assertions of authority".[48]

There is doubt that the Commission has the statutory authority that it claims to discipline attorneys.[49] In my own view, such power violates constitutional rights to due process and effective assistance of counsel. At any rate, one would at least expect that the Commission would exercise that power with restraint. On the contrary, however, in one case it was necessary for an attorney to go to the United States Court of Appeals to obtain reversal of a two-year suspension on a charge of improper conduct five years previously.[50] Although the court ultimately found the Commission's evidence to be insufficient to support a finding of impropriety, and directed the Commission to vacate its order against the attorney, the intimidating effect of such abuses of power is plain. Indeed, simply for the Commission to commence disciplinary action against an attorney constitutes, in itself, a severe penalty. As acknowledged by Commissioner Sommer, the Commission "know[s] full well" that an injunction action against a professional can have a "profound adverse effect", very often "far more profound and devastating" than a similar action against a business person.[51] Despite that awareness on the part of the Commission (or, perhaps, because of it) the SEC has sought to expand even further its disciplinary powers and the destructive impact of those powers. In a proposed amendment to its Rules of Practice, the Commission has proposed that its disciplinary inquiries should be made public at the outset. The result of that action, of course, would be to seriously damage or destroy an attorney's practice even if the attorney should ultimately be found innocent of any improper conduct.

Disciplinary action by the Securities and Exchange Commission against its own adversaries is perhaps the most extreme and obvious instance of conflict of interest in disciplinary proceedings. However, as indicated earlier in this chapter, there are innumerable cases in which disciplinary powers have been abused in order to impair or to destroy the professional careers of attorneys representing clients or causes unpopular with those exercising disciplinary authority. In addition, a number of critics, each with a different "public interest" concern, have sought to discourage or limit zealous and effective advocacy on behalf of a contrary point of view.

What those critics overlook is that zealous and effective advocacy is essential to the adversary system, which itself serves the public interest in a uniquely important way. It is instructive as well as ironic that it was former President Nixon's Chief Justice who so vigorously denounced attorneys for maintaining that their clients' trials were political, and that it was Mr. Nixon's attorney who subsequently was so vigorously attacked for serving as a "political mouthpiece". In attacking zealous advocacy, we not only do damage to the public interest, but we also endanger a precious safeguard that any one of us may have occasion to call upon if we should come to need our own champion against a hostile world.

Footnotes

[1] AMERICAN BAR ASSOCIATION, CANONS OF PROFESSIONAL ETHICS 15. *See also,* AMERICAN BAR ASSOCIATION, CODE OF PROFESSIONAL RESPONSIBILITY, CANON 7.

[2] Trial of Queen Caroline 8 (1821).

[3] NAACP v. Button, 371 U.S. 415, 83 S. Ct. 328, 9 L. Ed. 2d 405 (1963). The *Button* case and the general problem of advertising are discussed in Chapter 10 *infra.*

[4] EC 2-26.

[5] EC 5-2; DR 5-101.

[6] N.Y. Times, March 18, 1974, at 29, col. 1.

[7] AMERICAN BAR ASSOCIATION, STANDARDS RELATING TO THE DEFENSE FUNCTION 150 (1971).

[8] EC 7-1. *See also,* AMERICAN BAR ASSOCIATION, STANDARDS RELATING TO THE DEFENSE FUNCTION, INTRODUCTION 148 (1971).

[9] EC 7-4.

[10] *Id.*

[11] DR 7-102 (A) (2).

[12] Sacher v. United States, 343 U.S. 1, 9, 72 S. Ct. 451, 96 L. Ed. 717, 723 (1952).

[13] Anders v. California, 386 U.S. 738, 744, 87 S. Ct. 1396, 18 L. Ed. 2d 493, 498, *reh. den.,* 388 U.S. 924, 87 S. Ct. 2094, 18 L. Ed. 2d 1377 (1967).

[14] Comment, *Controlling Lawyers By Bar Associations and Courts,* 5 HARV. CIV. RIGHTS-CIV. LIB. L. REV. 301 (1970).

[15] Burger, *The Necessity for Civility,* 52 F.R.D. 211, 212-14 (1971). The Chief Justice made similar observations in addresses to the American Bar Association in August, 1970, to the American Law Institute in May, 1971, and again to the American Bar Association in July, 1971.

[16] N.Y. Times, Aug. 9, 1971, at 1.

[17] N. DORSEN & L. FRIEDMAN, DISORDER IN THE COURT 6 (1974).

[18] E. MARJORIBANKS, FOR THE DEFENSE: THE LIFE OF SIR EDWARD MARSHALL HALL 45 (1931).

[19] D. LOUISELL & G. HAZARD, CASES AND MATERIALS ON PLEADING AND PROCEDURE, STATE AND FEDERAL (2d ed. 1968).

[20] This discussion is not intended, of course, as a thorough analysis of the many and complex issues in the Chicago Seven case.

[21] United States v. Dellinger, 69 Cr. 180 (N.D. Ill.), Tr. Sept. 24, 1969, at 24.

[22] *Id.,* Tr. Jan. 12, 1969, at 21707-10.

[23] *See,* AMERICAN BAR ASSOCIATION, CODE OF PROFESSIONAL RESPONSIBILITY, CANON 8.

[24] EC 8-1.

[25] *See,* pp. 91-94 *infra,* regarding the prosecutor's conflict of interest in such cases.

[26] 353 U.S. 252, 77 S. Ct. 722, 1 L. Ed. 2d 810 (1957).

[27] *Id.* at 268, n. 27, 268-69, 1 L. Ed. 2d at 822-23.

[28] *Id.* at 269, 1 L. Ed. 2d at 823.

[29] *Id.* at 273, 1 L. Ed. 2d at 825. *See also, In re* Sawyer, 360 U.S. 622, 79 S. Ct. 1376, 3 L. Ed. 2d 1473 (1959); Garrison v. Louisiana, 379 U.S. 64, 85 S. Ct. 209, 13 L. Ed. 2d 125 (1964); Willner v. Committee on Character and Fitness, 373 U.S. 96, 83 S. Ct. 1175, 10 L. Ed. 2d 224 (1963); Schware v. Board of Bar Examiners, 353 U.S. 232, 77 S. Ct. 752, 1 L. Ed. 2d 796 (1957).

[30] Freedman, *A Civil Libertarian Looks at Securities Regulation,* 35 OHIO ST. L. J. 251, 280 (1974); *Professional Responsibility in Securities Regulation,* N.Y.L.J., Apr. 24, 1974, at 1; *Securities Enforcement: A Reply to Critics,* N.Y.L.J., May 30, 1974, at 1.

[31] Almost none of the many lawyers with whom I have spoken was willing to be identified by name. That, in itself, is some indication of the unhealthy relationship between the Securities and Exchange Commission and the lawyers who practice before it. However, in each instance in which I refer to information obtained in an interview with a lawyer, I subsequently received confirmation from at least one reputable and experienced attorney that the information that I had received was consistent with his or her experience. In addition, since publication of the articles cited in the previous footnote, I have received numerous letters from experienced attorneys, most of them offering additional illustrations of serious abuses of power by the Commission, and virtually all of them requesting that their names not be used, for fear of retaliation against themselves or their clients.

[32] "The Commission and the Bar: Forty Good Years", address by A. A. Sommer, Jr., Session of Corporation, Banking and Business Law of the American Bar Association, 97th Annual Meeting, Honolulu, Hawaii, Aug. 14, 1974, at 4.

[33] Sommer, *Emerging Responsibilities of the Securities Lawyer*, N.Y.L.J., Jan. 30, 1974, at 4:6.

[34] Sommer, *supra* note 31, at 10.

[35] *In re* Emanuel Fields, 2 S.E.C. Docket 1, at 4-5, n. 20 (July 3, 1973).

[36] *Id.*

[37] Sommer, *supra* note 32, at 4:5.

[38] Sommer, *supra* note 32, at 4:6.

[39] N.Y. Times, June 23, 1974, 4, at 9, cols. 1-4.

[40] "New Directions in Professional Responsibility", address by Ray Garrett, Jr., American Bar Association, Washington, D.C., Oct. 11, 1973, at 15.

[41] *Id.* at 10.

[42] Freeman, *Administrative Procedures*, 22 Bus. Law. 891, 895 (1967).

[43] Business Week, Aug. 10, 1974, at 102-03.

[44] *Id.*

[45] Sonde, *The Responsibility of Professionals Under the Federal Securities Law—Some Observations,* 68 Nw. U. L. Rev. 1 (1973).

[46] SEC v. Spectrum, Ltd., 54 F.R.D. 70 (S.D. N.Y. 1971).

[47] 17 C.F.R. 201.2 (e).

[48] Sommer, *supra* note 31, at 13.

[49] Brodsky, *SEC Disciplinary Proceedings Against Attorneys—Private or Public?,* N.Y.L.J., Aug. 21, 1974, at 1.

[50] Kivitz v. SEC, 475 F.2d 956 (D.C. Cir. 1973).

[51] Sommer, *supra* note 31, at 7.

Chapter 3

PERJURY: THE CRIMINAL DEFENSE LAWYER'S TRILEMMA

Is it ever proper for a criminal defense lawyer to present perjured testimony?

One's instinctive response is in the negative. On analysis, however, it becomes apparent that the question is an exceedingly perplexing one. My own answer is in the affirmative.

At the outset, we should dispose of some common question-begging responses. The attorney, we are told, is an officer of the court, and participates in a search for truth. Those propositions, however, merely serve to state the problem in different words: As an officer of the court, participating in a search for truth, what is the attorney obligated to do when faced with perjured testimony? That question cannot be answered properly without an appreciation of the fact that the attorney functions in an adversary system of criminal justice which, as we have seen in the two previous chapters, imposes special responsibilities upon the advocate.

First, the lawyer is required to determine "all relevant facts known to the accused",[1] because "counsel cannot properly perform their duties without knowing the truth".[2] The lawyer who is ignorant of any potentially relevant fact "incapacitates himself to serve his client effectively", because "an adequate defense cannot be framed if the lawyer does not know what is likely to develop at trial".[3]

Second, the lawyer must hold in strictest confidence the disclosures made by the client in the course of the professional relationship. "Nothing is more fundamental to the lawyer-client relationship than the establishment of trust and confidence."[4] The "first duty" of an attorney is "to keep the secrets of his clients".[5] If this were not so, the client would not feel free to confide fully, and the lawyer would not be able to fulfill the obligation to ascertain all relevant facts. Accordingly, defense counsel is required to establish "a relationship of trust and confidence" with the accused, to explain "the necessity of full disclosure of all facts", and to explain to the client "the obligation of confidentiality which makes privileged the accused's disclosures".[6]

Third, the lawyer is an officer of the court, and his or her conduct before the court "should be characterized by candor".[7]

As soon as one begins to think about those responsibilities, it becomes apparent that the conscientious attorney is faced with what we may call a trilemma—that is, the lawyer is required to know everything, to keep it in confidence, and to reveal it to the court. Moreover, the difficulties presented by those conflicting obligations are particularly acute in the criminal defense area because of the presumption of innocence, the burden upon the state to prove its case beyond a reasonable doubt, and the right to put the prosecution to its proof.

Before addressing the issue of the criminal defense lawyer's responsibilities when the client indicates to the lawyer the intention to commit perjury in the future, we might note the somewhat less difficult question of what the lawyer should do when knowledge of the perjury comes after its commission rather than before it. Although there is some ambiguity in the most recent authorities, the rules appear to require that the criminal defense lawyer should urge the client to correct the perjury, but beyond that, the obligation of confidentiality precludes the lawyer from revealing the truth.

In an opinion of major importance under the old Canons, an eminent panel of the American Bar Association Committee on Professional Ethics and Grievances, headed by Henry Drinker, held that if the client falsely tells the judge that he has no prior record, the lawyer should remain silent despite knowledge to the contrary.[8] The majority of the panel distinguished the situation in which the attorney has learned of the client's prior record from a source other than the client. William B. Jones, then a trial lawyer and now a judge in the United States District Court for the District of Columbia, wrote a separate opinion in which he asserted that in neither event should the lawyer expose the client's lie.

The relevant provision of the new Code of Professional Responsibility[9] is DR 7-102(B)(1). As originally drafted, in 1969, that provision is in two clauses—a main clause and an "and if" clause. The main clause provides that when the lawyer learns that a client has "perpetrated a fraud upon a person or tribunal", the lawyer "shall promptly call upon his client to rectify" the fraud. The second clause reads: ". . . and if his client refuses or is unable to do so, he shall reveal the fraud to the affected person or tribunal". Thus, the American Bar Association at first appeared to take a position in favor of disclosure by the lawyer contrary to the client's interest and in violation of confidentiality.

The District of Columbia was the first jurisdiction in the United States in which the practicing bar focused upon that particular provision and passed judgment upon it specifically.

On my motion, DR 7-102(B)(1) was amended when the Code was adopted in the District, so as to delete the "and if" clause entirely. On a mail referendum of the bar, the amendment carried by 74 percent of the vote, or virtually three to one. Similarly, the Quebec Bar Association, which has adopted substantial portions of the ABA Code, has rejected DR 7-102(B).[10] In addition, the Law Society, which oversees the conduct of solicitors in England, has taken the position that a solicitor must maintain confidentiality even upon learning from the client after the conclusion of a civil case that a witness has been paid by the client to commit perjury.[11] Finally, the American Bar Association itself recognized the impropriety of requiring a breach of confidentiality. In 1974, the ABA added a third clause to DR 7-102(B)(1), so that the attorney is called upon to reveal the client's fraud "except when the information is protected as a privileged communication".

Of course, DR 7-102(B) is not limited to perjury in the context of criminal litigation. Indeed, the bar of the District of Columbia was adverting specifically to the obligations of the civil practitioner in a divorce case or a tax case.[12] Entirely apart from any consensus of the bar relative to civil practice, however, divulgence by the defense attorney in a criminal case would be controlled by such constitutional provisions as the right to counsel, the privilege against self-incrimination, the right to trial by jury, and the right to due process. Thus, the ABA Standards, referring to the original draft of DR 7-102(B) (1), state flatly that that provision "is construed as not embracing the giving of false testimony in a criminal case".[13] That is, even in those jurisdictions that may not yet have adopted the ABA's amendment to DR 7-102(B), that clause does not apply to the criminal defense lawyer.

With respect to the case where the lawyer has foreknowledge of the perjury, another section of the Code appears, at first reading, to be unambiguous. According to DR 7-102(A)(4), a lawyer must not "knowingly use perjured testimony or false evidence".[14] The difficulty, however, is that the Code does not indicate how the lawyer is to go about fulfilling that obligation. What if the lawyer advises the client that perjury is unlawful and, perhaps, bad tactics as well, but the client nevertheless insists upon taking the stand and committing perjury in his or her own defense? What steps, specifically, should the lawyer take? Just how difficult it is to answer that question becomes apparent if we review the relationship between lawyer and client as it develops, and consider the contexts in which the decision to commit perjury may arise.

If we recognize that professional responsibility requires that an advocate have full knowledge of every pertinent fact, then the lawyer must seek the truth from the client, not shun it. That means that the attorney will have to dig and pry and cajole, and, even then, the lawyer will not be successful without convincing the client that full disclosure to the lawyer will never result in prejudice to the client by any word or action of the attorney. That is particularly true in the case of the indigent defendant, who meets the lawyer for the first time in the cell block or the rotunda of the jail. The client did not choose the lawyer, who comes as a stranger sent by the judge, and who therefore appears to be part of the system that is attempting to punish the defendant. It is no easy task to persuade that client to talk freely without fear of harm.

However, the inclination to mislead one's lawyer is not restricted to the indigent or even to the criminal defendant. Randolph Paul has observed a similar phenomenon among a wealthier class in a far more congenial atmosphere. The tax adviser, notes Mr. Paul, will sometimes have to "dynamite the facts of his case out of unwilling witnesses on his own side— witnesses who are nervous, witnesses who are confused about their own interest, witnesses who try to be too smart for their own good, and witnesses who subconsciously do not want to understand what has happened despite the fact that they must if they are to testify coherently".[15] Mr. Paul goes on to explain that the truth can be obtained only by persuading the client that it would be a violation of a sacred obligation for the lawyer ever to reveal a client's confidence. Of course, once the lawyer has thus persuaded the client of the obligation of confidentiality, that obligation must be respected scrupulously.

Assume the following situation. Your client has been falsely accused of a robbery committed at 16th and P Streets at 11:00 p.m. He tells you at first that at no time on the evening of the crime was he within six blocks of that location. However, you are able to persuade him that he must tell you the truth and that doing so will in no way prejudice him. He then reveals to you that he was at 15th and P Streets at 10:55 that evening, but that he was walking east, away from the scene of the crime, and that, by 11:00 p.m., he was six blocks away. At the trial, there are two prosecution witnesses. The first mistakenly, but with some degree of persuasiveness, identifies your client as the criminal. At that point the prosecution's case depends upon that single witness, who might or might not be believed. The second prosecution witness is an elderly woman who is somewhat nervous and who wears glasses. She testifies truthfully and accurately that she saw

your client at 15th and P Streets at 10:55 p.m. She has corrobo-
rated the erroneous testimony of the first witness and made conviction extremely likely. However, on cross-examination her relia-
bility is thrown into doubt through demonstration that she is
easily confused and has poor eyesight.* Thus, the corroboration
has been eliminated, and doubt has been established in the
minds of the jurors as to the prosecution's entire case.

The client then insists upon taking the stand in his own
defense, not only to deny the erroneous evidence identifying him
as the criminal, but also to deny the truthful, but highly damaging, testimony of the corroborating witness who placed him
one block away from the intersection five minutes prior to the
crime. Of course, if he tells the truth and thus verifies the corroborating witness, the jury will be more inclined to accept the
inaccurate testimony of the principal witness, who specifically
identified him as the criminal.

In my opinion, the attorney's obligation in such a situation
would be to advise the client that the proposed testimony is
unlawful, but to proceed in the normal fashion in presenting the
testimony and arguing the case to the jury if the client makes
the decision to go forward. Any other course would be a betrayal
of the assurances of confidentiality given by the attorney in order
to induce the client to reveal everything, however damaging it
might appear.

A frequent objection to the position that the attorney must
go along with the client's decision to commit perjury is that the
lawyer would be guilty of subornation of perjury. Subornation,
however, consists of willfully procuring perjury, which is not the
case when the attorney indicates to the client that the client's
proposed course of conduct would be unlawful, but then accepts
the client's decision.** Beyond that, there is a point of view,
which has been expressed to me by a number of experienced
attorneys, that the criminal defendant has a "right to tell his
story". What that suggests is that it is simply too much to expect
of a human being, caught up in the criminal process and facing
loss of liberty and the horrors of imprisonment, not to attempt
to lie to avoid that penalty. For that reason, criminal defendants
in most European countries do not testify under oath, but simply
"tell their stories". It is also noteworthy that subsequent perjury
prosecutions against criminal defendants in this country are
extremely rare. However, the judge may well take into account

---

* The question of the propriety of cross-examining an accurate and
truthful witness is considered in Chapter 4 *infra*.

** The analysis at pp. 5-6 *supra*, regarding the applicability of criminal
statutes generally to the lawyer-client relationship, is also applicable here.

at sentencing the fact that the defendant has apparently committed perjury in the course of the defense.[16] That is certainly a factor that the attorney is obligated to advise the client about whenever there is any indication that the client is contemplating perjury.

The discussion thus far has focused only on the lawyer's obligation when the perjury is presented by the client. Some authorities indicate a distinction between perjury by the criminal defendant, who has a right to take the stand, and perjury by collateral witnesses.[17] I agree that there is an important distinction, and that the case involving collateral witnesses is not at all as clear as that involving the client alone. In one case, however, a new trial was ordered when the trial court discovered that the defendant's attorney had refused to put on the defendant's mother and sister because the attorney was concerned about perjury.[18] Certainly a spouse or parent would be acting under the same human compulsion as a defendant, and I find it difficult to imagine myself denouncing my client's spouse or parent as a perjurer and, thereby, denouncing my client as well. I do not know, however, how much wider that circle of close identity might be drawn.

In a criticism of my position, Professor John Noonan of Boalt Hall argued that the true function of the advocate is to assist the trier of fact to reach a "wise and informed decision".[19] Upon analysis, however, that proposition only compounds the problem. For example, I have suggested that a criminal defendant is privileged to lie to the court in pleading "not guilty" even when the defendant knows that the plea is contrary to fact. Professor Noonan responded that the not-guilty plea, as used in the context of a court proceeding, is not a lie, because it is understood by everyone to mean: "I cannot be proved guilty of the charge by the ordinary process of law".[20] The "ordinary process of law", however, unquestionably includes the constitutional right to suppress relevant and truthful evidence that has been obtained in violation of constitutional rights—even though a wise and informed judgment might thereby be sacrificed. Thus, in order to justify or rationalize the false plea of not guilty, Professor Noonan is thrown back to a recognition of those aspects of the system that are inconsistent with his rationale. Certainly it is unlikely that Professor Noonan would suggest that attorneys should relinquish their clients' constitutional rights where those rights conflict with truth-seeking. Yet he does argue that attorneys should forego long-accepted trial tactics (*e.g.,* cross-examination of the relevant and truthful witness), because: "Repeated acts of confidence in the rationality of the trial system are necessary if the decision-making process is to approach rationality."[21] That seems to mean that the fortunes, liberty, and lives of today's clients can properly be jeopardized for the sake of creating a more rational system for tomorrow's litigants.

Moreover, Professor Noonan's general proposition does not decide specific cases. Like other critics who express disapproval of the idea that a lawyer might knowingly present perjured testimony, Professor Noonan does not suggest what a lawyer should do, as a practical matter, in the course of conferring with the client and presenting the case in court. For example, how would Professor Noonan's proposition resolve the following case? The prosecution witness testified that the robbery had taken place at 10:15, and identified the defendant as the criminal. However, the defendant had a convincing alibi for 10:00 to 10:30. The attorney presented the alibi, and the client was acquitted. The alibi was truthful, but the attorney knew that the prosecution witness had been confused about the time, and that his client had in fact committed the crime at 10:45. (Ironically, that same attorney considers it clearly unethical for a lawyer to present the false testimony on behalf of the innocent defendant in the case of the robbery at 16th and P Streets.) Should the lawyer have refused to present the honest alibi? How could he possibly have avoided doing so? Was he contributing to wise and informed judgment when he did present it?

The most obvious way to avoid the ethical difficulty is for the lawyer to withdraw from the case, at least if there is sufficient time before trial for the client to retain another attorney. The client will then go to the nearest law office, realizing that the obligation of confidentiality is not what it has been represented to be, and withhold incriminating information or the fact of guilt from the new attorney. In terms of professional ethics, the practice of withdrawing from a case under such circumstances is difficult to defend, since the identical perjured testimony will ultimately be presented. Moreover, the new attorney will be ignorant of the perjury and therefore will be in no position to attempt to discourage the client from presenting it. Only the original attorney, who knows the truth, has that opportunity, but loses it in the very act of evading the ethical problem.

The difficulty is all the more severe when the client is indigent. In that event, the client cannot retain other counsel, and in many jurisdictions it is impossible for appointed counsel or a public defender to withdraw from a case except for extraordinary reasons. Thus, the attorney can successfully withdraw only by revealing to the judge that the attorney has received knowledge of the client's guilt,* or by giving the judge a false or misleading reason for moving for leave to withdraw. However, for the attorney to reveal knowledge of the client's guilt would be a gross violation of the obligation of confidentiality, particularly since it is entirely possible in many jurisdictions that the same judge who permits the attorney to withdraw will subsequently hear the case and sentence the defendant.[22] Not only will the judge then have personal knowledge of the defendant's guilt before the trial begins, but it will be knowledge of which the newly appointed counsel for the defendant will very likely be ignorant.

Even where counsel is retained, withdrawal may not be a practical solution either because trial has begun or it is so close to trial that withdrawal would leave the client without counsel, or because the court for other reasons denies leave to withdraw.[23] Judges are most reluctant to grant leave to withdraw during the trial or even shortly before it because of the power that that would give to defendants to delay the trial date or even to cause a series of mistrials.

Another solution that has been suggested is that the attorney move for leave to withdraw and that, when the request is denied, the attorney then proceed with the case, eliciting the defendant's testimony and arguing the case to the jury in the ordinary fashion. Since that proposal proceeds on the assumption that the motion will be denied, it seems to me to be disingenuous. If the attorney avoids the ethical problem, it is only by passing it on to the judge. Moreover, the client in such a case would then have grounds for appeal on the basis of deprivation of due process and denial of the right to counsel, since the defendant would have been tried before, and sentenced by, a judge who had been informed by the defendant's own lawyer that the defendant is guilty both of the crime charged and of perjury. The prejudice inherent in such a situation is illustrated by a federal appellate case in which the majority voted to remand the case to determine whether the defendant had been denied certain due process rights. One judge dissented, however, expressly basing his opinion in part on incriminating information that had been put into the record by the defendant's own counsel.**

---

* The typical formula is for the attorney to advise the judge of "an ethical problem". The judge understands that to mean that the client is insisting upon a perjured alibi over the lawyer's objections. In one case, the judge incorrectly drew that inference when the lawyer's ethical concern was with the fact that the client wanted to enter a guilty plea despite the fact that he was innocent.

** Holmes v. United States, 370 F.2d 209, 212 (D.C. Cir. 1966) (Danaher, J.):

"Finding the Holmes testimony at variance from the opening statement made by his trial attorney, the latter in the absence of the jury ad-

Another unsucessful effort to deal with the problem appears in the ABA Standards Relating to the Defense Function. The Standards first attempt to solve the problem by a rhetorical attack, unsupported by practical analysis or verifiable research, upon those who are concerned with maintaining confidentiality. Thus, the Standards state that it has been "universally rejected by the legal profession" that a lawyer may be excused for acquiescing in the use of known perjured testimony on the "transparently spurious thesis" that the principle of confidentiality requires it. While "no honorable lawyer" would accept that view and "every experienced advocate can see its basic fallacy as a matter of tactics apart from morality and law", the "mere advocacy" of such an idea "demeans the profession and tends to drag it to the level of gangsters and their 'mouthpiece' lawyers in the public eye". The Standards conclude that that concept is "universally repudiated by ethical lawyers", although that fact does not fully repair the "gross disservice" done by the few who are "unscrupulous" enough to practice it.[24]

One hundred thirty-two pages later, however, the Standards express a very different assessment of lawyers' attitudes regarding perjury by the client. Although "some lawyers" are said to favor disclosure of the perjury, the Standards recognize that other attorneys (not characterized in the pejorative terms of the earlier passage) hold that the obligation of confidentiality does not permit disclosure of the facts learned from the client. To disclose the perjury, it is noted, "would be inconsistent with the assurances of confidentiality which counsel gave at the outset of the lawyer-client relationship".[25] Thus, the Standards acknowledge a genuine "dilemma" in the forced choice between candor and confidentiality.[26]

Since there are actually three obligations that create the difficulty—the third being the attorney's duty to learn all the facts—there is, of course, another way to resolve the difficulty. That is, by "selective ignorance". The attorney can make it clear to the client from the outset that the attorney does not want to hear an admission of guilt or incriminating information from

---

dressed the court: 'For purposes of the record, Your Honor, about half of what the defendant said on the stand was a complete surprise to me.'

"He added that in the course of 'numerous interviews' the appellant had 'consistently told me' a different story. The attorney asked Holmes no further questions.

"From the foregoing, some idea can be gleaned as to why I do not join my colleagues in thinking there even possibly could have been 'prejudice.'" (Emphasis added.)

the client.* That view, however, puts an unreasonable burden on the unsophisticated client to select what to tell and what to hold back, and it can seriously impair the attorney's effectiveness in counselling the client and in trying the case.

For example, one leading attorney, who favors selective ignorance to avoid the trilemma, told me about one of his own cases in which the defendant assumed that the attorney would prefer to be ignorant of the fact that the defendant had been having sexual relations with the chief defense witness. As a result of the lawyer's ignorance of that fact, he was unable to minimize its impact by raising it with potential jurors during jury selection and by having the defendant and the defense witness admit it freely on direct examination. Instead, the first time the lawyer learned about the illicit sexual relationship was when the prosecutor dramatically obtained a reluctant admission from the defense witness on cross-examination. The defense attorney is convinced that the client was innocent of the robbery with which he had been charged, but the defendant was nevertheless found guilty by the jury—in the attorney's own opinion because the defendant was guilty of fornication, a far less serious offense for which he had not been charged.

The question remains: what should the lawyer do when faced with the client's insistence upon taking the stand and committing perjury? It is in response to that question that the Standards present a most extraordinary solution. If the lawyer knows that the client is going to commit perjury, Section 7.7 of the Standards requires that the lawyer "must confine his examination to identifying the witness as the defendant and permitting him to make his statement". That is, the lawyer "may not engage in direct examination of the defendant . . . in the conventional manner". Thus, the client's story will become part of the record, although without the attorney's assistance through direct examination. The general rule, of course, is that in closing argument to the jury "the lawyer may argue all reasonable inferences from the evidence in the record".[27] Section 7.7 also provides, however, that the defense lawyer is forbidden to make any reference in closing argument to the client's testimony.

---

* The ABA Standards again employ harsh rhetoric in criticizing a viewpoint of which they disapprove: "The most flagrant form of the practice of 'intentional ignorance' on the part of defense lawyers is the tactic, occasionally advocated by unscrupulous lawyers both in private and in practice manuals and seminars, of advising the client at the outset not to admit anything to the lawyer which might handicap the lawyer's freedom in calling witnesses or in otherwise making a defense." According to the Standards, that tactic is "most egregious" and constitutes "professional impropriety". ABA STANDARDS RELATING TO THE DEFENSE FUNCTION, COMMENTARY b to § 3.2, at 205.

There are at least two critical flaws in that proposal. The first
is purely practical: The prosecutor might well object to testimony
from the defendant in narrative form rather than in the conventional manner, because it would give the prosecutor no
opportunity to object to inadmissible evidence prior to the jury's
hearing it. The Standards provide no guidance as to what the
defense attorney should do if the objection is sustained.

More importantly, experienced trial attorneys have often noted
that jurors assume that the defendant's lawyer knows the truth
about the case, and that the jury will frequently judge the
defendant by drawing inferences from the attorney's conduct in
the case.[28] There is, of course, only one inference that can be
drawn if the defendant's own attorney turns his or her back on
the defendant at the most critical point in the trial, and then,
in closing argument, sums up the case with no reference to the
fact that the defendant has given exculpatory testimony. As
held by a federal court:

> . . . The failure to argue the case before the jury, while
> ordinarily only a trial tactic not subject to review, manifestly
> enters the field of incompetency when the reason assigned is
> the attorney's conscience. *It is as improper as though the
> attorney had told the jury that his client had uttered a false-
> hood in making the statement.* The right to an attorney
> embraces effective representation throughout all stages of the
> trial, and where the representation is of such low caliber as to
> amount to no representation, the guarantee of due process
> has been violated.[29]

Similarly, Professor Addison Bowman of Georgetown Law Center
(an experienced trial lawyer, and a member of the Legal Ethics
Committee of the District of Columbia Bar) has stated: "I do
not believe it is proper for defense counsel to present the defendant's testimony in a fashion that may lead the jury to conclude that counsel does not believe his client."[30] Ironically, the
Standards reject any solution that would involve informing the
judge,[31] but then propose a solution that, as a practical matter,
succeeds in informing not only the judge but the jury as well.

It would appear that the ABA Standards have chosen to resolve
the trilemma by maintaining the requirements of complete knowledge and of candor to the court, and sacrificing confidentiality.
Interestingly, however, that may not in fact be the case. I say that
because the Standards fail to answer a critically important question: Should the client be told about the obligation imposed by
Section 7.7? That is, the Standards ignore the issue of whether the
lawyer should say to the client at the outset of their relationship:

"I think it's only fair that I warn you: If you should tell me anything incriminating and subsequently decide to deny the incriminating facts at trial, I would not be able to examine you in the
ordinary manner or to argue your untrue testimony to the jury."
The Canadian Bar Association, for example, takes an extremely
hard line against the presentation of perjury by the client, but it
also explicitly requires that the client be put on notice of that
fact.[32] Obviously, any other course would be a betrayal of the
client's trust, since everything else said by the attorney in attempting to obtain complete information about the case would
indicate to the client that no information thus obtained would
be used to the client's disadvantage.[33]

On the other hand, the inevitable result of the position taken
by the Canadian Bar Association would be to caution the client
not to be completely candid with the attorney. That, of course,
returns us to resolving the trilemma by maintaining confidentiality
and candor, but sacrificing complete knowledge—a solution which,
as we have already seen, is denounced by the Standards as "unscrupulous", "most egregious", and "professional impropriety".[34]

Thus, the Standards, by failing to face up to the question of
whether to put the client on notice, take us out of the trilemma
by one door only to lead us back by another.

Earlier in this chapter we noted that the Code appears to be
unambiguous in proscribing the known use of perjured testimony, but that the Code does not indicate how the lawyer is to go
about fulfilling that obligation. Analysis of the various alternatives that have been suggested shows that none of them is wholly
satisfactory, and that some are impractical and violate basic
rights of the client. In addition the ABA Standards rely upon
unsupported assertions of what lawyers "universally" think and
do. It is therefore relevant and important to consider the actual
practices of attorneys faced with the ethical issue in their daily
work.

A survey conducted among lawyers in the District of Columbia
is extremely revealing. The overall conclusion is that "less than
5% of practicing attorneys queried consistently acted in a manner
the legal profession claims that members of the Bar act, and, under
the new Code of Professional Responsibility, demands that they
act".[35] Specifically, when asked what to do when the client indicates an intention to commit perjury, 95% indicated that they
would call the defendant, and 90% of those attorneys responded
that they would question the witness in the normal fashion.[36]*

---

* The attorneys in the survey reflected, as a group, an ambivalence similar to that expressed above at p. 32 regarding the propriety of putting on a
perjurious witness other than the defendant. Only a bare majority (52%)

That striking discrepancy between published standards and professional action is perhaps best explained by attorneys' re-actions to being asked to participate in the survey. Virtually all of the attorneys personally interviewed refused to make an on-the-record statement, although without exception they were will-ing to participate in an anonymous interview.[37] Senior partners of two of Washington's most prestigious law firms, after refusing to allow the circulation of the questionnaire among the firm's mem-bers, permitted personal interviews on the condition that neither their names, names of the other members in the firm interviewed, nor the name of their firm would be published. Both attorneys, after apologizing for their insistence upon anonymity, explained that many of the local judges with whom they dealt daily would not look favorably upon their true views about the role of the defense attorney in a criminal case, especially if aired publicly. Their reason for not complying with the ABA's rules relating to the presentation of perjury was that those standards would com-promise their role as advocates in an adversary system.[38]

In view of those findings, which stem in substantial part from the impracticality of the published standards, we might return to the relevant provisions of the Code with a somewhat more critical eye to consider whether the rules really mean what they appear at first reading to say.*

The cases cited by the codifiers provide important clues as to what is intended. The strongest of the cases against confiden-tiality is *In re Carroll*,[39] which held that an attorney "should not sit by silently and permit his client to commit what may have been perjury, and which certainly would mislead the court and the opposing party". Two important observations can be made about that case. First, it was not a criminal case, but involved a divorce. Second, the husband, whom the attorney represented, testified that he did not own certain property, but the same at-torney had been authorized by the husband to claim ownership of the property in another judicial proceeding. Thus, the bond of confidentiality had already been loosened by the client's author-

---

answered in the affirmative, although a substantial number of those in the negative responded on tactical, not ethical, grounds. Friedman, *infra* note 34, at 69, 82. Unfortunately, the question was not broken down to distinguish between testimony by a spouse or parent as against, say, a casual acquaintance.

  * DR 7-102 (A) (4), which deals with the use of perjured testimony, turns upon whether the lawyer acts "knowingly". As we will see in a later chapter, that word is a term of art—or, put less charitably, a term of evasion—in the area of legal ethics. There are those who say that the lawyer never "knows" that the client is guilty or lying. For those lawyers the ethical question never arises, and the provisions of the Code and the Standards therefore never come into play.

ization. Third, assuming that *Carroll* does stand as unqualified
authority on behalf of divulgence, it is significant that the case is
cited as a footnote to an Ethical Consideration (which is only "aspirational in character") and not a Disciplinary Rule (which is
"mandatory in character", stating a "minimum level of conduct
below which no lawyer can fall without being subject to disciplinary action").[40]

The case citation to the applicable Disciplinary Rule, DR 7-
102, is significantly different. That case, *Hinds v. State Bar*,[41] also
involved a divorce rather than a criminal matter. Most important, the attorney had participated in preparing the perjured affidavit that was at issue. (Also, the attorney was shown to
have altered the client's deed to make the attorney's daughter a
grantee, and apparently perjured himself in testifying in connection with the disciplinary proceeding.) Putting the *Carroll* and
Hinds cases together, therefore, we may infer that the rule—in
civil cases—is that an attorney is urged (by an Ethical Consideration) to divulge the client's fraud on the other party, at least
when the client has authorized disclosure of the truth for other
purposes, but the attorney is required to divulge the client's
perjury, under sanction of a Disciplinary Rule, only when the
attorney has participated in creation of the perjury.

There is another relevant citation in the notes to Canon 7.
That case is *Johns v. Smyth*,[42] which, unlike the other two cases
in point, is a criminal case. *Johns* is in a note to the opening
sentence of EC 7-1, which reads: "The duty of a lawyer, both to
his client and to the legal system, is to represent his client zealously *within the bounds of the law, which includes Disciplinary
Rules. . . .*"[43] The case held that a defendant's constitutional rights
had been violated because the attorney, believing his client to be
guilty, did not argue the case in the ordinary manner.

Taking into account, therefore, the lack of practical guidance
in the Code, the practical and constitutional difficulties en-
countered by any of the alternatives to strict maintenance of
confidentiality, the consensus and the practice of the Bar, and the
implications of *Carroll, Hinds* and *Johns,* which are the three
key cases cited in the notes to Canon 7, I continue to stand with
those lawyers who hold that "the lawyer's obligation of confidentiality does not permit him to disclose the facts he has learned
from his client which form the basis for his conclusion that the
client intends to perjure himself".[44] What that means—necessarily, it seems to me—is that the criminal defense attorney, however unwillingly in terms of personal morality, has a professional
responsibility as an advocate in an adversary system to examine

the perjurious client in the ordinary way and to argue to the jury, as evidence in the case, the testimony presented by the defendant.

Footnotes

[1] AMERICAN BAR ASSOCIATION, STANDARDS RELATING TO THE DEFENSE FUNCTION, § 3.2 (a) (1971) [hereinafter cited as ABA STANDARDS].

[2] AMERICAN BAR ASSOCIATION, COMMITTEE ON PROFESSIONAL ETHICS AND GRIEVANCES, OPINION 23 (1930).

[3] ABA STANDARDS, COMMENTARY a, at 204-05.

[4] ABA STANDARDS, COMMENTARY a, at 201.

[5] *Id.*, quoting Taylor v. Blacklow, 3 Bing. N.C. 235, 249, 132 Eng. Rep. 401, 406, C.R. (1836).

[6] ABA STANDARDS, § 3.1 (a).

[7] AMERICAN BAR ASSOCIATION, CANONS OF PROFESSIONAL ETHICS, CANON 22 (1908).

[8] AMERICAN BAR ASSOCIATION, COMMITTEE ON PROFESSIONAL ETHICS AND GRIEVANCES, OPINION 287 (1953).

[9] AMERICAN BAR ASSOCIATION, CODE OF PROFESSIONAL RESPONSIBILITY (1970) [hereinafter cited as THE CODE].

[10] BAR OF QUEBEC, CODE OF ETHICS (Revised Draft, 1974).

[11] T. LUND, A GUIDE TO THE PROFESSIONAL CONDUCT OF SOLICITORS 105 (1960).

[12] The argument for the amendment stated in part: "The effect of the Code provision can be illustrated by a divorce case. At the husband's deposition he produces his tax return and testifies that it is complete and accurate. Through confidential communications from his client, the husband's attorney learns that the husband has additional, unreported income. The attorney urges him to correct his false testimony, and he refuses to do so. The proposed DR subjects the attorney to discipline if he does not reveal the unreported income to the wife and her attorney, to the court, and to the IRS. . . ."

[13] ABA STANDARDS, SUPPLEMENT, at 18.

[14] *See also,* DR 7-102 (A) (5), (7) and (8); EC 7-26.

[15] Paul, *The Responsibilities of the Tax Adviser,* 63 HARV. L. REV. 377, 383 (1950).

[16] *Cf.* United States v. Hendrix, Docket No. 74-1603 (2d Cir., Sept. 15, 1974).

[17] *See, e.g.,* DR 7-102 (B); ABA STANDARDS, COMMENTARY a to § 7.5; Bowman, *Standards of Conduct for Prosecution and Defense Personnel: An Attorney's Viewpoint,* 5 AM. CRIM. L. Q. 28, 30 (1966).

[18] *See,* Washington Post, Oct. 31, 1971, § D, at 3.

[19] Noonan, *The Purposes of Advocacy and the Limits of Confidentiality,* 64 MICH. L. REV. 1485 (1966). Professor Noonan drew his rationale from *Professional Responsibility: Report of the Joint Conference,* 44 A.B.A.J. 1160-61 (1958).

[20] *Id.* at 1491-92, n. 28.

[21] *Id.* at 1487-88.

[22] *Accord,* ABA STANDARDS, at 12.

[23] ABA STANDARDS, at 275. *See also,* Freedman, *Professional Responsibility of the Criminal Defense Lawyer: The Three Hardest Questions,* 64 MICH. L. REV. 1469, 1476-77 (1966).

[24] ABA STANDARDS, at 142.

[25] *Id.* at 276.

[26] *Id.*

[27] ABA STANDARDS, § 7.8.

[28] *See,* Burger, *A Sick Profession?,* 27 FED. B. J. 228, 229-30 (1967).

[29] Johns v. Smyth, 176 F. Supp. 949, 953 (E.D. Va. 1959) (emphasis added) (cited, THE CODE, at 29, n. 3).

[30] Bowman, *supra* note 16, at 28, 30.

[31] ABA Standards, at 12, 227.

[32] Canadian Bar Association, Code of Professional Conduct, Ch. VIII, ¶ 9, at 59-60, 62-64 (Special Committee on Legal Ethics, Preliminary Report, June, 1973).

[33] *See,* Orkin, *Defence of One Known to be Guilty,* 1 Crim. L. Q. 170, 174 (1958). Unless the lawyer has told the client at the outset that knowledge of guilt will require the lawyer to withdraw, "it is plain enough as a matter of good morals and professional ethics" that the lawyer should not withdraw on that ground. American Bar Association, Committee on Professional Ethics and Grievances, Opinion 90 (1932).

[34] *See,* pp. 35-36 *supra.*

[35] Friedman, *Professional Responsibility in D.C.: A Survey,* 1972 Res Ipsa Loquitur 60 (1972).

[36] *Id.* at 81.

[37] *Id.* at 60.

[38] *Id.* at 60, n. 3.

[39] 244 S.W.2d 474 (Ky. Ct. App. 1951).

[40] The Code, Preliminary Statement.

[41] 19 Cal. 2d 87, 119 P.2d 134 (1941).

[42] 176 F. Supp. 949 (E.D. Va. 1959).

[43] Emphasis added.

[44] ABA Standards, Commentary to § 7.7, at 276.

Chapter 4

CROSS-EXAMINATION: DESTROYING
THE TRUTHFUL WITNESS

More difficult than the question of whether the criminal defense lawyer should present known perjury, is the question of whether the attorney should cross-examine a witness who is testifying accurately and truthfully, in order to make the witness appear to be mistaken or lying. The issue was raised effectively in a symposium on legal ethics through the following hypothetical case.[1]

The accused is a drifter who sometimes works as a filling station attendant. He is charged with rape, a capital crime. You are his court-appointed defense counsel. The alleged victim is the twenty-two-year-old daughter of a local bank president. She is engaged to a promising young minister in town. The alleged rape occurred in the early morning hours at a service station some distance from town, where the accused was employed as an at-tendant. That is all you know about the case when you have your first interview with your client.

At first the accused will not talk at all. You assure him that you cannot help him unless you know the truth and that he can trust you to treat what he says as confidential. He then says that he had intercourse with the young woman, but that she "con-sented in every way". He says that he had seen her two or three times before when he was working the day shift at the station, and that she had seemed "very friendly" and had talked with him in a "flirting way". He says that on the night in question she came in for gas; they talked; and she invited him into the car. One thing led to another and, finally, to sexual intercourse. They were interrupted by the lights of an approaching vehicle which pulled into the station. The accused relates that he got out of the young woman's car and waited on the customer. The young woman hurriedly drove off.

The accused tells you he was tried for rape in California four years ago and acquitted. He has no previous convictions.

At the grand jury proceedings the victim testifies that she was returning to her father's house in town from the church camp, where her fiancé was a counselor, when she noticed that her fuel gauge registered empty. She stopped at the first station along the road that was open. The attendant, who seemed to be in sole charge of the station, forced his way into her car, terrified her with threats, and forcibly had sexual intercourse with her. She says he was compelled to stop when an approaching car turned into the station. The alleged victim's father testified as to her timely complaint. No other testimony is presented. The grand jury returns a true bill.

You learn that the victim has had affairs with two local men from good families. Smith, one of these young men, admits that the victim and he went together for some time, but refuses to say whether he had sexual intercourse with her and indicates he has a low opinion of you for asking. The other, Jones, apparently a bitterly disappointed and jealous suitor, readily states that he frequently had intercourse with the victim, and describes her behavior toward strange men as scandalous. He once took her to a fraternity dance, he says, and, having noticed she had been gone for some time, discovered her upstairs with Smith, a fraternity brother, on a bed in a state of semi-undress. He appears eager to testify and he states that the girl got what she'd always been asking for. You believe Jones, but are somewhat repelled by the disappointed suitor's apparent willingness to smear the young woman's reputation.

Suppose the accused, after you press him, admits that he forced himself on the victim and admits that his first story was a lie. He refuses to plead guilty to the charge or any lesser charge. He says that he can get away with his story, because he did once before in California.

Should the defense lawyer use the information supplied by Jones to impeach the young woman and, if necessary, call Jones as a witness?

One of the panelists who spoke to that question was Chief Justice (then Judge) Burger. The Chief Justice first discussed the question in terms of "basic and fundamental rules". One of those rules, which he characterized as "clear-cut and unambiguous", is that "a lawyer may never, under any circumstances, knowingly . . . participate in a fraud on the court". That rule, he said, "can never admit of any exception, under any circumstances", and no other consideration "can ever justify a knowing and conscious departure" from it. Moreover, only the "naive and inexperienced" would take a contrary position, which is a "perversion and prostitution of an honorable profession". Indeed, the Chief Justice held any other view to be "so utterly absurd that one wonders why the subject need even be discussed among persons trained in the law".[2]

After that powerful rhetoric, Chief Justice Burger's response to the question posed is a matter of some astonishment. The function of an advocate, and "particularly the defense advocate in the adversary system", is to use "all the legitimate tools available to test the truth of the prosecution's case". Therefore, he concluded, "the testimony of bad repute of the complaining witness, being recent and not remote in point of time, is relevant to her credibility".[3] The Chief Justice was even more explicit in the question period following the panel discussion: he considers it ethical to cast doubt on the woman's credibility by destroying her reputation, even though the lawyer knows that she is telling the truth.

That, of course, is sanction for nothing less than a deliberate attempt to perpetrate a fraud upon the finder of fact. The lawyer knows that the client is guilty and that the prosecutrix is truthful. In cross-examining, the lawyer has one purpose, and one purpose only: to make it appear, contrary to fact, that the prosecutrix is lying in testifying that she was raped.

There is only one difference in practical effect between presenting the defendant's perjured alibi—which the Chief Justice considers to be clearly improper—and impeaching the truthful prosecutrix. In both cases, the lawyer participates in an attempt to free a guilty defendant. In both cases, the lawyer participates in misleading the finder of fact. In the case of the perjured witness, however, the attorney asks only nonleading questions, while in the case of impeachment, the lawyer takes an active, aggressive role, using professional training and skills, including leading questions, in a one-on-one attack upon the client's victim. The lawyer thereby personally and directly adds to the suffering of the prosecutrix, her family, and the minister to whom she is engaged. In short, under the euphemism of "testing the truth of the prosecution's case", the lawyer communicates, to the jury and to the community, the most vicious of lies.

That case takes us to the heart of my disagreement with the traditional approach to dealing with difficult questions of professional responsibility. That approach has two characteristics. First, in a rhetorical flourish, the profession is committed in general terms to all that is good and true. Then, specific questions are answered by uncritical reliance upon legalistic norms, regardless of the context in which the lawyer may be acting, and regardless of the motive and the consequences of the act. Perjury is wrong, and therefore no lawyer, in any circumstance, should knowingly present perjury. Cross-examination, however, is good, and therefore any lawyer, under any circumstances and regardless of the consequences, can properly impeach a witness through cross-examination. The system of professional responsibility that I have been advancing, on the other hand, is one that attempts to deal with ethical problems in context—that is, as part of a functional sociopolitical system concerned with the administration of justice in a free society—and giving due regard both to motive and to consequences. In that respect, the debate returns us to some fundamental philosophical questions that have not been adequately developed in the literature of professional responsibility.

The classic exposition of a legalistic, anti-utilitarian ethical system is that of Immanuel Kant.[4] In assessing moral worth, Kant rejects any concern with motive or purpose, but relies exclusively upon fulfillment of duty as expressed in a maxim of conduct. Thus, says Kant, "the moral worth of an action does not lie in the effect expected from it, nor in any principle of action which requires to borrow its motive from this expected effect".

Kant's only test of the validity of a maxim is whether one is prepared to will the maxim to be a universal law. Referring specifically to lying, Kant suggests that it is improper to reason: "I should not lie, because then no one would thereafter believe me." The error in that, Kant says, is that one would then be telling the truth "from apprehension of injurious consequences", rather than from duty to principle. Assume, for example, that one is in a difficult situation which can be avoided only by telling a lie. One might say that everyone may tell a lie in order to escape a difficulty that otherwise cannot be avoided. However: "I presently become aware that while I can will the lie, I can by no means will that lying should be a universal law." From there, Kant reasons that telling the truth is a universal law, and that it cannot be violated under any circumstances. Thus, if a victim is fleeing from a would-be murderer, one must answer the murderer truthfully when asked where the victim is hiding. Lying—violation of principle—cannot be justified by mere expediency.

In response to that proposition, it would seem to be adequate to observe that there is something wrong with a system of morality that places a higher value upon one's moral rectitude with respect to lying, than upon the preservation of an innocent person's life. The legalistic mind, however, does not recognize such conflicts of principle; for example, what if one had already promised the victim to give him protection, and could only be truthful to the murderer by breaking one's word to the victim? That difficulty, of course, precisely parallels the problems faced by the criminal defense lawyer who has entered into an obligation of trust with the client, and who can avoid violating that trust only by presenting the client's perjury. One can agree with Chief

Justice Burger that lying is wrong, and still not know the answer to the question of whether it is worse to lie to the client or to lie to the court.*

There is an extremely important aspect of Kant's rejection of utilitarianism, however, which is frequently overlooked. That is, in holding that one must obey a maxim without regard to consequences, Kant is speaking at the level of personal morality. When he leaves the level of personal morality, and addresses himself to morality in systemic terms, Kant is entirely pragmatic. Thus, the fundamental question of whether a maxim is valid in the first instance (as distinguished from whether a valid maxim should be obeyed) is determined by the utilitarian concern with whether that maxim can be universalized, that is, with whether that maxim can be embodied into a viable system. For example, Kant determines that lying in order to extricate oneself from a difficulty cannot be universalized, because "with such a law there would be no promises at all, since it would be in vain to allege my intention in regard to my future actions to those who would not believe this allegation, or if they over-hastily did so, would pay me back in my own coin". Hence, he concludes, "my maxim, as soon as it should be made a universal law, would necessarily destroy itself". In short, in judging the morality of a maxim, considerations of disadvantage "to myself or even to others" are irrelevant, but disadvantage to the system—whether the maxim can "enter as a principle in a possible universal legislation"—is vital.

One of the major flaws in the traditional approach to legal ethics is that it seeks to answer the difficult questions in a legalistic fashion at the personal level, but begs completely the critical questions raised at the systemic level. Thus, if you say to a lawyer: "Lawyers are under a moral duty not to participate in the presentation of perjury, and therefore you are required to act in a way contrary to your client's interest if the client insists upon committing perjury", the lawyer is entitled to respond: "Let us consider your maxim. If it is embodied into the system as a universal law to be applied to all lawyers in all circumstances, would the maxim destroy itself and be destructive of the system?"

---

* Although Chief Justice Burger shares Kant's legalistic approach to obedience to norms, the Chief Justice does not reject, as Kant does, all selfishly pragmatic concerns. Thus, Kant singles out for condemnation one who says: "I ought not to lie if I would retain my reputation." Chief Justice Burger, on the other hand, has frequently stressed, at least as a secondary concern, that a lawyer who places confidentiality over candor will suffer in reputation and thereby in effectiveness as an advocate. *See, e.g.,* Burger, *infra* note 2, at 11, 13.

As we have seen in the previous chapters, the system requires the attorney to know everything that the client knows that is relevant to the case. In order to enable the lawyer to obtain that information, the system provides for an obligation of confidentiality, designed to protect the client from being prejudiced by disclosures to the attorney. In addition, the attorney is required to impress upon the client the obligation of confidentiality in order to induce the client to confide freely and fully.

Let us return, then, to the case involving the street robbery at 16th and P Streets, in which the defendant has been wrongly identified as the criminal, but correctly identified by the nervous, elderly woman who wears eyeglasses, as having been only a block away five minutes before the crime took place. If the woman is not cross-examined vigorously and her testimony shaken, it will serve to corroborate the erroneous evidence of guilt. On the other hand, the lawyer could take the position that since the woman is testifying truthfully and accurately, she should not be made to appear to be mistaken or lying. But if a similar course were to be adopted by every lawyer who learned the truth through confidential disclosures from the client, such disclosures would soon cease to be made. The result, for practical purposes, would be identical with the practice, disapproved in the ABA Standards, of "selective ignorance", in which the client is warned not to reveal to the lawyer anything that might prove embarrassing and prevent the lawyer from doing a vigorous job of presenting evidence and cross-examining.[5] Of course, if that is the result we want, it would be far better that lawyers take a direct and honest approach with their clients, telling them to be less than candid, rather than lying to their clients by impressing upon them a bond of trust that the lawyers do not intend to maintain. Thus, when we examine the problem in a systemic context, we reach the conclusion that Chief Justice Burger was correct, although for the wrong reason, in supporting cross-examination of the prosecutrix in the rape case.

Obviously, however, the rape case is a much harder one, because the injury done to the prosecutrix is far more severe than the more limited humiliation of the public-spirited and truthful witness in the case of the street robbery. In addition, in the rape case, the lawyer is acting pursuant to a manifestly irrational rule, that is, one that permits the defense to argue that the prosecutrix is the kind of person who would have sexual intercourse with a stranger because she has had sexual relations with two men whom she knew in wholly different social circumstances. Irrational or not, however, in those jurisdictions in which the defense of unchastity is still the law, the attorney is bound to provide it on the client's behalf.[6] For the lawyer who finds the presentation of that defense, and perhaps others in rape cases, to go beyond what he or she can in good conscience do, there are two courses that should be followed. The first is to be active in efforts to reform the law in that regard; the second is to decline to accept the defense of rape cases, on the grounds of a conflict of interest (a strong personal view)[7] that would interfere with providing the defendant with his constitutional right to effective assistance of counsel.

Footnotes

[1] Symposium, *Standards of Conduct for Prosecution and Defense Personnel*, 5 Am. Crim. L. Q. 8 (1966).

[2] Burger, *Standards of Conduct for Prosecution and Defense Personnel: A Judge's Viewpoint*, 5 Am. Crim. L. Q. 11, 12 (1966).

[3] *Id.* at 14-15.

[4] The discussion that follows is based primarily upon I. Kant, Fundamental Principles of the Metaphysics of Morals (T. K. Abbott, transl. 1949).

[5] *See,* pp. 35-36 *supra.*

[6] DR 7-101 (A) (1).

[7] DR 5-101 (A); EC 5-1, 5-2.

Chapter 5

WHAT DOES A LAWYER REALLY "KNOW": THE EPISTEMOLOGY OF LEGAL ETHICS

The discussion in the preceding chapters, regarding what a lawyer should do when the lawyer knows that the client is guilty, has proceeded on a premise that has not been adequately examined. That is, does the lawyer ever "really know" that a client is guilty? If not, then any discussion of legal ethics, based upon an assumption of "knowing", is of no practical significance. Thus, in a speech to a group of law students in 1966, Edward Bennett Williams professed to have experienced no ethical difficulty regarding the presentation of perjury, on the assertion that: "I never know whether a client is guilty." On the other hand, a former associate of Mr. Williams subsequently remarked: "I've been there. Believe me, you know."

There are three frequently quoted observations, two by Samuel Johnson and one by Baron Bramwell, regarding what a lawyer can know about a case. In response to Boswell's question: "But what do you think of supporting a cause which you know to be bad?" Dr. Johnson replied: "Sir, you do not know it to be good or bad till the Judge determines it."[1] Similarly, Baron Bramwell wrote: "A man's rights are to be determined by the Court, not by his attorney or Counsel. It is for the want of remembering this that foolish people object to lawyers that they will advocate a case against their own opinions. A client is entitled to say to his Counsel, 'I want your advocacy, not your judgment; I prefer that of the Court.' "[2] And Dr. Johnson again: "A lawyer has no business with the justice or injustice of the cause which he undertakes, unless his client asks his opinion, and then he is bound to give it honestly. The justice or injustice of the cause is to be decided by the Judge. . . . A lawyer is not to tell what he knows to be a lie; he is not to produce what he knows to be a false deed; but he is not to usurp the province of the jury and of the Judge and determine what shall be the effect of evidence. . . . If lawyers were to undertake no causes till they were sure they were just, a man might be precluded altogether from a trial of his claim, though, were it judicially examined, it might be found a very just claim."[3]

There are at least four ways of understanding those statements. The first is that both Johnson and Bramwell were addressing them-

selves to the ultimate justness of a particular cause in either a
moral or legal sense, and not to whether the facts as represented
by the client were true. That is, their concern may have been with
"good or bad" as distinguished from "true or false". Thus, Dr.
Johnson said: "A lawyer is not to tell what he knows to be a
lie. . . ." In the same sentence, however, he added: ". . . he is
not to usurp the province of the jury and of the Judge and
determine what shall be the effect of evidence. . . ." At any
rate, whatever may have been the intent of Johnson and Bramwell,
their remarks have been widely accepted as going to the situation
where the lawyer has knowledge of incriminating facts, rather
than the case where the lawyer merely has an opinion as to the
legal or moral merits.[4]

A second understanding of the proposition that a lawyer
does not know the truth, is the idea that information communi-
cated by another person—even a confession of a crime—is a less
than certain basis for "knowing". For example, a leading English
authority suggests that the lawyer should bear in mind that cases
have been known to occur in which people, "possibly through
some twist of the mind", have admitted offenses even though
they were innocent. People may also confess "perhaps for the
sake of notoriety", or because "they believe that they are protecting someone else".[5] If one makes such speculative possibilities
controlling, however remote they might appear, then again, the
ethical issue will never arise. In my own view, however, such
reasoning is morally irresponsible.

Suppose that a client comes to a lawyer seeking advice. The
client has been summoned into an alley by a man who dresses
poorly, speaks ungrammatically, and acts furtively, but who
insists that a pair of heavy, antique, sterling silver candelabra have
been in his family for generations. He is willing to sell them to
the client for $25. Of course, the client realizes that the candelabra
might have been stolen, but he does not know that to be a fact,
and, indeed, the man in the alley expressly says otherwise. There
is no doubt, however, what the lawyer will advise. If the client
were to purchase the candelabra, he would seriously risk being
found guilty of receiving stolen goods, even though that crime
requires scienter. In short, there is such a thing as "knowing"
for legal purposes, even in the face of contradictory statements.
Are lawyers, then, less capable of knowing than are their clients?
On the contrary, the ABA Standards require that the lawyer
must "know all that his client knows".[6] Of course, we are not
here concerned necessarily with knowledge in the legal sense,
but in the area of ethical responsibility the same reasoning would
seem to be even more clearly applicable. Surely there is such a

thing as knowing to a moral certainty or, at least, of being placed upon moral notice.

The idea, therefore, that a lawyer does not really know what the facts are can also be taken as a response at a level of personal morality, specifically, as a rejection of personal moral responsibility. When one of the Watergate principals was asked by a young associate why large sums of Republican campaign funds were being turned over to Gordon Liddy, he has been quoted as responding: "I don't want to know, and you don't want to know." That attitude does not appear to be adequate to the concerns of the conscientious attorney who, whether wanting to know or not, is compelled to admit: "I've been there. Believe me, you know."

There is yet another way, one that I believe is more honest and more useful, of understanding what is meant when one says that the lawyer does not know that the client is guilty. That is, by viewing the propositions in systemic rather than in personal terms. Thus, when Dr. Johnson says that a lawyer "is not to usurp the province of the jury and of the Judge", we can understand him as speaking in terms of the determination of guilt in accordance with established procedures, as distinguished from the fact of guilt as perceived by any particular person. The point, therefore, is not that the lawyer cannot know the truth, or that the lawyer refuses to recognize the truth, but rather that the lawyer is told: "You, personally, may very well know the truth, but your personal knowledge is irrelevant. In your capacity as an advocate (and, if you will, as an officer of the court) you are forbidden to act upon your personal knowledge of the truth, as you might want to do as a private person, because the adversary system could not function properly if lawyers did so."

I am inclined to believe, although not without reservations, that that is an accurate reflection of what is meant, or what should be meant, when we talk about whether and what the lawyer knows. If that is correct, then there are at least two advantages to saying so directly. First, we can avoid a good deal of confusion and nonsense that result from the several different meanings that are connoted by the concept of "knowing". Second, we can begin to focus upon whether the systemic command applies in all instances. For example, does it apply equally to the question of whether to accept a client as it does to the question of whether to withdraw from a case at a point at which the client would be prejudiced or a mistrial would be required? Does it apply equally to knowledge regarding perjury by a client and perjury by other witnesses? Does it apply equally in both civil and criminal cases? It would appear that the answers to those questions should be no.

A lawyer should be able to refuse a client for any reason, including mere suspicion of dishonesty (except in the extreme and unlikely circumstance that the client would thereby be left with no attorney available at all). Also, the attorney's responsibility will vary, constitutionally and otherwise, depending upon whether the perjury is that of the client or another witness, and depending upon whether the case is civil or criminal. As explained in Chapter 3, the criminal defense lawyer is compelled by reasons of practicality and constitutional requirements to present and argue the client's perjury if the client insists upon so testifying. In a civil proceeding between private parties, however, the practical and constitutional context is significantly different, and different answers to many of the same questions might well be required.

Let me be frank to concede, however, that I am not prepared to say precisely where and how those lines should be drawn, nor do I think that that task can be accomplished by means of anything less than careful analysis of a multitude of situations by a number of thoughtful attorneys with experience in all areas of practice. Moreover, once a decision were made that in some defined circumstances the lawyer should act upon knowledge of incriminating facts (by withdrawing, by informing the other party, by informing the court, by informing the prosecutor, etc.), further questions would then have to be specifically focused upon, for example, whether the standard of knowledge should be based upon certainty, belief beyond a reasonable doubt, clear and convincing evidence, etc. In addition, if a lawyer were to be required to act upon knowledge in some circumstances, under penalty of disciplinary action, should the test then be a subjective or an objective one?

Because there has been a failure to deal with those issues in systemic terms over the centuries, the suggested rules of professional responsibility that we do have lack any coherent pattern in dealing with the underlying difficulties. Thus, we do not have rules saying directly that there are occasions when a lawyer knows the truth but is forbidden to act upon that knowledge as would a private person of good conscience. Instead, there are rules that purport to require the lawyer in such circumstances to act inconsistently with the role of advocate, but which then define what it means to "know" in such a restrictive fashion as to ensure that the occasion will never arise. The example has already been given of the English authority who purports to forbid the attorney to present evidence of innocence when there is such a "clear confession" that the attorney is "really irresistibly driven" to a conclusion of guilt. That extreme situation is unlikely to develop, however, since even a confession is not to be taken as sufficient to establish knowledge, because people sometimes confess for the sake of notoriety or to protect others. The same authority also holds that an attorney would not be justified in drawing a conclusion of guilt when the client has given "perhaps a whole series of contradictory statements". The result of that kind of sophistry, of course, is the same as saying that a criminal defense lawyer is required to present whatever factual defense the client wants, even though the lawyer is reasonably certain that the evidence is false.

Similarly, we have already discussed the proposal of Section 7.7 of the ABA Standards that the lawyer must not present perjury by the client but, rather, must allow the client to testify only in narrative fashion, and must refrain from arguing to the jury the facts as stated by the defendant.[7] That circumstance, however, is conditioned upon two events. First, the defendant must have admitted facts establishing guilt. Second, the lawyer must have established that the admissions are true by means of an "independent investigation", implying that the corroborating evidence must have been obtained by the lawyer entirely independent of any leads provided by the client's admissions. At least, the careful phrasing of the Standards invites that interpretation, because the Supreme Court has held[8] that it would be "inconsistent with ethical standards" to permit the use of evidence resulting directly or indirectly from a violation of the defendant's constitutional rights; such evidence can be used only if it derives, untainted, from an "independent source".* In view of the difficulty of fulfilling that second requirement, therefore, it is most unlikely that any lawyer will actually have to perform the charade set forth in Section 7.7.**

---

* Section 4.1 of the Standards, which deals with the duty to investigate, refers to the obligation of making an "effective investigation" and an "adequate investigation", but only Section 7.7 refers to an "independent investigation". *See,* ABA STANDARDS, at 225-28.

** One is reminded of the Biblical commandment regarding the stubborn and rebellious son, who is to be denounced at the gates of the city and stoned to death. *Deuteronomy* 21:18. The rabbinical commentaries provide, however, that in order for the law to operate, the son must be of an age between thirteen years and one day, and thirteen years and three months. Moreover, since the parents are to denounce him by saying, "he will not obey our voice", it was decided that the parents must be indistinguishable from each other in voice, stature, and facial features. *Sanhedrin* 53a, 68b-72a; *cf., The Code of Maimonides, Book 14, The Book of Judges,* at 157-61 (A. M. Hershman transl. 1949). Thus: "There never has been a 'stubborn and rebellious son,' and there never will be." Why then, the rabbis asked, was the law written? And the rabbinical answer was: "That you may study it and receive reward [in the act of studying]"—which may or may not be an adequate reason for incorporating similar sophistries into standards relating to the defense function.

Although the Code of Professional Responsibility does not resort to unrealistically narrow definitions of knowing, the provisions that require some form of knowledge as a standard of conduct give every indication of having been drafted haphazardly, with no conscious effort having been made to analyze and weigh the varying standards adopted in one or another provision. At least half a dozen times, a purely subjective standard is used, in rules relating to advancing unwarranted claims,[9] failing to make a disclosure required by law,[10] using perjury,[11] participating in the presentation of perjury,[12] assisting in illegal or fraudulent conduct,[13] and personally making a false statement.[14] On a subjective standard of knowing, of course, disciplinary action would rarely, if ever, be taken.

There are also at least four variations of an objective standard in the Code. The most easily met appears to be in the provision that a lawyer must reveal a fraud committed by a client or another witness when the lawyer receives information "clearly establishing" the fraud.[15] The section permitting a lawyer to reveal a client's intention to commit a crime expresses no standard of knowledge at all, but an accompanying footnote suggests that the lawyer is obligated to report the client's intention to commit a crime only when the lawyer has facts indicating "beyond reasonable doubt" that a crime will be committed.[16] A third objective standard is found in the provision that the lawyer should not present evidence when he or she knows or "should know" that the evidence is false, fraudulent, or perjured.[17] The "should know" standard is vague and might be considered the most easily satisfied, but the accompanying footnote quotes from *In re Carroll*,[18] where the lawyer unquestionably knew that the client's testimony was inaccurate because the lawyer was representing the client in another case in which the client was taking a contrary position on the same fact. That would appear to be a rather limiting criterion of what a lawyer "should know". Finally, in several instances the Code uses the word "obvious" as a standard of what the lawyer is bound to act upon. That standard is found in such varied provisions as those dealing with advancing a claim merely for purposes of harassment,[19] prosecuting a criminal case where there is no probable cause,[20] creating or preserving false evidence,[21] and even continuing with a case where to do so would result in violation of any other Disciplinary Rule.[22]

Whatever sense might be made of those varying standards as applied to those undifferentiated circumstances, it seems clear that no effort has been made by the codifiers to distinguish between civil cases and criminal cases (where constitutional rights are likely to have a major bearing), or among the kinds of conduct at issue (*e.g.*, unwillingly going along with the client's decision to commit perjury, creating or preserving false evidence, assisting the commission of illegal conduct, or making a false statement one-self). Even if one rejects the suggestion put forth earlier in this chapter—that there are some circumstances in which the lawyer must go forward irrespective of knowledge to a certainty—it seems clear that some more rational pattern should be established in the Code for those situations in which specific requirements of conduct are imposed on the basis of what the attorney "knows".

To summarize, the statement that a lawyer "never knows that a client is guilty" may be meant in at least three different ways. First, it may be meant in the epistemological sense that knowledge is always uncertain in nature. That, however, is not a premise that we accept otherwise in our formulation of either legal or ethical rules. Second, it may be meant as a rejection of moral responsibility on a personal level: "I don't know, because I don't want to know." Third, it may be meant as a systemic response. In the adversary system, it is not the role or function of the advocate to act upon conclusions of ultimate facts such as guilt or in-nocence. That function is assigned to the judge or jury, which bases its decision on the adversaries' presentation of their clients' cases. Thus, the fact of guilt or innocence is irrelevant to the role that has been assigned to the advocate. At least in the context of criminal litigation, the attorney is required, by the defendant's constitutional rights and by considerations of practicality, to pre-sent and to argue the client's perjury if the client insists upon that course.[23]

Although the ABA Standards appear to reject that conclusion, for practical purposes they reach the same result, by setting a disingenuous test for determining when the lawyer "knows". The lawyer is thereby placed under an apparent, but really nonex-istent, obligation to violate the client's trust. The Code of Pro-fessional Responsibility illustrates another undesirable aspect of the traditional approach by using the concept of knowing in a vague and undifferentiated way. As a result, we are left without any significant guidance in drawing possible distinctions between criminal and civil litigation, and among different kinds of conduct that might be improper.

Footnotes

[1] 2 J. Boswell's Life of Samuel Johnson 47 (G.B. Hill ed. 1887).

[2] Johnson v. Emerson, L.R. 6 Ex. 329, 367 (1871).

[3] J. Boswell, Tour to the Hebrides, Aug. 15, at 175.

[4] *See, e.g.*, J. Singleton, Conduct at the Bar 31-33 (1969); D. Mellin-koff, The Conscience of a Lawyer 156-57, 164 (1973).

[5] T. Lund, A Guide to the Professional Conduct of Solicitors 106 (1960).

6 AMERICAN BAR ASSOCIATION, STANDARDS RELATING TO THE DEFENSE FUNCTION 145 (1971).

7 *See*, pp. 36-38 *supra*.

8 *See*, Nardone v. United States, 308 U.S. 338, 340, 60 S. Ct. 266, 84 L. Ed. 307, 311 (1939); Silverthorne Lumber Co. v. United States, 251 U.S. 385, 392, 40 S. Ct. 182, 64 L. Ed. 319, 321-22 (1920).

9 DR 7-102 (A) (2).

10 DR 7-102 (A) (3).

11 DR 7-102 (A) (4).

12 EC 7-26.

13 DR 7-102 (A) (7).

14 DR 7-102 (A) (5).

15 DR 7-102 (B).

16 DR 4-101 (C) (3), and n. 16.

17 EC 7-26.

18 244 S.W.2d 474 (Ky. Ct. App. 1951).

19 DR 2-110 (B) (1); 7-102 (A) (1); 2-109.

20 DR 7-103 (A).

21 DR 7-102 (A) (6).

22 DR 2-110 (B) (2).

23 *See*, Chapter 3 *supra*.

Chapter 6

COUNSELLING THE CLIENT: REFRESHING RECOLLECTION OR PROMPTING PERJURY?

When I first attempted to analyze problems of professional responsibility several years ago, I suggested that the question of interviewing and counselling the client prior to trial is probably the most difficult of all.[1] As I have thought about issues of legal ethics and discussed them with others over the ensuing years, I have become more and more persuaded that it is indeed the most difficult question, and I have become less and less satisfied with my original resolution of it. Unquestionably, one of the lawyer's principal functions is to advise the client about the law, and that advice must include an understanding of what facts are relevant to the case and why. But when, if ever, does it become improper for the attorney to perform that function because the client might put that legal advice to unlawful purposes?

The particular focus of this chapter is on giving advice that might induce the client to commit perjury. That, however, is only one aspect of a broader question relating to counselling. It might be useful, therefore, to begin with some of the more general aspects of that problem. Assume, for example, that a lawyer has an annual retainer on behalf of an appliance store located near the state line. The client does not open on Sundays, because there is a state Blue Law forbidding it to do so. However, less than a mile away, in the adjoining state, several discount stores operate on Sunday. As a result, the client is suffering a crippling decline in its sales. The client, therefore, asks the attorney what the penalty would be for remaining open on Sunday. The attorney researches the issue and informs the client that the prescribed penalty is $25 for each violation, and that the highest court of the state has interpreted "violation" to refer to each day that business is done, rather than to each sale that is made. The client then opens the store regularly on Sundays, and, as it develops, is never prosecuted or even asked to pay the penalty, despite the notorious nature of the act.

Predictably, then, the client has used the attorney's legal advice as the basis for a decision to break the law. Should the lawyer have refused to answer the client's question, or, having answered it and seen the client use the legal advice to an illegal purpose, should the lawyer terminate the retainer?

Even though the client's only interest in knowing the applicable law would relate to a possible decision to break the law, it seems absurd to hold broadly that a lawyer cannot tell a client what is in a public statute and in relevant decisions of the highest court of the state. One experienced and respected practitioner, who is now on the faculty of one of our leading law schools, said that he would answer a client if asked which countries in the Western Hemisphere do not have extradition treaties with the United States. "In that situation," he said, "I am simply a law book." Another member of the same faculty disagreed, saying that he would refuse to give the information, but he added that he would not consider it appropriate to forbid lawyers to do so; rather, he said, it is a matter that should be left to the personal judgment of each lawyer.

The Code of Professional Responsibility is ambiguous on the issue. The Code provides that an attorney "shall not . . . Counsel or assist his client in conduct that the lawyer knows to be illegal. . . ."[2] However, the Code also provides that when the client "seeks to pursue an illegal course of conduct",[3] withdrawal from the case by the attorney is "permissive" (*sic*) but not "mandatory". It appears, therefore, that the words "Counsel or assist" refer to an active kind of participation in the client's illegal act, going beyond merely giving advice about the law.* Moreover, by making withdrawal permissible, the Code leaves the decision to the personal judgment of each attorney in all cases.

In the Blue Law case, and even in the one involving extradition treaties, that seems to be a satisfactory position. That solution appears less appropriate, however, in other contexts. For example, what if the lawyer is asked whether the penalty for armed robbery of a bank is any greater if an automatic weapon is used, or whether federal penalties can be avoided in a kidnapping if the child is not transported across state lines? In those cases, the "I am a law book" response is not satisfactory. Unfortunately, however, the Code does not suggest any distinction between the Blue Law case and the kidnapping case. In fact, as we have seen earlier, the Code is similarly ambiguous with respect to the lawyer's obligation to withhold or to reveal the intention of the client to commit a crime; the Code simply leaves it to the discretion of the individual attorney, without suggesting any cri-

---

* *Compare* the decision of Judge Learned Hand, interpreting a statute relating to aiding and abetting a crime: "It is not enough that he does not forego a normally lawful activity, of the fruits of which he knows that others will make an unlawful use; he must in some sense promote the venture himself, make it his own, have a stake in its outcome." United States v. Falcone, 109 F.2d 579 (2d Cir. 1940), *aff'd*, 311 U.S. 205, 61 S. Ct. 204, 85 L. Ed. 129 (1940).

teria for making that judgment.[4] Here again, I think that distinctions should be made in terms of the gravity of the offense, and that in some situations—at least those relating to violence to the person and other offenses involving moral turpitude—the lawyer should be forbidden to give the advice. At the other extreme, however, I would agree with the Code in leaving the decision to the individual attorney in situations such as the Blue Law case and the extradition case. In neither of those situations is there a victim in the ordinary sense.*

The Code is also ambiguous with respect to whether the lawyer should give the client legal advice that may induce the client to commit perjury. The Code provides that a lawyer shall not "participate in the creation" of evidence when he or she knows or it is obvious that the evidence is false.[5] There again, however, the degree of participation is unclear. For example, what if a client in an uncontested divorce case asks a lawyer which states provide the quickest divorces and what evidence must be presented in each jurisdiction in order to obtain a divorce? It is unlikely that the codifiers intended to forbid the lawyer to explain the requirements of domicile, even though the attorney should "know" (or, at least, it is "obvious" enough to me) that the client is shopping for a forum rather than for a permanent residence.** Once again, therefore, I would conclude that the intention of the Code is to forbid active participation by the attorney in creating the perjury, but not to proscribe merely giving relevant legal advice. Clearly, however, such a fundamental and pervasive issue should not be left to uncertain inferences from vague standards.

In fact, the general problem of prompting perjury is far more complex than is recognized by the superficial treatment it receives in the Code. As noted at the beginning of this chapter, perhaps the most difficult area for the practicing attorney relates to inter-

---

* Moreover, in the extradition case, the client, who may be guilty of a crime, is at least paying the penalty of self-imposed exile.

** Compare the following situation: An elderly client of Lawyer *A* shortly after a serious heart attack decides to make a sizeable gift to his son. *A* advises the client to develop evidence that the gift was not made in contemplation of death but with a lifetime motive, to avoid paying a higher tax.

That case was used in a pre-test in a study of ethical conduct among lawyers. The case was not retained for use in the final survey, however, because the lawyer's conduct was so generally approved by lawyers who were regarded as ethical. (J. E. CARLIN, LAWYERS' ETHICS: A STUDY OF THE NEW YORK CITY BAR 46 (1966). For a critical review of the book, *see,* Freedman, Book Review, 16 AM. U. L. REV. 177 (1966).) Despite the high likelihood of a consensus among tax lawyers that Lawyer *A* acted properly, Lawyer *A*'s conduct appears rather clearly to involve a degree of active participation in the creation of false evidence that would constitute a violation of DR 7-102 (A) (6).

viewing and counselling a client or other witness prior to trial. In broad outline, it is reasonably clear what a lawyer is required to do. In specific situations, however, there is little guidance at all on either a practical or ethical level.

Let us begin by observing those aspects of the lawyer's counselling function that appear to be beyond controversy. There are three published works that are particularly useful for that purpose, because they have been chosen as the first three articles in SELECTED WRITINGS ON THE LAW OF EVIDENCE AND TRIAL.[6] That book was compiled under the sponsorship of the Association of American Law Schools by a committee of the nation's leading authorities on the law of evidence. The purpose was to gather together in one volume much of "the best legal thought" on evidence for the "benefit of the legal profession, as well as to assist law students and teachers. . . ."[7] Therefore, those three works, by Lloyd Paul Stryker, Harry S. Bodin, and Edward W. Cleary,[8] can fairly be said to represent a consensus of the most prestigious authorities as to the proper manner to interview and prepare witnesses for trial.

In discussions with nonlawyers I have been surprised to find how common the belief is that it is improper for an attorney to prepare or coach a witness prior to trial. The rule of practice, of course, is precisely the contrary. As Professor Cleary says: "No competent attorney dreams of calling witnesses who have not previously been interviewed."[9] The lawyer must try to elicit all relevant facts and to help the client—who, typically, is not skilled at articulation—to marshal and to express his or her case as persuasively as possible. For example, the poorly educated day laborer who has suffered an injury, and who can only say, "It hurts bad", must be helped to articulate what the pain is like, when it is present, and how it interferes with work, sleep, family life, and recreation. In addition, the statement "I hurt myself while I was working", will not be enough. The relevant details must be elicited through skilled questioning, and the witness must then be sufficiently rehearsed to assure that no important evidence will be overlooked in testimony at trial, where leading questions will not be permitted.

In discussing the technique of interviewing the client, Mr. Bodin notes that it is generally advisable to let the client tell his or her own story while the lawyer just listens. If the attorney insists upon getting only answers to specific questions, important points may be screened out, because a lawyer cannot possibly anticipate all the facts in every case.[10] Having gotten the client's story in narrative fashion, the lawyer must then seek additional facts that may have been omitted. That is done by asking questions and by explaining to the client how important the additional information may be to the case. "If the client can be made to understand your thoughts, he may tell you facts which otherwise would have been inadvertently overlooked or consciously and erroneously discarded by him as immaterial."[11] At the same time it is recognized that the client's story will be affected by a "subconscious suppression, psychologically induced by the wish to put one's best foot forward or by nature's trick of inducing forgetfulness of what one does not like to remember".[12] That is, people will, in perfectly good faith, relate past events in a way that they believe (rightly or wrongly) to be consistent with their own interests. Necessarily, therefore, in pressing the client for additional information, and in explaining the relevance and importance of that information, the lawyer will be affecting the ultimate testimony. As emphasized by Professor Cleary, although it is improper to prompt or suggest an answer to one's witness during the actual testimony, the interview "affords full play to suggestion . . . and evokes in advance of trial a complete verbalization, the importance of which cannot be overlooked".[13]

The process of preparing or coaching the witness, of course, goes far beyond the initial eliciting of facts. In the course of polishing the client's testimony, Mr. Stryker recommends as many as fifty full rehearsals of direct and cross-examination. During those rehearsals, the testimony is developed in a variety of ways. The witness is vigorously cross-examined, and then the attorney points out where the witness has been "tripped" and how the testimony can be restructured to avoid that result. The attorney may also take the role of witness and be cross-examined by an associate. The attorney's "failures" in simulated testimony are then discussed, and the attorney then may conduct a mock cross-examination of the associate. In that way, "new ideas are developed while all the time the client is looking on and listening. He probably is saying, 'Let me try again.' And you will then go through the whole process once more." By that time, as one might expect, the client "does far better".[14] In fact, after many weeks of preparation, "perhaps on the very eve of trial", the client may come up with a new fact that "may perhaps make a difference between victory and defeat".[15]

Nowhere in those three selections relating to preparation of witnesses is there any analysis of the ethical implications of the model practices that are set forth. Mr. Stryker does say that in repeatedly going over the "hard spots" and the "awkward places" and in showing the client how to "surmount his difficulties", the witness is "still staying well within the truth, the whole truth, and nothing but the truth".[16] Saying that, however, does not make it so. If people do respond to suggestion, and if the lawyer helps the client to "fill in the gaps" and to avoid being "tripped", by developing "new ideas" in the course of repeated rehearsals, it is reasonably clear that the testimony that ultimately is presented in court will have been significantly affected by the lawyer's prompting and by the client's self-interest. Whether the end product is "well within the truth, the whole truth and nothing but the truth", is therefore subject to considerable doubt.

In fact, one finds in the three selections an astonishing disregard of the ethical implications of the preparation of testimony. It is difficult to believe that one with Stryker's experience and sophistication is unaware of the impact of suggestion, which is recognized in the article by Cleary. Similarly, Cleary concerns himself only with the problem of how rules of evidence—but not the rules of legal ethics—might be reformed to take into account the psychological realities that he discusses. Bodin also recognizes the "psychologically induced" inclination to remember or forget in a way consistent with one's own interests. However, he ignores the implications of that fact when he discusses how important it is for the lawyer to make the client aware of the importance and significance of information that may have been left out of the client's original narrative.

In addition, the Bodin article (unlike Cleary's) reflects the general ignorance within the legal profession of psychological learning regarding memory. For example, Bodin says that: "Experienced trial lawyers have learned that even an honest and rational client, who will not *invent* 'facts,' may nevertheless *suppress* facts."[17] Experiments by psychologists, however, indicate that those experienced trial lawyers (whoever they may be) are wrong: invention is no less common than suppression. Bodin also states that: "Of first importance in any action are the *facts*—the *exact* facts and *all* the facts."[18] He then explains how the lawyer must seek to elicit "all the important facts" by probing the client's memory with "detailed questioning".[19] What Bodin does not seem to realize is that the effort to obtain *"all* the facts" is virtually certain to result in obtaining something very different from "the *exact* facts".

One of the most common misconceptions about memory is that it is a process of recollection or reproduction of impressions, closely analogous to the functioning of a phonograph record or tape recorder—"the mental imprint left by perception of objective happenings", as distinguished from a "subjective reconstruction".[20] In that respect, legal thinking is centuries out of date, proceeding as if highly relevant experiments in behavioral psychology had never taken place. St. Augustine referred to "the great harbour of memory", from which experience "may be reproduced and brought back again when the need arises". Thus, experiences are "stored up in the memory . . . ready at hand for thought to recall". (Confessions, Book X, Ch. 8.) Similarly, John Locke, in the first edition of his ESSAY CONCERNING HUMAN UNDERSTANDING, referred to memory as "the storehouse of our ideas". David Hume distinguished memory from imagination in part on the ground that "memory is in a manner tied down . . . without any power of variation". (TREATISE OF HUMAN NATURE, Book I, Part I, Section III.)[21]

In fact, perceiving is not merely "the passive reception of stimuli", and remembering is not "the simple reduplication of the patterns thus formed", as if they were "lifeless, fixed and unchangeable memory traces".[22] Rather, memory is much more a process of reconstruction than one of recollection or recall. Moreover, the process is a highly creative one, affecting what is "remembered" as much as what is "forgotten".

Thus, contrary to Bodin's assertion,[23] an honest and rational client will invent facts as readily as suppress them. Indeed, even before the process of remembering begins, what goes into the supposed "mental storehouse" is significantly influenced by the personality and previous experiences of the observer. As noted by F.C. Bartlett, who is probably the leading experimental psychologist concerned with memory, "temperament, interests, and attitudes often direct the course and determine the content of perceiving". In addition, "a great amount of what is said to be perceived is in fact inferred", a process that Bartlett calls "inferential construction".[24] Experiencing a situation that is unclear in part or ambiguous, an observer typically "fills up the gaps of his perception by the aid of what he has experienced before in similar situations, or, though this comes to much the same thing in the end, by describing what he takes to be 'fit,' or suitable, to such a situation". As observed by another authority, "recall brings greater symmetry or completeness than that which was actually observed".[25] Moreover, the process of unconscious reconstruction continues with the passage of time, probably increasing considerably as the event is left farther behind.[26]

Nor is any dishonesty involved in that process. "He may do this without being in the least aware that he is either supplementing or falsifying the data of perception. Yet, in almost all cases, he is certainly doing the first, and in many cases he is demonstrably doing the second."[27] The "vast majority" of testimonial errors are those of the "average, normal honest man", errors "unknown to the witness and wholly unintentional". Such testimony has been described as *"subjectively* accurate but *objectively* false".[28]

An interesting illustration of the tendency to eliminate situational ambiguities in remembering was provided in the Senate Watergate hearings. John Dean was testifying regarding a meeting with Herbert Kalmbach. Dean had no incentive whatsoever to lie about that particular incident. In fact, it was extremely important to him to state the facts with as much exactness as possible. He testified that he had met Kalmbach in the coffee shop of the Mayflower Hotel in Washington, D.C., and that they had gone directly upstairs to Kalmbach's room in the same hotel. Dean was pressed several times on that point, in a way that implied that his questioners had reason to believe that he was lying as to whether the meeting had taken place at all. Each time, Dean confidently reaffirmed his clear recollection about the incident. Finally, it was revealed that the register of the Mayflower Hotel indicated that Kalmbach had not been staying at the hotel at the time in question. Dean nevertheless remained certain of the occurrence, putting forth the unlikely theory that Kalmbach had been using an alias. The difficulty was cleared up when someone realized that there is a Mayflower Doughnut Coffee Shop in the Statler Hilton Hotel in Washington—and Kalmbach was found to have been registered there, under his own name, on the day in question. Thus, Dean's basic story was confirmed. Without realizing it, however, Dean had inaccurately resolved the ambiguity created by the coincidence of the two names by confidently "remembering" the wrong hotel, and by inventing the use of an alias by Kalmbach, despite the fact that he had had every incentive to report those details correctly, and had come close to being seriously discredited because of his unconscious error.

As Bartlett summed it up, remembering is "not the reexcitation of innumerable fixed, lifeless and fragmentary traces". Rather, it is "an imaginative reconstruction or construction", "built out of the relation of our attitude towards the whole active mass of organized past reactions or experience".[29] Moreover, because remembering is "rapidly affected by unwitting transformations", "accurate recall is the exception and not the rule". That is true even when material is arranged in a short series, is small in bulk and simple in objective structure, and when it is so given that an observer knows that he or she will be asked to describe it later.[30] Accordingly, in certain parts of "ostensibly factual reporting", we can be sure that "a large proportion of the details will be incorrect, even though presented with the utmost certitude and in good faith".[31] "Victims of assault are notoriously unreliable witnesses regarding the description of their assailants", notes Professor Talland, "but then so are onlookers who watched in safety." An event need not stir up emotional reactions in order to be "grossly misrepresented" in recollection.[32]

Questioning is, of course, an essential part of interviewing and preparing a witness for trial. It is particularly noteworthy, therefore, that questions, even "straightforward questions of fact", may play a very strong part in inducing "importation of detail" into the process of remembering,[33] and that leading questions, when purposefully used to induce error, succeed in doing so to a startling degree.[34] A recent study by Elizabeth Loftus showed that witnesses' estimates of the speed of an automobile involved in an accident will vary in accordance with the verb used by the questioner in describing the impact: "smashed" (40.8 mph), "collided" (39.3 mph), "bumped" (38.1 mph), "hit" (34.0 mph), and "contacted" (31.8 mph). In addition, twice as many witnesses reported seeing nonexistent broken glass on the ground when the questioner used the word "smashed" instead of "hit". Dr. Loftus concluded that "memory itself undergoes a change" as a result of the type of question asked.[35]

Moreover, memory in general, and responses to questions in particular, will be affected by "preferential psychological reactions"—that is, there is a natural and honest tendency to remember-reconstruct in ways that are "strongly determined by an active subjective bias of the nature of interest".[36] Indeed, the unconscious impact of reward and punishment has been observed even at the level of perception, before memory even begins. For example, in one experiment a group of people were shown sets of varying numbers of dots, and required to estimate the numbers. They were rewarded proportionately to the number estimated, provided that the estimate was correct, but they were penalized for incorrect estimates. Up to the twentieth trial, the people in that group produced more overestimates than did another group of observers who were rewarded for correct responses irrespective of the number estimated. However, as it became apparent that overestimates were not proving effective in winning rewards, overestimation disappeared entirely.[37]

A further significant aspect of remembering is the "witness's readiness to respond and his self-confidence when in fact he ought to be cautious and hedge his statements".[38] In an experiment conducted by Bartlett relating to remembering faces, the person who unconsciously invented more detail than any other in the test group was "completely confident throughout". In another case, referred to by Bartlett as a brilliant example of obviously constructive remembering of a narrative, he noted that "it was precisely concerning his inventions that the subject was most pleased and most certain".[39] Moreover, when our "recall" is occasioned by a mental "visual image", the appearance of the visual image is followed by an increase of confidence "entirely out of proportion to any objective accuracy that is thereby secured".[40]

To sum up, the process of remembering is not one dependent upon "memory traces", which can be played back as if by placing a stylus into the groove of a phonograph record. Rather, the process is one of active, creative reconstruction, which begins at the moment of perception. The reconstructive process is significantly affected by the form of the questions asked and by what we understand to be in our own interest—even though, on a conscious level, we are responding as honestly as we possibly can.

Those conclusions might seem to suggest that the conscientious lawyer should avoid giving a client or other witness an understanding of what is relevant and important and should rely only upon narrative statements unassisted by questions that seek to elicit critical facts. However, anyone who has conducted interviews will immediately recognize that such a procedure would be highly impractical. An untrained and perhaps inarticulate person cannot be expected to relate all that is relevant without a substantial amount of direction. That is why one of the most important functions of the lawyer is to provide an awareness of what is legally relevant. Moreover, the same psychological authorities support the necessity of prompting in order to maximize recall. What prompting can do is to trigger recognition, which is a less complex process than remembering.[41] Bartlett notes, for example, that in any experimental series, "only a relatively small portion of the material that can be recognized can, as a rule, be recalled".[42] Another authority observes similarly that narrative is "the most accurate" but "the least complete" of all forms of recall.[43] That is, if we rely only upon unprompted narrative, many important facts will be omitted, facts which can be accurately reported if memory is prompted by recognition, such as through leading questions. Obviously, therefore, we are faced with another dilemma. On the one hand, we know that by telling the client that a particular fact is important, and why it is important, we may induce the client to "remember" the fact even if it did not occur. On the other hand, important facts can truly be lost if we fail to provide the client with every possible aid to memory. Furthermore, since the client's memory is inevitably going to be affected by reconstruction consistent with self-interest, a client who has a misunderstanding of his or her own legal interest could be psychologically inclined to remember in a way that is not only inconsistent with the client's case, but also inaccurate.

The complexity of the difficulty is heightened, both on a practical and an ethical level, if we reconsider at this point the attorney's professional responsibility to "know all the facts the client knows",* and if we pose again the question, raised in the previous chapter, of when the lawyer "knows" sufficiently to be on moral notice. In the area of counselling, those two aspects of knowing are tightly interrelated. It is nevertheless useful to keep in mind that they are different in important respects. When we speak of the obligation to know everything that the client knows, we refer to the importance of being as fully informed as possible, for tactical purposes, in order most effectively to counsel and to represent the client in an adversarial situation. On the other hand, when we speak of knowing in the sense of being on moral notice, we refer to a state of awareness that is sufficient to compel the conscientious person to recognize that a moral choice has been presented—that there is, in short, a situation in which a conscious refusal to make a choice is itself a moral decision.

Particularly effective in illustrating the difficulty is the so-called *Anatomy of a Murder* situation.[44] The lawyer who has received from his client an incriminating story of murder in the first degree, says, in effect: "If the facts are as you have stated them, you have no legal defense, and you will probably be electrocuted. On the other hand, if you acted in a blind rage, there is a possibility of saving your life. Think it over, and we will talk about it tomorrow." A number of lawyers have sought to avoid the implications of that case by arguing that the lawyer's principal fault was in not counselling the client in a manner that would have avoided the lawyer's knowing too much too soon. That is, the criticism is that the attorney could have given the legal advice (which ultimately prompted the perjurious defense) at a significantly earlier point, so that the lawyer would have been in a more effective position to claim that he did not really "know" the incriminating facts before channelling the client's story in the desired direction. Most of those same lawyers would recognize, however, the tactical importance of getting a substantial part of the client's narrative version of the facts

---

* *See,* Chapter 1 *supra.*

before any suggestive or directive prompting by the lawyer begins. Otherwise, as we have seen in reviewing the psychological literature, the lawyer may well close off information that would be essential to developing a sound tactical position. Can the lawyer, then, have it both ways? Is it possible to know enough of the incriminating truth for tactical purposes and not, at the same time, come to know enough to be placed upon moral notice that the lawyer's advice about the law is likely to do more than simply prompt remembering-reconstructing in accordance with self-interest, and enter the area of prompting a conscious decision to commit perjury?

Before attempting to deal directly with the *Anatomy of a Murder* situation, in which the facts are unambiguous and the lawyer is suggesting a defense based upon radically different facts from those related by the client, let us deal with some situations in which there is necessarily a degree of ambiguity about facts that are relevant under applicable law. For example, there are innumerable instances in which a person's "intent" is crucial, despite the fact that he or she may have had no intent at all in the sense contemplated by rules of law. For example, a German writer, considering the question of intention as a test of legal consequences, suggests the following situation.[45] A young man and a young woman decide to get married. Each has $1,000. They decide to begin a business with those funds, and the young woman gives her money to the young man for that purpose. Was the intention to form a joint venture or a partnership? Did they intend that the young man be an agent or a trustee? Was the transaction a gift or a loan? Most likely, the young couple's state of mind did not conform to any of the modes of "intention" that the law might look for. Thus, if the couple should subsequently visit a tax attorney and discover that it is in their interest that the transaction be viewed as a gift, they might well "remember" that to have been their intention. On the other hand, should their engagement be broken and the young woman consult an attorney for the purpose of recovering her money, she might "remember", after proper counselling, that it had been her intention to make a loan.

The foregoing is not intended in a cynical way. As in many other instances, the rules of law require determinations of "fact" where the facts are truly ambiguous. Moreover, as we have seen, in the normal process of remembering-reconstructing, the client's honest recollection is inevitably going to be affected by what the client assumes to be in his or her best interest. In such an ambiguous situation, therefore, it would be absurd for the lawyer to insist that the client state a conclusion as to whether the intent had been to make a gift or to make a loan, without first explaining to the client what the applicable law is and what the significance would be of each of the possible responses.

Similarly, there are issues of judgment or degree that will also be colored by the client's understanding (whether correct or incorrect) of his or her own interest. For example, assume that your client, on trial for his life in a first-degree murder case, has killed another man with a penknife but insists that the killing was in self-defense. You ask him: "Do you regularly carry the penknife in your pocket, do you carry it frequently or infrequently, or did you take it with you only on that particular occasion?" He replies: "Why do you ask me a question like that?" It is entirely appropriate to inform him that his carrying the knife only on that occasion, or infrequently, might support an inference of premeditation, while if he carried the knife invariably, or frequently, the inference of premeditation would be negated. Thus, your client's life may depend upon his recollection as to whether he carried the knife frequently or infrequently. Despite the possibility that the client or a third party might infer that the lawyer was prompting the client to lie, the lawyer must apprise the defendant of the significance of his answer. There is no conceivable ethical requirement that the lawyer trap the client into a hasty and ill-considered answer before telling him the significance of the question. As observed by Professor John Noonan of Boalt Hall (in an article otherwise generally critical of my position): "A lawyer should not be paternalistic toward his client, and cannot assume that his client will perjure himself." Professor Noonan continued: "Furthermore, a lawyer has an obligation to furnish his client with all the legal information relevant to his case; in fulfilling this duty to inform his client, a lawyer would normally not violate ethical standards."[46]

Up to this point, the analysis presented in this chapter parallels that in my earliest article, in the *Michigan Law Review*.[47] I now believe, however, that I erred in going on to conclude that the *Anatomy of a Murder* situation is "essentially no different"[48] from those just discussed. I reached that conclusion in the Michigan article in part by following the penknife case with a case in which the client has given the lawyer incriminating information before being fully aware of its significance. Assume that a man consults a tax lawyer and says: "I am fifty years old. Nobody in my immediate family has lived past fifty. Therefore, I would like to put my affairs in order. Specifically, I understand that I can avoid substantial estate taxes by setting up a trust. Can I do it?" The lawyer informs the client that he can successfully avoid the estate taxes only if he lives at least three years after establishing the trust or, should he die within three years, if the trust should be found not to have been created in contemplation of death. The client then might ask how to go about satisfying the Internal Revenue Service or the courts that the trust was not in contemplation of death.

At that point, the lawyer can either refuse to answer the question, or he can tell the client, first, that he should never again tell anyone that he is concerned about an early death, and, second, that he should write letters and have conversations with relatives and friends indicating that he is setting up the trust for reasons that have nothing to do with imminent death or a desire to "put his affairs in order". On the assumption that virtually every tax attorney in the country would answer the client's question (and subsequently present in court the letters and the testimony about the client's conversations), I concluded that it should not be unethical for the lawyer to give the advice. Although I did not articulate it at the time, I also had in mind the "I am a law book" rationale, that is, that the attorney would be doing no more than informing the client of what is in the applicable statutes and court decisions. After considerable reflection, I now consider that decision to have been wrong. The lawyer in the tax case is, purely and simply, the active instrument in establishing—and, ultimately, presenting—a fraudulent case. (It is the same as if, in the penknife case, the defendant had in fact bought the knife the very day of the killing, and the lawyer had advised him to say instead that he had been carrying it daily for several months.) Although a probable consensus of the tax bar is not irrelevant to making an ethical judgment, it should not be conclusive in such a blatant case of manufactured evidence.

As noted earlier in this chapter, the Code of Professional Responsibility is ambiguous on the general question of whether the attorney may give advice that might induce perjury. The applicable Disciplinary Rule provides only that the lawyer should not "participate in the creation" of evidence when the lawyer knows or it is obvious that the evidence is false.[49] The relevant Ethical Considerations are of only limited assistance, in part because they are intended to be only "aspirational", and do not have the binding force of disciplinary rules. Ethical Consideration 7-5 provides that a lawyer should not "knowingly assist the client to engage in illegal conduct", and that a lawyer should never "encourage or aid" the client to commit criminal acts or "counsel his client on how to violate the law and avoid punishment therefor". However, the footnote to the Code at that point suggests the extreme situation in which the lawyer is representing "a syndicate notoriously engaged in the violation of the law for the purpose of advising the members how to break the law and at the same time escape it". Ethical Consideration 7-6 says that the lawyer may properly assist the client in "developing and preserving evidence of existing motive, intent, or desire", but adds that, "obviously", he may not do "anything" furthering the creation or preservation of false evidence. That last proscription is extremely broad. The same Ethical Consideration also notes, however, that in many cases a lawyer may not be "certain" as to the client's state of mind, and holds that in those situations the lawyer "should resolve reasonable doubts in favor of the client". Even under that more lenient test, in the tax case suggested above, it would seem to require what Professor Noonan called "brute rationalization"[50] to claim that there is any genuine uncertainty or any reasonable doubt in the lawyer's mind as to why the client has come to the lawyer to set up a trust.

Referring specifically to the *Anatomy of a Murder* case, I suggested additional reasons for telling the client about a factual defense that would have more chance of success than the facts narrated by the client. I argued that that is information which the lawyer would have, without advice, were the lawyer in the client's position, and that the client is entitled to have that information about the law and to make his own decision as to whether to act upon it. To withhold the advice, I said, would not only penalize the less well-educated defendant, but would also prejudice the client because of his initial truthfulness in telling his story in confidence to the attorney.

The fallacy in that argument is that the lawyer is giving the client more than just "information about the law", but is actively participating in—indeed, initiating—a factual defense that is obviously perjurious. To suggest that the less well-educated defendant is entitled to that extent of participation by the attorney in manufacturing perjury carries the "equalizer" concept of the lawyer's role too far. Moreover, even though the client has initially been truthful in telling his story to the attorney in confidence, it does not follow that there is any breach of confidentiality if the lawyer simply declines to create a false story for the client.* Accordingly, I do not believe that this is one of those situations in which the lawyer should in effect be told: "What you know to be the fact is irrelevant to your role as an advocate in an adversary system."** The concerns of policy that

---

* That is a very different matter from accepting a client's decision to commit perjury, and presenting that perjury to the court, recognizing that to do otherwise would undermine the confidential relationship. *See,* Chapter 3 *supra.*

** *See,* Chapter 5 *supra.*

would justify that directive in other contexts are not present in this one.

Before attempting to draw the analysis to a conclusion, two more situations would be worth discussing, because both are very close to the line that has been suggested thus far. Assume that Jurisdictions X and Y are adjacent to each other and that many lawyers practice in both jurisdictions. In Jurisdiction X, there are a large number of workmen's compensation cases in which workers strain themselves while lifting, and recover compensation. In Jurisdiction Y there is an equivalent number of such cases, but in all of them the workers who strain themselves while lifting also slip or trip on something in the process. That coincidence is fortunate, because in Jurisdiction X it is sufficient for compensation simply that the strain be work-related, while in Jurisdiction Y the applicable law requires that the injury be received in the course of an "accident", such as a slip or a trip. Obviously, the same lawyers whose clients are not slipping or tripping in Jurisdiction X are prompting their clients to recall a slip or trip when the injury is received in Jurisdiction Y.

In those cases, there are no issues of intent or of judgment, but only of objective fact. Nevertheless, even if the client's initial narrative of the incident should omit any reference to slipping or tripping, I believe that the lawyer's obligation is to explain to the client in Jurisdiction Y that one of the legal requirements for recovery is an accident, such as a trip or slip. As we have seen in the earlier discussions of experiments by behavioral psychologists, a factual detail of that sort might very well be omitted in a narrative of the incident. Moreover, the narrator's understanding (whether accurate or inaccurate) of his or her own self-interest will affect the remembering-reconstruction of the incident entirely apart from any conscious dishonesty. Thus, the client who incorrectly assumes that tripping or slipping might preclude recovery (perhaps because it might imply care-lessness) might unconsciously screen out that fact. Despite the risk, therefore, that a dishonest client might consciously invent a trip or slip to meet the needs of the occasion, the attorney is obligated to prod the client's remembering-reconstruction by explaining the relevance and importance of that factual element.

A further risk that the lawyer thereby takes, of course, is the tactical one of being misinformed about that factual element of the case. However, that kind of risk is unavoidable—the lawyer may also be misinformed because of a *failure* to prompt the client's memory on that point. That unavoidable tactical risk is very different, however, from the one that is created when a lawyer indicates to a client that the lawyer prefers not to know any incriminating information, because the lawyer is seeking to avoid the moral responsibility that might result from knowing too much.

The workmen's compensation situation, in which a crucial slip or trip may have been omitted from the client's original narrative, suggests how the client may unconsciously remember-reconstruct the facts in accordance with what is assumed to be self-interest. In addition, a client may well make a quite conscious decision to tell the lawyer a false story initially, because the client mistakenly believes the truth to be more incriminating than it is in fact. For example, in Chapter 1, an actual case was mentioned in which the client was reluctant to tell her lawyer that her husband had attacked her with a knife, because that fact tended to confirm that she had shot him. Had the client known that self-defense is a legal defense, she would have had no hesitation at the outset in telling the lawyer what had happened.

In interviewing, therefore, the attorney must take into account the practical psychological realities of the situation. That means, at least at the earlier stages of eliciting the client's story, that the attorney should assume a skeptical attitude, and that the attorney should give the client legal advice that might help in drawing out useful information that the client, consciously or unconsciously, might be withholding. To that extent—but on a different, and more limiting, rationale—I adhere to my earlier position that there are situations in which it may be proper for the attorney to give the client legal advice even though the attorney has reason to believe that the advice may induce the client to commit perjury. There does come a point, however, where nothing less than "brute rationalization" can purport to justify a conclusion that the lawyer is seeking in good faith to elicit truth rather than actively participating in the creation of perjury.

Frequently, the lawyer who helps the client to save a losing case by contributing a crucial fact is acting from a personal sense of justice: the criminal defense lawyer who knows that prison is a horror and who believes that no human being should be subjected to such inhumanity; the negligence lawyer who resents the arbitrary rules that prevent a seriously injured and impoverished individual from recovering from an insurance company; the prosecutor who does not want to see a vicious criminal once again turned loose upon innocent citizens because of a technical defense; or the tax attorney who resents an arbitrary and unfair system that leaves Peter with his wealth while mulcting Paul. I have sometimes referred to that attitude (with some ambivalence) as the Robin Hood principle. We are our clients' "champions against a hostile world", and the desire to see justice done, despite some inconvenient fact, may be an overwhelming one. But Robin Hood, as romantic a figure as he may have been, was an outlaw. Those lawyers who choose that role, even in the occasional case under the compulsion of a strong sense of the justness of the client's cause, must do so on their own moral responsibility and at their own risk, and without the sanction of generalized standards of professional responsibility.

Footnotes

1 Freedman, *Professional Responsibility of the Criminal Defense Lawyer: The Three Hardest Questions,* 64 MICH. L. REV. 1469, 1478 (1966).

2 DR 7-102(A)(7).

3 DR 2-110(C)(1)(b).

4 DR 4-101 (C) (3). *See,* p. 6 *supra.*

5 DR 7-102(A)(6).

6 SELECTED WRITINGS ON THE LAW OF EVIDENCE AND TRIAL (W. Fryer ed. 1957) [hereinafter cited as FRYER].

7 *Id.* at v.

8 L.P. STRYKER, THE ART OF ADVOCACY (1954); H.S. BODIN, MARSHALLING THE EVIDENCE (1954); Cleary, *Evidence as a Problem in Communicating,* 5 VAND. L. REV. 275, 277 (1952).

9 Cleary, *supra* note 8, as quoted in FRYER, at 30.

10 BODIN, *supra* note 8, as quoted in FRYER, at 13.

11 *Id.*

12 *Id.* at 14.

13 Cleary, *supra* note 8, as quoted in FRYER, at 30.

14 STRYKER, *supra* note 8, as quoted in FRYER, at 4.

15 *Id.* at 3.

16 *Id.* at 3.

17 BODIN, *supra* note 8, as quoted in FRYER, at 13 (emphasis in the original).

18 *Id.* (emphasis in the original).

19 *Id.* at 13-14.

20 *See,* E. MORGAN, J. MAGUIRE, & J. WEINSTEIN, CASES AND MATERIALS ON EVIDENCE 230 (3d ed. 1951).

21 The quotations from St. Augustine, John Locke, and David Hume are found in D. LOCKE, MEMORY (1971).

22 F.C. BARTLETT, REMEMBERING: A STUDY IN EXPERIMENTAL AND SOCIAL PSYCHOLOGY 33, 46 (1967) [hereinafter cited as BARTLETT].

23 BODIN, *supra* note 8, as quoted in FRYER, at 13.

24 BARTLETT, at 33. *See also,* Buckout, *Eyewitness Testimony,* SCIENTIFIC AMERICAN, Dec. 1974, at 23.

25 Moore, *Elements of Error in Testimony,* 28 ORE. L. REV. 293, 295 (1949).

26 BARTLETT, *supra* note 22, at 58, 63 *et seq.,* 80, 93.

27 BARTLETT, at 14.

28 Gardner, *The Perception and Memory of Witnesses,* 18 CORNELL L. Q. 391 (1933) (emphasis in the original).

29 BARTLETT, at 213.

30 *Id.*

31 G.A. TALLAND, DISORDERS OF MEMORY AND LEARNING 18-19 (1969).

32 *Id.*

33 BARTLETT, at 58; TALLAND, *supra* note 31, at 19.

34 *See,* Gardner, *supra* note 28, at 403.

35 E. Loftus, in PSYCHOLOGY TODAY, Dec. 1974, at 117, 119.

[36] BARTLETT, at 38, 191.

[37] M.D. VERNON, THE PSYCHOLOGY OF PERCEPTION 206-07 (1962).

[38] TALLAND, *supra* note 31, at 19.

[39] *Id.* at 78.

[40] *Id.* at 60.

[41] *See, e.g.,* BARTLETT, at 195.

[42] *Id.*

[43] Gardner, *supra* note 28, at 404.

[44] *See,* J. VOELKER (R. Traver, pseudonym), ANATOMY OF A MURDER (1958).

[45] WURZEL, DAS JURISTISCHE DENKEN 82 (1904), translated in L. FULLER & R. BRAUCHER, BASIC CONTRACT LAW 67 (1964).

[46] Noonan, *The Purposes of Advocacy and the Limits of Confidentiality,* 64 MICH. L. REV. 1485, 1488 (1966).

[47] Freedman, *supra* note 1, at 1478-80.

[48] *Id.* at 1481.

[49] DR 7-102 (A) (6).

[50] Noonan, *supra* note 45, at 1488.

Chapter 7

SOME ETHICAL PROBLEMS OF THE PROSECUTOR

It is generally recognized that prosecution and defense attorneys have significantly different roles and functions, and that their ethical difficulties and the solutions to them must vary accordingly. Those differences derive principally from important distinctions between the government and the individual citizen who is prosecuted. One such distinction is the paramountcy and the sanctity of the individual in our society. Another is the awesome power of the government, a power that the founders of our nation had good reason to circumscribe in the Bill of Rights and elsewhere in the Constitution. A third difference is the majesty and dignity of our government. Conduct that may be tolerable in individuals may be reprehensible when done "under color of law" on behalf of the nation or a state. In addition, the prosecutor has extraordinary discretion in directing investigations, defining the crime to be charged, affecting the punishment, and even in deciding whether to prosecute at all. In the course of exercising that discretion, the prosecutor is frequently called upon to make decisions which, in private litigation, would be made by a client rather than by the lawyer. Thus, to say that the prosecutor has special responsibilities in wielding the huge discretionary powers of government, is simply to recognize that the prosecutor is the attorney who has that discretionary power to wield. Further, defense counsel has special professional responsibilities deriving from the importance, to the adversary system, of confidentiality between attorney and client, the presumption of innocence, the constitutional right to counsel, and the constitutional privilege against self-incrimination. The prosecutor, who does not represent a private client, is not affected by those considerations in the same way.

For example, the defense attorney may be professionally bound to withhold evidence: there is nothing unethical in keeping a guilty defendant off the stand and putting the government to its proof. The Constitution guarantees the defendant nothing less than that. Obviously, however, it does not follow that the prosecutor is similarly privileged to withhold material evidence, and the constitutional command is, of course, precisely the contrary.[1] Similarly, it is ethical for defense counsel to cross-examine a prosecution witness to make the witness appear to be inaccurate or untruthful, even when the defense attorney knows that the witness is testifying accurately and truthfully.[2] Even those who assert that counsel should never mislead the court in any way agree with that conclusion.[3] They reach that result on the reasoning that the defense is entitled to "put the government to its proof",[4] and to "test the truth of the prosecution's case",[5] whereas I base the same conclusion on the necessities of the obligation of confidentiality. None of those rationales, however, would justify a prosecutor in obtaining a conviction by making a defense witness appear to be lying when the prosecutor knows that the witness is testifying truthfully. The defendant, who is presumed innocent, does not have a burden of proof to be tested, nor does the prosecutor function under the burden of an obligation of confidentiality in conducting the trial.

In recognition of the different roles of defense counsel and prosecutor, the American Bar Association and the Association of American Law Schools, in their Joint Conference Report on Professional Responsibility, concluded that: "The public prosecutor cannot take as a guide for the conduct of his office the standards of an attorney appearing on the behalf of an individual client. The freedom elsewhere wisely granted to partisan advocacy must be severely curtailed if the prosecutor's duties are to be properly discharged."[6] Similarly, the Code of Professional Responsibility states that the responsibility of a public prosecutor "differs from that of the usual advocate; his duty is to seek justice, not merely to convict".[7] In addition, the ABA Standards Relating to the Prosecution and the Defense Function are divided into a separate body of rules for each. The Standards also emphasize the unique role of the prosecutor: "Although the prosecutor operates within the adversary system, it is fundamental that his obligation is to protect the innocent as well as to convict the guilty, to guard the rights of the accused as well as to enforce the rights of the public." The prosecutor is not just an advocate, but an "administrator of justice". He is an administrator "in the sense that he acts as a decision-maker on a broad policy level and over a wide range of cases as director of public prosecution. . . . Since his is a large share of the responsibility for what cases are taken into the courts, the character, quality and efficiency of the whole system is shaped in great measure by the manner in which he exercises his broad discretionary powers."[8]

Unfortunately, however, both the Code and the Standards fail to establish rules of ethical conduct that are adequate to the high purposes that have been set forth. The problem is illustrated by a debate a few years ago over the propriety of government prosecutions of peace activists and civil rights militants, as in the Chicago conspiracy trial and in prosecutions of Black Panthers. In response to the charge that it is unethical for a prosecutor to make a political decision to "get" members of dissident groups, no less an authority than the late Professor Alexander M. Bickel of Yale Law School defended the practice. Professor Bickel wrote that such an exercise of prosecutorial discretion is "unexceptional" as long as the prosecutor succeeds in developing a "plausible" case, even though that case should ultimately prove to be "quite flimsy".[9] Professor Bickel later emphasized that he had said that the crime for which one is thus "gotten" should be one "that has exposed and would expose others to arrest and prosecution".[10] That observation, however, is not responsive to the problem. There are very few of us against whom a determined prosecutor could not make a "plausible" case once the mighty investigatory resources of the government have been brought to bear—and, of course, the plausible (albeit flimsy) case would be for some conduct generally recognized as criminal, or else we would not really have been gotten. Although it surely was not Professor Bickel's intention, his standard could readily be taken as sanctioning the establishment of an Enemies List, compiled for the purpose of "getting" or, in John Dean's word, "screwing" those in political disfavor.

The first major issue of prosecutorial discretion, therefore, relates to the decision to investigate. Justice Robert Jackson (a former Attorney General) called that "the most dangerous power of the prosecutor", because it enables the prosecutor to "pick people he thinks he should get rather than pick cases that need to be prosecuted". Justice Jackson went on to observe that, with the law books filled with a great assortment of crimes, a prosecutor stands a fair chance of pinning at least a technical violation of some act on the part of almost anyone. In such a case, he observed, it is "not a question of discovering the commission of a crime and then looking for the man who has committed it, it is a question of picking the man and then searching the law books or putting investigators to work, to pin some offense on him". At that point, law enforcement "becomes personal, and the real crime becomes that of being unpopular with the predominant or governing group, being attached to the wrong political views, or being personally obnoxious to or in the way of the prosecutor himself".[11]

How then is that "most dangerous power" of the prosecutor dealt with in the ABA's Code of Professional Responsibility or in its Standards Relating to the Prosecution Function? The answer is: not at all. It is essential, therefore, that immediate attention be given to developing appropriate standards.

To begin with, it should be recognized that motive is a principal element of ethical concern. Contrary to the implication of Professor Bickel's standard, the propriety of an Enemies List does not turn upon the success or failure of the prosecutor in ultimately developing a case. That is, "selective prosecution"— when the selection derives from improper motives—constitutes an abuse of official power and a violation of fundamental rights, and is therefore unethical conduct. One form of such conduct is illustrated by *Yick Wo v. Hopkins*.[12] There a San Francisco ordinance made it unlawful for any person to maintain a laundry in a wooden building without securing a license from the Board of Supervisors. Yick Wo was convicted of violating the ordinance and imprisoned for nonpayment of the fine. The record in the case showed that virtually all applications for licenses that were filed by Chinese were denied, and that virtually all licenses requested by non-Chinese applicants had been granted. Thus, the prosecutions of Yick Wo and others were founded in discriminatory treatment deriving from improper motives. The Supreme Court held: "Though the law itself be fair on its face and impartial in appearance, yet, if it is applied and administered by public authority with an evil eye and an unequal hand, so as practically to make unjust and illegal discriminations between persons in similar circumstances, material to their rights, the denial of equal justice is still within the prohibition of the Constitution."*

Unambiguous cases like *Yick Wo* are the easy ones (although it should be borne in mind that the case was not only prosecuted but carried on appeal as far as the Supreme Court). A more difficult case was presented by the campaign of Robert Kennedy, as Attorney General, against James Hoffa. Kennedy was known to have circulated among the United States Attorneys' offices a special list that included the names of Hoffa and Roy Cohn, both of whom had earned Kennedy's enmity in years past. Within the Justice Department there was a Get-Hoffa squad (it was actually called that) which succeeded, during Kennedy's tenure, in bringing more prosecutions against Hoffa than there were civil rights cases in the entire state of Mississippi, and more prosecutions against officers of the Teamsters Union than there were civil rights cases in the entire country. In view of the fact that Kennedy was

---

* Also of interest is Lenske v. United States, 383 F.2d 20 (9th Cir. 1967), in which an Internal Revenue agent recommended prosecution in a report emphasizing that the defendant, a lawyer who represented "left wing causes", was thought to be a Communist. Only one member of the court relied on that improper motive in reversing the conviction, but one hopes that under what Mr. Agnew has called the "post-Watergate morality", there would be a greater sensitivity to such a case.

said to have a "commitment" to civil rights, his devotion to putting Hoffa in jail bordered on obsession. The first product of that extraordinary diversion of government resources was a two-month trial of Hoffa on a misdemeanor charge.[13]

I have previously taken the position that James Hoffa was a marked man from the day he told Robert Kennedy that he was nothing but a rich man's kid who had never had to earn a nickel in his life, and that when Kennedy became Attorney General, satisfying that grudge became the public policy of the United States. Professor H. Richard Uviller of Columbia Law School has replied: ". . . [I]f Robert Kennedy as Attorney General, was convinced that the Teamsters Union and Hoffa in particular was destructive to trade unionism and a powerful, dangerous, and gangster-ridden force in the economy of the nation, would not his pursuit of Hoffa seem more ethical than if . . . Kennedy resolved to imprison Hoffa in revenge for a trivial personal insult . . .?"[14]

There is obvious merit in Professor Uviller's response. Motive is, of course, a primary consideration in making judgments regarding the ethical quality of conduct. Nevertheless, a resolution of the ethical problem raised by the Kennedy-Hoffa problem lies elsewhere. We are concerned here with the attorney as public official, wielding enormous governmental powers, and responsible for assuring not only that justice be done but that it appear to be done. It does not matter, therefore, whether I am right in believing that Kennedy was bent upon satisfying a personal grudge, or Professor Uviller right in suggesting a worthier motive. Rather, the significant possibility that professional duty might be affected by personal interest created a conflict of interest, even if only in appearance, which required that Kennedy abstain from any direct or indirect role in Justice Department actions against Hoffa. As stated in DR 5-101(A) of the Code, a lawyer "shall not" act professionally if the exercise of professional judgment will be or "reasonably may be" affected by "personal interests". In addition, Canon 9 provides that a lawyer should avoid "even the appearance" of professional impropriety. Similarly, the ABA Standards provide that: "A prosecutor should avoid the appearance . . . of a conflict of interest with respect to his official duties."[15] The Commentary to that section adds that: "It is of the utmost importance that the prosecutor avoid participation in a case in circumstances where any implication of partiality may cast a shadow over the integrity of his office." When a conflict of interest may arise, the prosecutor is required by the Standards to withdraw from the case and make appropriate arrangements for appointment of a special prosecutor.[16]

Several years ago I argued that the prosecution of Al Capone for tax evasion was improper, because the motive was to punish Capone for other crimes that the prosecution suspected but was unable to prove.[17] That is, I put the Capone case into Justice Jackson's category of "picking the man and then searching the law books or putting investigators to work, to pin some offense on him". On reflection, I think that position was wrong. Again, we are principally concerned with motive, and what I had overlooked is that Capone was being pursued for nothing other than criminal activity, and that the tax evasion was uncovered in the course of proper investigations of his suspected criminal conduct. Thus, the Capone prosecution would fall within a proposed standard drafted by Professor Uviller: "The prosecutor should affirmatively seek the evidence to support a prosecution where, in his judgment, the well-being of the community is seriously threatened by illegal enterprise or by the criminal activities of an identifiable person or persons, notwithstanding the fact that such crime or criminal has thus far escaped detection or arrest."[18] With the addition of a conflict-of-interest provision that would deal with the Kennedy-Hoffa kind of situation, Professor Uviller's proposal would seem to have considerable merit. I would also add the following corollary: "The prosecutor should not seek evidence to support a prosecution unless, in his or her reasonable judgment, the well-being of the community is threatened by illegal enterprise or by the criminal activities of an identifiable person or persons."

The second part of the issue of prosecutorial discretion relates to the standard that should be applied in deciding whether to proceed with the criminal trial process, beginning with seeking an indictment.

At the outset, it is important to note that merely to be charged with a crime is a punishing experience. The defendant's reputation is immediately damaged, usually irreparably, despite an ultimate failure to convict. Anguish and anxiety become a daily presence for the defendant, and for the defendant's family and friends. The emotional strains of the criminal trial process have been known to destroy marriages and to cause alienation or emotional disturbance among the accused's children. The financial burden can be enormous, and may well include loss of employment because of absenteeism due to pretrial detention or time required away from work during hearings and the trial, or because of the mere fact of having been named as a criminal defendant. The trial itself, building up to the terrible anxiety during jury deliberations, is a torturing experience. All that, and more, the prosecutor sets into motion simply by exercising the awesome discretionary power to seek an indictment against a fellow citizen. Expressing the idea that the government seeks justice, not convictions, it is said that the government wins its point even when a not-guilty verdict is returned. That is true also in a less idealistic, more cynical sense: the prosecution wins even when the defendant is found innocent because, typically, the defendant will carry for life the severe scars of that encounter with justice.

Recognizing those facts, conscientious prosecutors do not put the destructive engine of the criminal process into motion unless they are satisfied beyond a reasonable doubt that the accused is guilty. In a thoughtful and candid exploration of the exercise of prosecutorial discretion, Professor John Kaplan of Stanford Law School has observed that the "first and most basic standard" is that, "regardless of the strength of the case", a prosecutor who does not "actually believe" that the accused is guilty does not feel justified in prosecuting. In Professor Kaplan's experience as a prosecutor, the attitude "was more than a mere question of prosecutorial policy". The "great majority, if not all" of the Assistant United States Attorneys took the position that it was "morally wrong" to initiate a prosecution unless one was "personally convinced" of guilt.[19] The same standard is followed by New York State Special Prosecutor Maurice Nadjari.[20] In addition, the Code of Professional Responsibility reminds us that "in our system of criminal justice the accused is to be given the benefit of all reasonable doubts".[21]

It is with considerable dismay, therefore, that one finds that both the Code and the ABA Standards Relating to the Prosecution Function propose rules that fall far short of the standard practiced in fact by Mr. Nadjari and the Assistant United States Attorneys with whom Professor Kaplan worked. Under the Code, contrary to its promise, the accused is not given "the benefit of all reasonable doubts" in the rules relating to whether a citizen should be put to the ordeal of a criminal prosecution. On the contrary, the standard set forth is that the charges be supported by "probable cause".[22] Probable cause, of course, may be based upon hearsay and may be satisfied by even less than a substantial likelihood of guilt. The only saving aspect of the Code provision is that the disciplinary standard is, although to a very limited extent, an objective one. That is, the prosecutor violates the rule whenever he or she knows "or it is obvious" that the charges are not supported by probable cause. That means that even if the prosecutor should deny knowing that probable cause was lacking to justify instituting prosecution, the prosecutor might nevertheless be disciplined upon a finding that the lack of probable cause was "obvious".

The ABA Standards are also patently inadequate. The test for instituting criminal charges is, again, probable cause.[23] The Standards, however, eliminate even the minimally objective test of the Code, by providing that the prosecutor violates the rule only when he or she "knows" that the charges are not supported by probable cause, and despite the fact that the lack of probable cause is obvious. Thus, for practical purposes, there is no ethical limitation imposed upon the prosecutor's discretion under the Standards. The only saving aspect of the Standards is that the prosecutor is told that he or she "should not" seek charges that the prosecutor cannot "reasonably support with evidence at trial".[24] The Commentary to that provision indicates that the prosecutor is thereby urged not to institute charges unless a "prima facie case" can be established. That standard is somewhat higher than probable cause, since it requires sufficient admissible evidence to make a minimal case on each element of the offense charged, but a prosecutor can well have that much evidence and nevertheless be virtually certain of the defendant's innocence. Finally, there is some small comfort for the conscientious prosecutor like Professor Kaplan or Mr. Nadjari, since the Standards do say that a prosecutor "may" decline to go forward when the prosecutor has "reasonable doubt that the accused is in fact guilty".

We have learned, of course, not to expect too much from the Code and the Standards in their treatment of the prosecutor's professional responsibilities. As noted earlier, a prosecutor could draw up a personal Enemies List for investigatory purposes without violating a Disciplinary Rule under the Code or committing unprofessional conduct under the Standards. Much more disappointing, therefore, is to find that Professor Richard Uviller has also sanctioned the notion that a prosecutor can properly go forward when he or she has reasonable doubt as to the guilt of the accused. Professor Uviller gives the following illustrative case. An elderly white person is suddenly grabbed from behind in a dimly lit vestibule by a black youth who shows a knife and takes the victim's wallet. The entire incident occupies thirty seconds. Some days later, the victim sees someone in the neighborhood whom he believes to have been the assailant and has him arrested. Although the prosecutor presses him hard, the victim swears he has picked the right man. There is nothing unusual about the defendant's appearance, the victim never saw him except during those few moments of terror in a dim light, and the victim admits that he does not know many black people personally. However, he remains certain because, he says, his attacker's face was "indelibly engraved on [his] memory". The defendant has an alibi: his mother will testify that at the time of the crime he was at home watching television with her. As Professor Uviller concedes, the prosecutor knows the fallibility of identification under such circumstances. Therefore, Professor Uviller acknowledges, reasonable doubt will be "clear" to the prosecutor. Professor Uviller also recognizes that "juries regularly convict in such cases". And yet, incredibly, he suggests that the prosecutor may properly, and perhaps even should, go forward in such a case.[25] Although Professor Uviller concedes that the prosecutor should not proceed when there is a "substantial likelihood" of innocence or when there is "good reason to believe" that a prosecution witness is lying about a material fact, he goes so far as to say that even when the issue "stands in equipoise" in the prosecutor's mind, there is "no flaw in the conduct of the prosecutor" who puts the accused to the burden of a criminal prosecution.

If we follow Professor Uviller's suggested case to its likely conclusion in fact, we touch upon another major area of abuse of prosecutorial discretion, that is, plea bargaining. Presumably, the charge in the case he posed will be armed robbery, which may carry a penalty ranging from thirty years to life in prison. The defendant firmly states his innocence. However, his lawyer explains to the young man that if he goes to trial on a charge involving use of a weapon, and if he is convicted, he may not get out of prison until he is a very old man, if ever. He will protest, of course, that conviction is impossible, because he is innocent and because his mother will confirm that he was at home. But the defense lawyer will know as well as Professor Uviller and the prosecutors do that "juries regularly convict in such cases". The defense lawyer will have to tell that to the defendant. The defendant will also learn that his lawyer will try to negotiate a plea of guilty to assault with intent to rob. The maximum penalty on that offense may be fifteen years, but if the defendant saves the government the expense of a trial, the judge may be lenient and give him only, say, three to nine years in prison. If the defendant is really lucky, he will be permitted to plead guilty to simple assault, for which the maximum penalty is only one year of his freedom, and he might actually be out of jail in a matter of months. Although the defendant is innocent, that presents no problem with the bargained plea. The law, in its even-handed majesty, permits the innocent as well as the guilty to plead guilty in order to avoid the coercive threat of extended imprisonment.[26]

Thus, although Professor Uviller rationalizes his conclusion on the ground that the prosecutor should not preempt the function of the judge and jury in a doubtful case, the fact is that eight or nine times out of ten that is precisely what will happen, through plea bargaining, in the case he suggests. I agree, therefore, with Professor Kaplan and Mr. Nadjari. A prosecutor cannot properly go forward with a case unless the prosecutor is satisfied beyond a reasonable doubt that the accused is guilty. In addition, a prosecutor should be professionally disciplined for proceeding with prosecution if a fair-minded person could not reasonably conclude, on the facts known to the prosecutor, that the accused is guilty beyond a reasonable doubt.

The practice of plea bargaining in a metropolitan court was described by the Department of Justice several years ago. The "great volume of business at the court makes rapid disposition of cases extremely important". That in turn requires that most defendants plead guilty and that they not "persist in demands for trials". One method of assuring a sufficient number of such pleas is to overcharge, that is, to charge a more serious offense or an accumulation of offenses and thereby "set the stage for subsequent bargaining". Commonly, cases are drawn up as felonies, with the prosecutor noting that a plea for some misdemeanor should be accepted. Thus, the prosecutor consciously coerces the defendant into foregoing the constitutional right to trial by jury. As noted in the Department of Justice report: "Negotiation in such cases is a formality."[27] Although the reason for this practice —"the great volume of business at the court"—is a serious practical problem, it does not justify the unethical practical effect of impairing a constitutional right by a combination of duress and trickery.

In fact, the situation is often far worse than that, because the prosecutor is knowingly participating with unscrupulous defense counsel in misleading the defendant into believing that a real plea bargain has been made, when in fact both attorneys know that the defendant was overcharged in the first instance. To quote again from the Department of Justice: "[I]n such a case no real bargain occurs, since both [attorneys] know that the original charges are too heavy to sustain." The defense lawyer, however, may not communicate that knowledge to the client, "who may feel that a reduction in charges is in all cases a disposition well worth a plea of guilty, and well worth the fee which the attorney demands for obtaining it". It is open to question, therefore, how many "real" felony cases—*i.e.,* those which the prosecutor believes can be successfully prosecuted as felonies—actually are compromised at the plea-bargaining session.[28]

Other instances can be cited in which prosecutors have failed to advise the court that the defendant has been denied the consti-

tutional right to effective assistance of counsel, and in which prosecutors have even taken conscious advantage of ineffective assistance
of counsel. Several years ago a defendant was prosecuted for
crimes arising out of his practice of law without a license.[29] In
the course of his trial, an experienced member of the prosecutor's
office testified that in a case in which he had served as prosecutor
and in which the imposter had served as defense counsel, it had
been the prosecutor's judgment that the imposter had not rendered effective assistance of counsel. The prosecutor admitted his
obligation to advise the court of ineffective assistance, but admitted further that he had not done so. In fact, he had taken the
trouble to praise defense counsel's ability in his summation to
the jury. When I suggested to a member of the United States
Attorney's Office that the comments in summation indicated
that the imposter had indeed rendered effective assistance, I was
told that it indicated precisely the contrary, since it was the
practice of members of the prosecutor's office to put favorable
comment about defense counsel into the trial record whenever
they were concerned that the issue of ineffective representation
might legitimately be raised on appeal.

Even more serious than those cases in which the prosecutor
fails to expose ineffective assistance of counsel, are those in
which the prosecutor purposefully seeks out a forum in which
defense counsel is likely to overlook defects in the prosecutor's
case. "It is not uncommon in the District [of Columbia] to
prosecute a case in General Sessions Court in order to avoid
problems which might be raised in a [United States] District
Court trial, where defense counsel and judges may be more
meticulous in their treatment of the case or, in some instances,
more likely to recognize flaws in the prosecution."[30] In other
words, in cases in which conviction might be precluded by an
adequate defense, some prosecutors have nevertheless pressed
charges in the hope that inadequate representation might result in
conviction.

Another serious prosecutorial abuse is the practice of deferred
sentencing, which permits the prosecutor to maintain a powerful
coercive hold on a witness who has pleaded guilty, but who will
not be sentenced until after having testified in a manner satisfactory to the prosecution in the trial of another defendant. Un-
happily, the practice is so commonplace that it is rarely viewed as
falling within the scope of professional ethics. Consider, however,
how promptly and properly disciplinary action would follow if a
defense attorney were to promise to compensate a defense witness
$10 contingent upon how helpful the witness' testimony proved to
be in the case. According to the ABA Code: "Witnesses should

always testify truthfully and should be free from any financial inducements that might tempt them to do otherwise."[31] The footnote to that provision quotes from a New York case which holds that attorneys "must keep themselves clear of any connection which in the slightest degree tends to induce witnesses to testify in favor of their clients".[32] The text of the Code expressly refers to payments of money, but the explanation of the rule relates more broadly to anything that "in the slightest degree" "tends to induce" witnesses to testify in a particular way. Unquestionably, ten years of freedom from imprisonment, which the prosecutor may give, is a far greater inducement than ten dollars, or any other amount of money, that a defense lawyer might be prepared to give.*

Another common form of coercion of witnesses by prosecutors is the use of prior convictions for impeachment of a defendant or of witnesses for the defense, where the prejudicial effect on the jury far outweighs the asserted justification of casting doubt on credibility. In one case, the prosecutor's true motive in using prior convictions to impeach defense witnesses was made manifest by his argument to the jury that they should consider the kind of person the defendant was in the light of the criminal records of the defense witnesses with whom he had been associating. Even without such argument, the prejudicial effect, and the prejudicial intention, is clear. As one prosecutor wrote to me: "I prefer to use [prior convictions] as heavy weights affixed to an object I intend to sink in deep water." A former prosecutor has also written that in his experience the opportunity to inform the jury of a prior conviction was considered "a strong weapon" for the state, "almost invariably" tipping the balance against the defendant.[33] Of course, the inevitable result of the prosecutor's practice of using prior convictions to impeach is to coerce the defendant from exercising the constitutional right to take the stand in his or her own defense. Thus, the jury listens to the prosecution's case, and then waits in vain for the defendant to deny the allegations. Presented with the Hobson's choice of either not testifying or else taking the stand and having the jury prejudiced by knowledge of prior convictions, defendants with prior records are under additional heavy pressure to plead guilty and forego their constitutional rights, for reasons unrelated to guilt or innocence.

---

* Of course, defense counsel can and does point up in cross-examination that the prosecution witness is awaiting sentencing—a point which the jury may or may not fully appreciate, since they will know that it is the judge who gives the sentence. By the same token, however, the prosecution could bring out the fact that the defense witness was hoping for compensation, but obviously that would not be an adequate or acceptable solution.

Another important area of unprofessional conduct by prosecutors relates to condoning and covering up police abuses, such as brutality, perjury, unlawful arrests, unlawful searches and seizures, and unlawful interrogation. Again, there is a practical difficulty at the root of the problem. The prosecutor must maintain a close working relationship with the police. The prosecutor's job can be made extremely onerous if there is not willing cooperation from the police, both in investigating and in presenting evidence in court. As a consequence, the prosecutor sometimes is under considerable compulsion either to present charges against members of the police department for unlawful conduct, which impairs cooperation, or to condone or cover up police crime.

The problem is a serious one. As stated by Judge Irving Younger (formerly a prosecutor and now a Professor of Law at Cornell University): "Every lawyer who practices in the criminal courts knows that police perjury is commonplace."[34] Similarly, Professor Uviller has noted that prosecutors have become so concerned about police perjury regarding unlawful searches in narcotics cases, that the New York County District Attorney recently joined with defense counsel in an unsuccessful attempt to have the New York Court of Appeals shift the burden of proof to the state when abandonment by the defendant is asserted in reply to a motion to suppress contraband drugs.[35] Although the District Attorney deserves credit for taking such action, one may infer, without undue cynicism, that the prosecutors have been presenting what they have reason to believe is police perjury in such cases.

A particularly revealing case occurred several years ago in the District of Columbia. Two black men were stopped, interrogated, and searched for no other apparent reason than that they were walking with a white woman. They disputed the propriety of that arrest and, as a result, were charged with disorderly conduct.[36] The police officers attempted to justify the initial arrest by swearing under oath that the men corresponded to a description of two burglars, broadcast over the squad-car radio that same evening. The police log book revealed, however, that no such burglary had taken place, and no such description had been broadcast. The prosecutor made strenuous efforts to prevent defense counsel from examining the log book, which indicates that the prosecutor was aware of the perjury and was attempting to prevent its exposure. A police trial board subsequently found the officers guilty of unlawful arrest and perjury. (It subjected them only to small fines, however, rather than to dismissal from the force.) Despite demands of civic organizations, the United States Attorney for the District of Columbia failed to prosecute the officers.* Nor, or course, was any disciplinary action ever taken against the prosecutor for attempting to cover up the police officers' perjury at the trial of the two men.

In many prosecutors' offices it is common practice to institute criminal prosecutions to retaliate against citizens who complain of police misconduct, or to condition a *nolle prosequi* on the defendant's release of civil claims against the arresting officers. Such practices have been condemned by the Virginia State Bar Legal Ethics Committee,[37] the President of the Board of Commissioners of the District of Columbia,[38] and the President's Commission on Crime in the District of Columbia.[39] In a case that arose in the District of Columbia after the practice had thus been condemned, the chief prosecutor admitted that the prosecution had been reinstituted, after having been dropped, solely because the defendant had made a complaint against the arresting police officer:[40] ". . . Three months later he comes in and makes a formal complaint. So we said, 'if you are going to play ball like that why shouldn't we proceed with our case?' . . . I had no reason to file until he changed back on his understanding of what we had all agreed on. *That is done in many criminal cases.*"** In the opinion of Chief Judge David Bazelon, the prosecutor thereby admitted to a "gross abuse of discretion".[41] In addition, the Code of Professional Responsibility forbids a lawyer to "present, participate in presenting, or threaten to present criminal charges solely to obtain an advantage in a civil matter".[42] Nevertheless, many prosecutors continue to institute criminal charges in order to coerce private citizens out of their rights to seek remedies for police abuse.[43]

In an unreported California case, it was stipulated that six prosecutors were prepared to testify that they considered it to be

---

* The United States Attorney sought to justify his failure to prosecute by saying that he could not obtain indictments from a grand jury. That explanation is inadequate, however, in view of the fact that "grand juries in the District of Columbia by and large follow the lead of the prosecutor. They are always theoretically free to ignore cases, but as a practical matter they do so only when the alternative is suggested to them." OFFICE OF CRIMINAL JUSTICE, U.S. DEPARTMENT OF JUSTICE, CRIMINAL JUSTICE IN A METROPOLITAN COURT 37 (1966). In view of the documentary evidence of the officers' perjury—the log book and the transcript of their testimony at the trial—it is difficult to believe that the case was effectively presented to the grand jury.

** The conduct thus admitted is criminal as well as unethical: "Whoever . . . threatens to accuse any person of a crime . . . with intent to extort from such person . . . any pecuniary advantage whatever, *or to compel the person accused or threatened to do or to refrain from doing any act,* and whoever with such intent publishes any such accusation against another person shall be imprisoned for not more than five years or be fined not more than one thousand dollars, or both." 22 D.C. CODE 2305 (1961) (emphasis added).

unmeritorious, and that they would not care to prosecute it. The case was nevertheless prosecuted because of the likelihood that the defendant would file a civil action against the police department. According to one prosecutor: "[T]he duty of the [prosecutor], in addition to prosecuting criminals, [is] to protect the police officers, and in so protecting the police officers . . . any [prosecutor] worth his salt would have at that point included any offense . . . on which the defendant could have been convicted."[44] That quote echoes the point made earlier, that the prosecutor has a special sense of obligation to the police, who are the prosecutor's daily working associates. As Professor Younger has commented, even if a police officer's lies are exposed in the courtroom, the police-man is as likely to be indicted for perjury by "his co-worker, the prosecutor", as he is "to be struck down by thunderbolts from an avenging heaven".[45]

The obvious solution to that difficulty is to recognize it for what it is, a classic instance of conflict of interest. In any case involving charges of police abuse, therefore, a special prosecutor, who is not in a daily working relationship with the police, should be appointed to handle both the police officer's charge against the citizen and the citizen's charge against the officer.

With regard to the general issue of conflict of interest on the part of the prosecutor, the ABA Standards are unsatisfactory because they are unspecific and vague. Section 1.2 reads simply: "A prosecutor should avoid the appearance or reality of a conflict of interest with respect to his official duties. In some instances, as defined in the Code of Professional Responsibility, his failure to do so will constitute unprofessional conduct." The Commentary provides a cross reference to DR 5-101(A), which is equally general, proscribing acceptance of employment if the exercise of the lawyer's professional judgment "will be or reasonably may be affected by his own financial, business, property, or personal interest".

Criticizing the Standards on that ground, Professor Uviller has drafted a substitute conflict of interest provision.[46] Although his accompanying text suggests that Professor Uviller did not have in mind the conflict of interest relating to charges against police officers, one section of his draft could be read to cover that situation. It refers to "any obligation to or association with any person or organization which has had or may have any material influence upon the course of his professional career and which is involved in or materially affected by the case in question". Unfortunately, however, Professor Uviller would provide a test of "self-appraisal" which is "not entirely subjective",[47] but which is not sufficiently objective. That is, the prosecutor must not participate in any phase of a criminal investigation or prosecution unless the prosecutor "reasonably believes" that his or her judgment will be entirely unaffected by the conflicting interest. Although there is an objective element to the requirement that the belief be reasonable, that is a significantly less stringent test than is ordinarily applied in a conflict of interest situation. In that respect, therefore, the Standards are substantially preferable, because they impose the traditional test that a prosecutor should "avoid the appearance" of conflict of interest, irrespective of whether there is a conflict in fact.

Another question of prosecutorial ethics was raised at a recent debate before the Association of the Bar of the City of New York.[48] Maurice Nadjari, the Special Prosecutor for New York State, was asked whether it is proper for a prosecutor to call a press conference to announce an indictment and to describe the substance of the charges. Mr. Nadjari professed to find "little problem" with "what it is you can and what you cannot give to the press". Noting that an indictment is a public record and that it therefore must be "exposed to the press", Mr. Nadjari contended, by implication at least, that the prosecutor is therefore under an obligation to hold press conferences to announce the contents of the indictment "and additional information as well, including the prior criminal record of the defendant". In my own view, such conduct by the prosecutor is reprehensible. Only two purposes, both of them improper, are served when a prosecutor calls in the television cameras to announce an indictment: the defendant is severely defamed, and the likelihood of an unprejudiced jury is reduced. (Imagine the impact of that televised announcement on the family and friends of the defendant, who is said to be presumed innocent, and who, many months later, may be found to be innocent.) On the other hand, any legitimate end asserted to be served by such an announcement is adequately achieved simply by making the indictment a matter of public record. (That alone, of course, can be seriously prejudicial to the defendant, but is essential to protect against the greater abuses of secret indictments.) Particularly in light of Mr. Nadjari's cavalier attitude regarding pretrial press conferences by prosecutors, that problem is one that requires the urgent attention of disciplinary boards.

Because the prosecutor should be barred from speaking publicly about the case before trial does not mean that the defendant or the defense attorney should, or can constitutionally, be similarly restricted. The defendant's plea of not guilty is neither as edifying nor as dramatic as is an indictment. Moreover, through the very act of filing the indictment, the prosecutor commits a privileged defamation of the defendant. The defendant must be permitted to counter that defamation as promptly and as effectively as possible. The prosecutor, as representative of the government, does not in that capacity have a First Amendment right to defame the defendant, but the defendant is not stripped of his or her First Amendment rights by being named in an indictment. On the contrary, it would be difficult to imagine a situation in which those rights could be more crucial.

Another ethical problem of the prosecutor, which is not at all uncommon, arises when a prosecutor makes prejudicial comments in argument to the jury. Unless the action is deliberate, of course, there is no violation of professional responsibility. In one case, for example, the court found the prosecutor's misconduct to have been "so persistent and prejudicial" as to require reversal on grounds of "plain and prejudicial error".[49] The court quite properly noted, however, that the prosecutor's actions might have been the result of "his zeal and the excitement of the trial" rather than "deliberate intention" on his part. That is perfectly understandable, and one might not expect disciplinary action to result where the attorney has acted in the heat of the trial in a way that the same lawyer might disapprove upon cooler reflection. On the other hand, cooler reflection too seldom takes place. Almost invariably, the prosecutor's office seeks affirmance of the conviction on appeal, prevents the defendant from obtaining release pending appeal, and imposes no intra-office sanction against the offending prosecutor. At that point, the improper trial conduct is in effect ratified and becomes official office policy, which does indeed rise to the status of unprofessional conduct.

An encouraging exception to that general practice occurred recently in New York. A defendant had been tried three times for murder. The first trial ended in a hung jury, the second ended in a mistrial, and the third resulted in a conviction for first-degree manslaughter, with the jury rejecting first- and second-degree murder charges. Beginning with his arrest, the defendant spent a total of 6½ years in prison. Finally, the defense discovered that the prosecution had suppressed the fact that an important prosecution witness in all three trials had psychiatric and criminal records, and the court vacated the conviction. At that point, Manhattan District Attorney Richard H. Kuh (who had not been District Attorney during the previous stages of the case) declined to appeal and requested the court to dismiss the indictment, on the ground that further prosecution "would strip the law of dignity and compassion".[50] It remains to be seen, however, whether any disciplinary action will be taken against the two prosecutors who violated their constitutional obligation to provide the information to the defense in the three trials.

In fact, it is extraordinarily rare that a prosecutor is disciplined for even the grossest misconduct short of serious criminal offenses. The attitude seems to be that an occasional reversal of a conviction on appeal is an adequate sanction, although of course it is not. Illustrative of the reluctance of disciplinary boards to take action against public prosecutors is the case of *Miller v. Pate*,[51] which involved the rape-murder of an eight-year-old girl. At trial the prosecutor introduced into evidence a pair of man's undershorts, allegedly the defendant's, and described them as being "heavily stained with blood". In fact, although there was some blood on the shorts, the dramatic stains that the prosecutor emphasized to the jury were red-brown paint—a fact unknown to defense counsel because the prosecutor had blocked defense efforts to examine the shorts. Despite a finding by the Supreme Court that the prosecutor had "deliberately misrepresented the truth" in securing the conviction, the Grievance Committee failed to recommend disciplinary action.[52]

There is, however, a significant exception to the general failure of disciplinary boards to deal with unprofessional conduct by prosecutors. Recently in the District of Columbia, the Court of Appeals found it necessary over a period of time to reverse several convictions obtained by the same prosecutor through the use of inflammatory language in summation. The reversals alone, however, were not sufficient to impress upon the prosecutor that his conduct had been improper. In a letter to the Bar Counsel, he protested that his trial tactics were highly professional. The decision of the Bar Counsel was to censure the individual prosecutor, and to admonish the United States Attorney that it is unprofessional for his office to seek affirmance on appeal of a conviction obtained by conduct that is clearly unethical on the part of a member of his office. In addition, the Association of the Bar of the City of New York has recently urged that when prosecutors engage in unprofessional conduct, the appropriate grievance committees "should be diligent in investigating and acting on the matter". Moreover, "Bar Associations should encourage defense lawyers and judges to report cases of prosecutorial misconduct and should follow up on these cases as vigorously as possible". The Association of the Bar specifically notes that alternative remedies, such as reliance upon intra-office sanctions or reversal on appeal, have proven inadequate. "Since every bar association has insisted that a prosecutor is, first and foremost, a lawyer, it follows that control by the profession should be invoked when he violates the standards established to guide his courtroom performance."[53]

Footnotes

[1] Brady v. Maryland, 373 U.S. 83, 87, 83 S. Ct. 1194, 10 L. Ed. 2d 215, 218-19 (1963).

[2] See, Chapter 4 supra.

[3] See, e.g., Burger, Standards of Conduct for Prosecution and Defense Personnel: A Judge's Viewpoint, 5 AM. CRIM. L. Q. 11, 14-15 (1966).

[4] Bress, Professional Ethics in Criminal Trials: A View of Defense Counsel's Responsibility, 64 MICH. L. REV. 1493, 1494 (1966).

[5] Burger, supra note 3, at 14.

[6] AMERICAN BAR ASSOCIATION-ASSOCIATION OF AMERICAN LAW SCHOOLS, JOINT CONFERENCE REPORT ON PROFESSIONAL RESPONSIBILITY (1958).

[7] AMERICAN BAR ASSOCIATION, CODE OF PROFESSIONAL RESPONSIBILITY, EC 7-13.

[8] AMERICAN BAR ASSOCIATION, STANDARDS RELATING TO THE PROSECUTION FUNCTION, COMMENTARY to § 1.1 [hereinafter cited as the ABA STANDARDS].

[9] Bickel, Judging the Chicago Trial, COMMENTARY, Jan., 1971, at 31, 36, 37, 39.

[10] COMMENTARY, May, 1971, at 14.

[11] Address by Justice Jackson, Second Annual Conference of U.S. Attorneys, April, 1940.

[12] 118 U.S. 356, 6 S. Ct. 1064, 30 L. Ed. 220 (1886).

[13] See, V. NAVASKY, KENNEDY JUSTICE, Ch. IX (1971).

[14] Uviller, The Virtuous Prosecutor in Quest of an Ethical Standard: Guidance from the ABA, 71 MICH. L. REV. 1145, 1152 (1973).

[15] ABA STANDARDS, § 1.2.

[16] See, ABA STANDARDS, COMMENTARY to § 1.2; § 2.10.

[17] Freedman, The Professional Responsibility of the Prosecuting Attorney, 55 GEO. L. J. 1030, 1034-35 (1967).

[18] Uviller, supra note 14, at 1154.

[19] Kaplan, The Prosecutorial Discretion—A Comment, 60 Nw. U. L. REV. 174, 178-79 (1965). Professor Kaplan notes some deviation from that standard in some special categories of cases.

[20] ASSOCIATION OF THE BAR OF THE CITY OF NEW YORK, PROFESSIONAL RESPONSIBILITY IN THE PRACTICE OF CRIMINAL LAW: THE MURKY DIVIDE BETWEEN RIGHT AND WRONG (May 8, 1974).

[21] EC 7-13.

[22] DR 7-103.

[23] ABA STANDARDS, § 3.9(a).

[24] Id. at § 3.9(e).

[25] Uviller, supra note 14, at 1157-59.

[26] North Carolina v. Alford, 400 U.S. 25, 91 S. Ct. 160, 27 L. Ed. 2d 162 (1970); McCoy v. United States, 124 App. D.C. 177, 363 F.2d 306 (D.C. Cir. 1966).

[27] OFFICE OF CRIMINAL JUSTICE, U.S. DEPARTMENT OF JUSTICE, CRIMINAL JUSTICE IN A METROPOLITAN COURT 34-35 (1966).

[28] Id. at 47-48.

[29] United States v. Morgan, Crim. No. 755-61 (D.D.C., May 1, 1964).

[30] OFFICE OF CRIMINAL JUSTICE, supra note 27, at 36.

[31] EC 7-28.

[32] In re Robinson, 151 App. Div. 589, 600, 136 N.Y.S. 548, 556-57 (1912), aff'd, 209 N.Y. 354, 103 N.E. 160 (1913).

[33] Letter from Howard D. Stave to the Editor of the New York Law Journal, Aug. 28, 1974.

[34] Younger, The Perjury Routine, 3 CRIM. L. BULL. 551 (1967).

[35] Uviller, supra note 14, at 1158, citing People v. Berrios, 28 N.Y.2d 361, 321 N.Y.S.2d 884, 270 N.E.2d 709 (1971).

[36] District of Columbia v. Mills, Crim. No. D.C. 3135-64 (D.C. Ct. Gen. Sess., Jan. 22, 1965).

[37] Opinion No. 131, approved by the Virginia State Bar Council, Oct. 25, 1963, reported in Virginia Bar News, Dec., 1963.

[38] Letter from President of Board of Commissioners of District of Columbia to the National Area Civil Liberties Union, Feb. 3, 1964.

[39] REPORT OF THE PRESIDENT'S COMMISSION ON CRIME IN THE DISTRICT OF COLUMBIA 338 (1966).

[40] District of Columbia v. Dixon, Nos. 4071, 4072 (D.C. Ct. App., June 13, 1967).

[41] Dixon v. District of Columbia, 394 F.2d 966 (D.C. Cir. 1968). *See also,* MacDonald v. Musick, 425 F.2d 373 (9th Cir. 1970), *cert. den.,* 400 U.S. 852, 91 S. Ct. 54, 27 L. Ed. 2d 90 (1970).

[42] DR 7-105(A).

[43] *See, e.g.,* Lansner, *Prosecution of Juvenile Delinquents,* N.Y.L.J., Sept. 24, 1974, at 1.

[44] Information supplied by counsel for defendant in *California v. MacDonald* (unreported).

[45] Younger, *supra* note 34, at 551.

[46] Uviller, *supra* note 14, at 1164.

[47] *Id.* at 1165.

[48] ASSOCIATION OF THE BAR OF THE CITY OF NEW YORK, *supra* note 20.

[49] King v. United States, 372 F.2d 383 (D.C. Cir. 1966).

[50] N.Y. Times, Aug. 24, 1974, at 1, 11.

[51] 386 U.S. 1, 87 S. Ct. 785, 17 L. Ed. 2d 690 (1967).

[52] *See,* Alschuler, *Courtroom Misconduct by Prosecutors and Trial Judges,* 50 TEX. L. REV. 629, 671-72 (1972).

[53] N. DORSEN & L. FRIEDMAN, DISORDER IN THE COURT 187-88 (1974).

Chapter 8

CERTIFICATION OF TRIAL LAWYERS

A common complaint with law schools and young lawyers has been expressed by trial attorney F. Lee Bailey:

> Most law schools teach little or nothing about cross-examination. There should be courses in the methods and principles of cross-examination, and the courses should be followed up with practice sessions. Instead, the new lawyer must learn cross-examination in real trials at the expense of real clients. To me, this makes about as much sense as it would make to let medical interns practice surgery on living people instead of cadavers.

Surprisingly, that quotation is from a description by Mr. Bailey of his own truly masterful cross-examination in the *Torso Murder Case*.[1] Although Mr. Bailey is unconscious of the irony, he achieved that feat of high professional artistry when he was only three months out of law school, and despite the fact that he had never previously cross-examined a witness before a jury. Unfortunately, a similar view has been expressed by Chief Justice Warren Burger, who has called for certification of litigating lawyers, based upon the estimate that "from one-third to one-half of the lawyers who appear in the serious cases are not really qualified to render fully adequate representation".[2]

Mr. Bailey and the Chief Justice remind me of my father's friend, Moe, whose opinions were such, my father once said, that if Moe had gotten to this country before his father did, and if his views had prevailed, Moe's father would never have been permitted to immigrate. Similarly, if Mr. Bailey's and Chief Justice Burger's restrictive views had been adopted before they entered the Bar, Mr. Bailey might never have defended his first case, and the graduate of an unaccredited night law school might never have had the opportunity to become Chief Justice of the United States.

Before I develop my disagreement with the Chief Justice and Mr. Bailey, I should stress those major issues on which we agree. First, the extent of ineffective assistance of counsel is outrageous and inexcusable. Second, the law schools bear a heavy responsibility for providing training in trial and appellate advocacy, as well as in related client-oriented skills such as interviewing and counselling.

It is clear, however, that a great deal of the current debate is being carried on in ignorance of how much legal education has progressed in the past ten or fifteen years, to say nothing of the past three or four decades. For example, a recent letter to the deans of New York law schools from the New York County Lawyers Association suggests that the issue might be explored of adjusting law school curricula to include, at least as an elective, a course in trial and appellate advocacy. In fact, of course, the law schools (in substantial part through the assistance of the Council on Legal Education for Professional Responsibility) have made enormous gains in developing methodology and courses to teach litigating skills. At Hofstra Law School, for example, which is not atypical in this regard, there are well over a dozen clinical programs and courses in advocacy, including a Neighborhood Law Office in which students, under faculty supervision, interview clients, draft pleadings, research and write briefs, and appear in court. In addition, lawyering skills and legal ethics are increasingly emphasized in traditional substantive law courses. My point is not that there is ground for complacency regarding needed improvements in legal education. Indeed, in New York the rules of the Court of Appeals severely restrict the law schools in their efforts to expand clinical legal education programs. It is nevertheless obvious that the principal opportunity for major reform in dealing with incompetent practitioners lies elsewhere than in further revision of law school curricula and methodology.

Nor is certification the proper cure for Chief Justice Burger's complaint—certainly not, at least, until several crucial questions have been satisfactorily answered. Who will do the certifying? Who will certify the certifiers? What will the standards be? How will exploitation of young lawyers (compelled to serve as apprentices to older lawyers) be avoided? What steps will be taken to eliminate the inadequate advocates from the ranks of "experienced" members of the Bar, particularly in view of the fact that the complaints have been directed against those already in practice?

To illustrate the last point, the members of the New York State Trial Lawyers Association may be one-third to one-half incompetent—if we are to accept the Chief Justice's authority on the matter—but they are certainly not stupid. Promptly following the Chief Justice's call for certification, the New York State Trial Lawyers Association proposed a certification program, complete with a grandfather clause which will have the effect of making certification unnecessary for the very lawyers whose past performance has given rise to the idea that certification is needed.

One of the oddest aspects of the current certification suggestions, is the emphasis on litigating attorneys. In fact, it has been urged that all certification be limited, at first, to admission to trial practice.[3] Surely it cannot be supposed, however, that the level of competence is higher among the large majority of lawyers who never go to court—those who do such office work as draft wills, plan estates, write contracts, counsel on business ventures, or prepare tax returns. In fact, in one critically important respect the litigating attorney is the lawyer *least* in need of certification, because only the litigating attorney operates in what the Chief Justice has called the "gold-fish bowl" of the courtroom,[4] under close and constant scrutiny by the public, other attorneys, and— most important—by the judges themselves.

Which brings me to my principal point. If one-third to one-half of the litigating lawyers are inadequate, and if it "happens regularly" that attorneys are unable to handle criminal cases assigned to them,[5] and if Chief Justice Burger in eighteen years on the Bench has indeed seen hundreds, if not thousands, of "miscarriages of justice",[6] caused by incompetent lawyers, then who is best able to do something about it? Who, in fact, has a constitutional and an ethical responsibility to do something about it? The answer is obvious: Chief Justice Burger, and his colleagues on the bench.[7]

On the contrary, however, not the Chief Justice nor virtually any other judge has accepted that fundamental responsibility. It is, indeed, extraordinary for a judge to seek disciplinary action against an attorney on grounds of incompetence, even though it is unprofessional for a lawyer to accept a case that he or she is not competent to handle,[8] and even though a judge is bound to prevent unprofessional conduct[9] and to guard against the violation of constitutional guarantees such as the right to effective assistance of counsel.[10]

In fact, the courts have gone in precisely the opposite direction. They have placed such a "heavy burden"[11] upon a defendant to maintain a claim of ineffective assistance of counsel, that innumerable cases are never appealed, and in most of those that are appealed, the inadequate attorney is "vindicated". That heavy burden requires the client to prove not simply that counsel was ineffective or incompetent but that counsel was "horribly inept", and nothing less than showing a "farce and mockery" will do.[12] Even if a defendant's attorney was demonstrably "mentally incapacitated and of unsound mind", that "may" be grounds for reversal, but does not assure it.[13] In one case, for example, the defendant's attorney did not have an office, was a chronic alcoholic, and had to be summoned to court by a bench warrant. Since the panel on appeal was one of the most liberal in the country, the defendant had the satisfaction of a dissenting vote on the court when his conviction was affirmed.[14]

Thus, the judges' failure to expose incompetency of counsel is compounded by (and probably motivated by) an unwillingness to reverse convictions where there has been a denial of the constitutional right to counsel. That aspect of the problem is illustrated by a "decertification" practice in the United States District Court for the Southern District of New York.[15] A Criminal Justice Act Panel, composed of federal judges, has notified some attorneys that their handling of cases has been so bad that they will not be assigned further cases. But no defendants represented by any of those lawyers have ever had their convictions vacated on that ground (as should be done automatically), nor have any such defendants even been informed of the judges' opinion of their counsels' lack of competence.

It is true that the Second Circuit has recently announced an intention "to insure that defense counsel will observe their duties" under the Code of Professional Responsibility.[16] Unfortunately, however, the first two cases decided under that policy indicate how limited it will be in practice. In the first case, defense counsel was censured not for inadequate representation, but for undue zeal in summation.[17] In that regard, we might note Chief Judge Irving Kaufman's observation that: "The adversary process is not threatened by over-zealous advocates, but by complacent ones."[18] The second case was one in which the court was remanding the case on other grounds, so the finding of the attorney's incompetence had no practical impact on the defendant's rights.[19] There seems scant likelihood, therefore, of a significant change in the judicial practice of tolerating ineffective representation.

To summarize: (1) the law schools should continue to develop methodology and courses to train students more effectively in all areas of lawyering skills; (2) certification is a dubious remedy at best, but if it is adopted, it should apply to those now practicing as well as to those who have never yet had the opportunity to give cause for alarm; (3) the most effective remedy for dealing with incompetence of attorneys is for judges to accept their ethical and constitutional obligations "to criticize and correct unprofessional conduct" and "to support the federal Constitution and . . . fearlessly observe and apply fundamental . . . guarantees".[20] In short, the Chief Justice, who claims to have seen innumerable miscarriages of justice resulting from incompetence of counsel, but who appears to have taken no corrective action in any of them, might look closer to home for the best cure for his complaint.

Footnotes

[1] F.L. BAILEY & H. ARONSON, THE DEFENSE NEVER RESTS (1971), reprinted in GREAT COURTROOM BATTLES 43-44 (Rubenstein ed. 1973).

[2] Burger, *The Special Skills of Advocacy: Are Specialized Training and Certification of Advocates Essential to Our System of Justice?*, 42 FORDHAM L. REV. 227, 234 (1973).

[3] *Id.* at 239.

[4] Burger, *A Sick Profession?*, 27 FED. B. J. 228 (1967).

[5] Burger, *supra* note 2, at 231.

[6] *Id.* at 238.

[7] *See,* U.S. CONST., amend. VI; AMERICAN BAR ASSOCIATION, CANONS OF JUDICIAL ETHICS, CANONS 3, 11.

[8] DR 6-101(A)(1); EC 6-1, 3; EC 2-30.

[9] AMERICAN BAR ASSOCIATION, CANONS OF JUDICIAL ETHICS, CANON 11.

[10] *Id.,* CANON 3.

[11] Harried v. United States, 389 F.2d 281 (D.C. Cir. 1967) (Burger, J.).

[12] *See,* United States *ex rel.* Maselli v. Reincke, 383 F.2d 129, 132 (2d Cir. 1967).

[13] *See,* United States *ex rel.* Pugach v. Mancusi, 310 F. Supp. 691, 716 (S.D. N.Y. 1970), *aff'd,* 441 F.2d 1073 (2d Cir. 1971), *cert. den.,* 404 U.S. 849, 92 S. Ct. 156, 30 L. Ed. 2d 88 (1971).

[14] United States v. Simpson, Crim. No. 24,817 (D.C. Ct. App., Jan. 26, 1973) (opin. per cur., Wright and Leventhal, J.; dissent by Bazelon, C.J.).

[15] *See,* Burger, *supra* note 2, at 240, n. 24.

[16] *See, Second Circuit Court Critical of Defense Counsel,* N.Y.L.J., Jan. 22, 1974, at 1, col. 3.

[17] *Id.*

[18] N.Y.L.J., Dec. 7, 1973, at 5, col. 3.

[19] N.Y.L.J., Jan. 22, 1974, at 4, col. 5. *But, cf.,* the commendable decision by Bauman, J., in *Johnson v. Vincent,* reported in N.Y.L.J., Feb. 4, 1974, at 1, cols. 6-7.

[20] AMERICAN BAR ASSOCIATION, CANONS OF JUDICIAL ETHICS, CANONS 3, 11.

Chapter 9

THE MYTH OF BRITISH SUPERIORITY

A recurring theme in commentaries on the American bar, and particularly in regard to proposals for certification of litigating attorneys, is the notion that the British lawyer, and especially the British barrister, is superior to the litigating attorney in the United States.[1] It has been suggested, for example, that British barristers are superior as a group not only in the quality of their advocacy, but also in their "ethics, manners and deportment".[2] On the basis of research,[3] discussions with English lawyers and judges, and personal observations, I disagree on both counts.

Although it has been noted that the present Lord Chief Justice of England is the son of a working man,[4] the sample of one person is a small one and, it happens, not at all typical. Class status and "knowing the old boy network" are primary considerations at the threshold of the profession. To become a solicitor, one must be selected as an articled clerk by a firm of solicitors; to become a barrister, one must be selected for pupillage by a set of Chambers (that is, a group of barristers sharing the same suite of offices). According to the Oxford University Appointment Board in its 1968 annual report, having "the right father" was often more important than any other factor in obtaining solicitor's articles,[5] and it is likely that the situation is even worse with respect to the Bar because the profession is so limited in number of practitioners and in sets of Chambers.[6]

As might be expected, therefore, there is substantial discrimination against those of humble origin, members of minority groups, and women.[7] I had occasion to visit one set of Chambers, and was struck with the interesting mixture of names. Some were African, some Indian, some Jewish, and some British. The barristers with the British names, I found, were women. I was told by one of the members of those particular Chambers that there were more minority-group and women members in that one set of Chambers than there were among all of the remaining barristers in the city of London. Although he may have been exaggerating, his point was made soberly and with chagrin.

In addition, the expenses of becoming a barrister are substantially higher than those incurred in entering any other profession in England. The bar student's expenses are compounded by the requirement of "keeping term", which means that a student must have dinner in the Hall of an Inn of Court (in effect, a club) for a specified number of times over a period of three years. That practice has virtually no educational value whatsoever.[8] After dinner, it is true, lectures are given or moot trials are conducted, and this "centuries-old . . . school of advocacy" has been noted as one of the reasons for British superiority.[9] Unfortunately, according to the testimony of one who actually suffered through the experience, the lectures and mock trials (unlike the dinners) are voluntary, and therefore are "avoided by the vast majority of the students, who leave the moment dinner is concluded".[10]

It has also been argued that the British bar student receives better training than the American law student because of the system of pupillage, under which law clerks are trained by practicing barristers. There is, however, a strong element of question-begging in that proposition. A pupillage can only be successful if the barrister conducting it has been well trained. In addition, the barrister must have the time as well as the ability to teach. I seriously doubt, however, that most English barristers would qualify for membership on the better American law faculties. Yet, under the pupillage system, a single barrister, in addition to practicing full-time, carries the load of an entire law school faculty, with all of its breadth and variety of expertise. Moreover, the barrister is supposed to do in as little as one year what an American law faculty devotes three years to achieving.

Advancement in the profession is also tightly controlled. A barrister is a "junior", regardless of age, until he or she is appointed Queen's Counsel. One who is Queen's Counsel does not thereby become a public official, but merely achieves a higher status within the private bar. Nevertheless, control over advancement from junior to Queen's Counsel is vested principally in a single public official, the Lord Chancellor (who consults with other judges, the Permanent Secretary, the Attorney General, and the Solicitor General). The selection process is "based on no objective basis or principle", and has been characterized as an annual "cattle market".[11] Finally, appointment to the Bench is almost invariably made from the ranks of Queen's Counsel.

As one might expect, therefore, the English bar is characterized by social homogeneity, conformity, and a lack of inclination to criticize either fellow lawyers or legal institutions.

Furthermore, the dual system of solicitors and barristers produces some extremely undesirable results, with little or none of the claimed advantages. Clients are charged more than they would otherwise have to pay, because they must retain two lawyers for one piece of litigation. The lawyer who prepares the case, the solicitor, is not the lawyer who handles the case in court, and the solicitor frequently works up the case without substantial guidance from the barrister. The barrister sees no witnesses, except the client, before examining them in court. In civil cases, there is far less pretrial discovery than in the United States, which means that cases are not as thoroughly prepared and that the game of surprise at trial, as distinguished from truth-seeking, is far more common. The trial brief prepared by the solicitor is often sloppily done, and the barrister may well not trouble to read it earlier than the evening before going to trial, yet criticism by one branch of the other's inadequate performance is rare. Because of the frequent lack of cooperation between solicitors and barristers, the conclusion has been reached that: "The client is getting the worst of both worlds. He pays for two teams of lawyers, without getting the benefit of double-checking or the advantages of pooling information."[12]

The dual system also produces some quaint rules regarding the relationships between barristers and solicitors, because the solicitors select the barristers for their clients. Thus, a barrister who is "in the habit of frequenting cafes or restaurants" with a solicitor's clerk "loses caste". Yet, some of a barrister's best friends may be solicitors: "Do not think for one moment that I am deprecating friendships between solicitors and members of the Bar. One branch of the profession is as good as the other and I dare say most of us have formed lasting friendships with solicitors. . . ."[13]

In the trial of criminal cases, there are special problems. Barristers in private practice are selected by the police to prosecute cases. Fees from such retainers can become an important, even an essential, part of the income of a barrister, particularly the younger one. Barristers do not exercise discretion regarding the decision to prosecute. They are hired guns and they prosecute as directed by the police. If, for whatever reason (including doubts regarding the defendant's guilt), a barrister does not prosecute with a zeal satisfactory to the police, that barrister will not be retained again. Even more seriously, a barrister who is unduly vigorous, in the eyes of the police, when serving for the defense, will thereafter be denied the valuable retainers for the prosecution. As a result of such problems, a prestigious group concerned with the administration of justice has recommended that England adopt the "Scottish system" of a public prosecutor who is independent of the police.[14]

What has been referred to as the good manners among members of the English bar may be, in another view, simply unprofessional work. As a result of the selection process for membership in the bar, the method of advancement within the bar and to the bench, and the resulting pressures to be a member of the "old boy club", a British barrister is far more tolerant of errors by opposing counsel and by the court than an American lawyer would be. I spoke with one experienced English barrister who had lived for two years in the United States, and who told me that he had once thought he would enjoy trying a case in this country. However, he said, after attending two or three American trials, he realized that he was not competent to litigate a case in this country. "I simply would not have been able to get out a line of questioning," he explained. "You're not as easy-going with each other as we are."

My own observation of British trials confirmed that comment. I was immediately and continually struck by the fact that counsel asked leading questions, argumentative questions, elicited hearsay and opinion, and made prejudicial asides to the jury, without a word of objection from opposing counsel or reaction from the judge. It may be, of course, that what is called "skill in advocacy" is simply a reference to the expeditiousness with which litigation is conducted (". . . their trials are conducted in a fraction of the time we expend . . .").[15] That kind of skill, however, would not seem to require the intricate training and certification that are now being called for. Moreover, when the administration of justice is at issue, one hesitates to make a *per se* equation of expedition with excellence.

In addition, when counsel is principally concerned with not offending the judge and the opposing attorney, the client's interest suffers. That result is rendered more acceptable to the barrister than to the litigating attorney in the United States, because the former is relatively remote from the client. Indeed, barristers consider their aloofness from their clients and from their clients' causes to be a mark of esteem. One barrister took pride in telling me that only once in his entire career did he have any concern with whether his client's case was won or lost. A frequent consequence of that aloofness is a sense of alienation and resentment on the part of clients, reflected in the complaint of solicitors that their rapport with their clients can be adversely affected when the barristers ("a bloodless lot") enter a case.

It has been suggested that a major advantage of the dual system of solicitor and barrister is that it eliminates one of the most difficult questions faced by an American lawyer, that is, whether the attorney can properly elicit known perjury. Since the barrister "takes the brief" from the solicitor and does not deal directly with the witnesses, the barrister is substantially insulated from such troublesome matters as contradictions in the case as it originally developed or admissions of incriminating information. However, discussions with barristers and solicitors confirmed what a moment's reflection would suggest: the problem of known perjury has not been eliminated by the dual system; it has simply been moved back one step. That is, there will be fewer instances in which the barrister knows or has reason to know that a witness is committing perjury, only because the barrister has been shielded by the solicitor. The solicitor, however, will still know if "inconsistent instructions" have been given. Thus, the barrister's skirts may be somewhat cleaner, but the difficulty has not been eliminated from the system.

Indeed, the practice of coaching the witness to fashion testimony in the most helpful manner, even to the point of shaving the truth, may be aggravated rather than eliminated by the dual system. Professor Michael Zander has observed: "The division of the profession encourages each side [*i.e.,* the solicitor and the barrister] to avoid taking responsibility for what happens. The solicitor may hint to the witness that his evidence will be more acceptable in one rather than another form, and can salve *his* conscience by the reflection that it is not his duty to examine the witness in court. The barrister may or may not suspect that the witness's story is not the full truth, but *he* can avoid the moral issue because he has not himself had any hand in the preparation of the witness for trial."[16]

In addition, the practice of "selective ignorance" (which has been characterized by the ABA Standards as "unscrupulous")[17] may be indulged by the barrister in conferences with the client (which are permitted in the presence of the solicitor). To quote Professor Zander again: "The barrister sometimes realizes during a conference that a particular line of questioning is leading in a direction which is potentially 'unhelpful'." Usually, if he realizes in time, "he indicates that he would rather not hear anything about that matter". Moreover, the barrister may frame questions in such a way as to avoid an "awkward response". As Professor Zander points out: "This is considered perfectly proper." He concludes: "In such cases it is difficult to be smug about the moral superiority of our system." Although the barrister "is not directly implicated in the client's lies or half-truths . . . neither is he wholly free from involvement".[18]

Nor are English attorneys above creating and producing false evidence in an appropriate case. Until recently, for example, the only ground for divorce was adultery. Thus developed the practice known as "going to Brighton". Solicitors would employ women to accompany the husband in an uncontested divorce case to the seaside resort of Brighton. There, the husband and the woman would check into a hotel, sit in the room together for about a half hour smoking cigarettes, and then return. The hotel register was then introduced as evidence of adultery, despite the fact that the barristers knew as well as the solicitors did what was going on. One well-regarded solicitor told me that it was never really necessary for the solicitor to go so far as to hire women to take the trip. Representing the wife in an uncontested divorce case, his practice was to advise the husband that a copy of an appropriate hotel record would make things easier. Subsequently (usually soon after the next following weekend), the husband would supply the solicitor with the record necessary to make out a case of adultery. The solicitor seemed amused, or perhaps bemused, when I suggested that he had either participated in the manufacture of false evidence, or else, of necessity, that he had induced the commission of the crime of adultery.

There has been no effort in England, as there has in the United States and in Canada, to codify rules governing professional responsibility. The Law Society has adopted six rules, four of them substantive, known as The Solicitor's Practice Rules. All of them are of the guild or trade association kind, proscribing such practices as advertising and charging less than a fixed fee. There are also a few short treatises on "professional conduct and etiquette", but those are, for the most part, superficial, providing little guidance and virtually no analysis.[19] Moreover, insofar as firm positions are taken on difficult questions, they frequently conflict with the rules expressed in the Code of Professional Responsibility and in the ABA Standards Relating to the Prosecution and the Defense Function.

As discussed in an earlier chapter, the Guide published by The Law Society virtually eliminates the issue of whether the lawyer should present known perjury, by taking the position that even a confession by the client to the lawyer may be disregarded. Only if the solicitor is "really irresistibly driven" to the conclusion that the client is guilty, should the solicitor refrain from presenting affirmative evidence inconsistent with a confession.[20] Even in a civil case, involving the subornation of perjury of a witness other than the client, The Law Society has taken a position against disclosure. In one case, solicitors who had recovered damages for a client were told by the client, after the case was concluded, that one of the witnesses had been paid by the client to give false evidence. The solicitors were advised by the Law Society that they should decline to act for that client in subsequent cases, but that they were not at liberty to disclose the perjury.[21]

The principal authority for barristers is a Guide written by W.W. Boulton, who is Secretary to the General Council of the Bar. Mr. Boulton states that: "Any deception of the Court must be avoided." Nevertheless, if a client informs the barrister after conclusion of a hearing, but before the court has rendered judgment, that the client has committed perjury, it would be "contrary to his duty to his client for counsel to inform the Court". The attorney is permitted to withdraw from the case at that point, but is not required to do so. Mr. Boulton also takes the position that counsel in a criminal case has no duty to correct any information given to the Court by the prosecution if the correction would be to the client's detriment.[22]

Oddly, Mr. Boulton does not even raise the question of how the lawyer should proceed upon learning that the client intends to commit perjury in a criminal case,* although he recognizes that "every accused person has the right to decide whether or not to give evidence in his own defense", and that "it is the accused himself who must make the decision".[23] When I asked him what the barrister should do if the client's decision is to commit perjury, Mr. Boulton gave me the clear impression that he had not given the question much thought, but did say that if the client persisted in that decision, he would seek leave to withdraw. If he were denied leave to withdraw, Mr. Boulton said, he was "not quite sure" what to do next. He finally indicated, however, that he would then go forward in the ordinary manner. The striking thing, of course, is not the merits of the particular conclusion that Mr. Boulton ultimately expressed, but that the Secretary to the General Council of the Bar, and the author of the authoritative Guide to Conduct and Etiquette at the Bar, has given so little attention to such a fundamental issue.

In sum, I think it is a myth that the English bar is superior to the American bar, either in professional skills or in professional ethics. With respect to litigating ability, it is my estimation that barristers, as a group, are inferior to litigating attorneys in the United States. Moreover, the same problems of ethics exist in England as in this country, and they are in no significant way mitigated by the dual system. In addition, there is no coherent body of rules dealing with professional conduct, and

---

* Mr. Boulton provides a single illustration relating to the presentation of perjury, under the heading, "Matrimonial Proceedings": ". . . Counsel is entitled to appear for a wife who admits that she has committed adultery and to present her case for desertion and adduce evidence in support of it. What he may not do is to set up an affirmative case that his client has not been guilty of adultery or call any evidence which he must know to be false, having regard to her admission." BOULTON, *infra* note 19, at 76.

the scant literature on the subject in England is generally unsophisticated and virtually devoid of practical analysis. Although
we in this country have little to be complacent about, we would
be mistaken to look to English practice as a guide.

Footnotes

[1] *See, e.g.*, Burger, *The Special Skills of Advocacy: Are Specialized Training and Certification of Advocates Essential to Our System of Justice?* 42
FORDHAM L. REV. 227, 227-30 (1973).

[2] *Id.* at 229.

[3] *See, e.g.*, M. ZANDER, LAWYERS AND THE PUBLIC INTEREST (1968); M.
ZANDER, CASES AND MATERIALS ON THE ENGLISH LEGAL SYSTEM (1973); Q.
JOHNSTONE & D. HOPSON, LAWYERS AND THEIR WORK (1967); Kaplan, *An
American Lawyer in the Queen's Court: Impressions of English Civil Pro-
cedure,* 69 MICH. L. REV. 821 (1971); Cohen, *The British Legal Association
at Bath,* 118 THE SOLICITOR'S J. 325 (1974).

[4] Burger, *supra* note 1, at 229, n. 5.

[5] ZANDER, *supra* note 3, at 31.

[6] *Id.*

[7] *Id.*

[8] *Id.* at 33-39.

[9] Burger, *supra* note 1, at 228.

[10] ZANDER, *supra* note 3, at 37.

[11] *Id.* at 132.

[12] *Id.* at 304-05; *see also,* Kaplan, *supra* note 3.

[13] J. SINGLETON, CONDUCT AT THE BAR 12 (1969).

[14] JUSTICE, THE PROSECUTION PROCESS IN ENGLAND AND WALES (1970).

[15] Burger, *supra* note 1, at 228.

[16] ZANDER, *supra* note 3, at 284-85.

[17] *See,* pp. 35-36 *supra.*

[18] *Id.* at 284-85.

[19] *See,* W.W. BOULTON, A GUIDE TO CONDUCT AND ETIQUETTE AT THE
BAR OF ENGLAND AND WALES (5th ed. 1970); T. LUND, A GUIDE TO THE
PROFESSIONAL CONDUCT OF SOLICITORS (1960); J. SINGLETON, CONDUCT AT THE
BAR (1969).

[20] LUND, *supra* note 19, at 106.

[21] *Id.* at 105.

[22] BOULTON, *supra* note 19, at 74, 76.

[23] *Id.* at 76.

Chapter 10

ACCESS TO THE LEGAL SYSTEM: THE
PROFESSIONAL OBLIGATION TO CHASE AMBULANCES

Ernest Gene Gunn, a five-year-old boy, was seriously injured as a result of negligent driving attributed to John J. Washek. Shortly after the accident, the boy's mother was visited at home by an adjuster from Mr. Washek's insurance company. The adjuster told her that there was no need to retain an attorney, because the company would make a settlement as soon as the boy was out of his doctor's care; if Ms. Gunn were not satisfied at that time, she could retain an attorney and file suit.

The boy's injuries were sufficiently severe to require a doctor's care for 23 months. At the end of that time Ms. Gunn made repeated efforts to reach the insurance company adjuster, but without success. She then retained a lawyer, who promptly filed suit for her. Ms. Gunn's boy never did have his day in court, however, because the attorneys for the insurance company successfully pleaded a two-year statute of limitations.[1]

The *Gunn* case illustrates two important issues of professional responsibility, which unfortunately, have never been adequately dealt with by the organized Bar. First, however, let us dispose of some preliminary issues of professional responsibility.

If counsel for the insurance company had no prior knowledge of the adjuster's actions, then it would not have been unprofessional to raise the defense of the statute of limitations. A client is entitled to have the benefit of the presentation of any lawful defense.[2] However, it would have been entirely proper—indeed, ethically required—for counsel at least to have urged the company to forego pleading the statutory bar because of the unjust circumstances of the case.[3] Moreover, an attorney would be justified in refusing to accept a retainer in such a case, because, contrary to popular belief, an attorney has no obligation to take a case (as distinguished from continuing in a case already under way) that would require the attorney to act in a way offensive to the attorney's personal judgment.[4] Indeed, if an attorney's personal objections are sufficiently strong about a particular matter, the attorney would be obligated to refrain from taking the case because of the potential conflict of interest.

Yet what if counsel was, in advance, aware of (or prompted) the adjuster's actions? For a lawyer to participate in a scheme to trick a lay person out of effective representation of counsel would constitute counselling or assisting the client in fraudulent conduct in violation of the Code of Professional Responsibility.[5] There is reason to believe, however, that it is not uncommon for some lawyers, acting alone or in connivance with insurance adjusters, to take advantage of claimants' ignorance and to mislead them into foregoing legal rights. Nevertheless, it is rare, if ever, that a lawyer has been disciplined for such perversion of professional knowledge and skills.

On the contrary, the thrust of Bar discipline has been directed toward restricting lay persons' knowledge of their rights and their access to legal redress. For example, not long after Ms. Gunn had lost her fight to overcome the effects of the insurance adjuster's deceitful actions, the Committee of Censors of the Philadelphia Bar Association undertook a $125,000 investigation —not of insurance adjusters, but of "unethical" solicitation of clients by plaintiffs' lawyers. The resulting report recognized the need on behalf of plaintiffs "to counter the activity of [insurance] carriers' adjusters", but casually suggested that that problem could be dealt with "by the exercise of restraint on the part of carriers".[6] The Report also acknowledged the propriety and "social value" of automobile wrecking companies listening to police calls in order to be the first to arrive at accident scenes to carry off the damaged vehicles, but it found no justification at all in a similar effort directed toward protecting the legal rights of the injured people.[7]

The basis for disciplinary action that interferes with lawyers' efforts to advise people of their rights are, of course, the ABA Code strictures against advertising and solicitation.[8] Those provisions continue long-standing rules against maintenance, champerty, and barratry—commonly referred to as ambulance chasing or stirring up litigation.

A common justification for such rules is that advertising would lead to abuses such as false and misleading claims. Why lawyers would be more prone to engage in that kind of dishonesty, however, than are sellers of other services or of commodities has never been articulated. Nor has it been explained why it is feasible to regulate the size and content of professional cards, which is done now,* but impossible to regulate false and misleading advertising by lawyers. What is clear is that the principal purpose of the anti-

---

* In the Province of Quebec, which includes Montreal, lawyers are permitted to advertise in newspapers and in the Yellow Pages. Regulation of such advertising includes a limitation that: "Such advertisements shall never exceed 16 square inches in size." REGULATION OF THE BAR OF QUEBEC, § 18, ¶ 72(2).

solicitation rules is to limit competition among lawyers. Illustrative is a case permitting a bar association to advertise its lawyer referral service in a newspaper.[9] The court expressly justified its decision on the ground that the real evil in advertising is competition among lawyers, which is not present when the Bar advertises as a whole.[10]

It is not surprising, therefore, that a number of leading authorities have criticized the anti-solicitation rules as unrelated to professional ethics as distinguished from what Harvard Law Professor Andrew Kaufman calls "the rules of a guild".[11] That is, they are directed against competition rather than for the maintenance of moral standards in the public interest. Other authorities have also emphasized the effect of those rules in protecting established lawyers and large firms from undesired competition from young lawyers and small firms.[12]

Nevertheless, there are those who object that advertising for clients would "degrade the profession", and the ABA Code informs us that: "History has demonstrated that public confidence in the legal system is best preserved by strict, self-imposed controls over, rather than by unlimited advertising."[13] No historical reference is provided, however, to support that assertion. Similarly, the Philadelphia Report, referred to above, suggests that solicitation of clients in violation of the rules has led to intense public dissatisfaction with the Bar.[14] In fact, the opposite may be true—that is, that dissatisfaction with the Bar stems in major part from lawyers' aloofness, and from their failure to reach out to those whom they purport to serve.

For example, in a survey conducted by two law professors at the University of Edinburgh for the Law Society of Scotland, people were asked whether they would resent or welcome an attorney who approached them to offer legal services in six situations (if you were in an accident; if you were considering buying a house; if you were going into a new business venture; etc.). The study revealed that less than two percent of the people in the survey would resent an attorney's contact, while about half would welcome the unrequested proffer of services by an attorney in all six cases.[15] Generally, about 70 percent fell in the "welcome" category. Moreover, the least well-educated people were those who, most of all, would welcome being solicited by attorneys. The study concludes: "The extraordinarily high proportions of people who would welcome the solicitor's initiating contact in the different situations we have posed must seriously question many commonly held assumptions about the correct stance for members of the profession. Taken with the data noted which showed that few members of the public have adequate knowledge of the services solicitors could provide, and would like to know about these (*i.e.*, want more advertisement), there is a coherent and very emphatic call for a more active and positive legal profession."[16]

A similar conclusion was reached by the Special Committee on Legal Ethics of the Canadian Bar Association. The Committee found that the increasing complexity and specialization in law make it more and more difficult for a potential client to have confidence in the selection of a lawyer. Accordingly, the committee recommended that the permitted forms of advertising by attorneys "should be enlarged and extended" to include "publication of professional cards, in an institutional form in newspapers, shopping center guides, and other like publications".[17]

Those who object to solicitation of clients are typically ignorant of the fact that the strictures against it are themselves only minor exceptions to the more fundamental rule of professional responsibility expressed in Canon Two of the Code of Professional Responsibility: "A Lawyer Should Assist the Legal Profession in Fulfilling Its Duty to Make Legal Counsel Available." The Code thus recognizes an affirmative obligation of the profession to provide access to the legal system—and that access, presumably, is for the benefit of all people, not just a select few.

Oddly enough, however, the solicitation limitation appears in the Disciplinary Rules under that same Canon Two. Disciplinary Rule 2-104 reads, in part: "A lawyer who has given unsolicited advice to a layman that he should obtain counsel or take legal action shall not accept employment resulting from that advice. . . ." Disciplinary Rule 2-103 says: "A lawyer shall not recommend employment as a private practitioner of himself, his partner, or associate to a non-lawyer who has not sought his advice."

Those rules appear on first reading to be broad and absolute. But they are practically meaningless—at least for a particular class of lawyers and clients—because of certain exceptions to the anti-solicitation rules. For example, DR 2-104 provides further that: "A lawyer [who has volunteered advice] may accept employment by a close friend, relative, [or a] former client. . . ." That refinement means that those who are accustomed to retaining lawyers, say, for their tax or estates work, and those who have attorneys as relatives and friends, are the kind of people who can be solicited despite the rule. As to that socioeconomic class of people, there is no impropriety in solicitation. In addition, consistent with DR 2-104, lawyers have been known to take tax deductions for membership fees in country clubs, on the ground that such fees are an ordinary and necessary business expense—

that is, a means for discreetly soliciting business. One prominent federal judge resigned from several exclusive clubs upon going on the Bench, explaining to friends that he no longer needed to attract clients.

Another device approved by the ABA for soliciting clients is the law list, such as in the impressive volumes of *Martindale-Hubbell*. This is purely and simply a self-laudatory advertisement, euphemistically called a "card", and directed to potential clients. Yet not every attorney is permitted to advertise his or her professional autobiography, prestigious associations, and important clients in *Martindale-Hubbell*. One must await an invitation from the publisher to apply for an "a" rating, which can be achieved only upon submission of favorable references from 16 judges and attorneys who have themselves already received an "a" rating. For all other members of the profession, *Martindale-Hubbell* is a closed book.

A similar service is *The Attorneys' Register*. Their brochure boasts that the register holds a certificate of compliance from the American Bar Association, and explains that: "The primary purpose of *The Attorneys' Register* is to continue to be a valuable forwarding medium aimed at securing SUBSTANTIAL legal business for our listees. . . ." (The word SUBSTANTIAL is written in capital letters throughout the brochure.) Further, it offers the attorney "an opportunity to be recognized in association with other reputable members of the Bar", and the publishers promise that they will do "everything they properly can to encourage active forwardings to our listees". The brochure also provides a partial list of "important corporations which . . . have requested, and will receive, a copy of our current edition . . . for use when seeking qualified . . . counsel". The list contains about 100 corporations, including Abbott Laboratories, American Sugar, Continental Can, DuPont, General Electric, and U.S. Plywood—corporations that will look for the attorney's name and qualifications in the paid advertisement in the register. In addition, the register is distributed free to "a careful selection of banks and trust companies, important industrial corporations, insurance companies, financing institutions, and the like, who are believed to be prolific forwarders of SUBSTANTIAL legal matters".

That is the way solicitation is carried on with impunity by lawyers seeking to represent those of wealth and privilege, such as John J. Washek's insurance company. The problem of impropriety arises, of course, only for those who seek to represent that other socioeconomic group typified by the mother of Ernest Gene Gunn or, say, by tenants as distinguished from landlords, or by consumers as distinguished from manufacturers. For such unsophisticates—that is for those who are most in need of that access to the legal system which is promised by Canon Two—the organized Bar, through its disciplinary rules and actions, discourages any realistic opportunity to take controversies "out of the streets and into the courtrooms".

Imagine, for example, the following situation. A woman arrives at a metropolitan courthouse holding a small boy by the hand. She speaks almost no English at all. She is intimidated by the imposing surroundings, and she is frightened and confused. All that she knows is that she is required to be some place in that building because her son has been arrested or her landlord is attempting to evict her family. People brush by her, concerned with their own problems. Then a man appears, smiles at her, and asks her in her own language whether he can help her. Through him, she meets and retains the man's employer, a lawyer who guides her to the proper place and who represents her interests. In my view, that lawyer should have been given a citation as Attorney of the Year. Instead, he was prosecuted as a criminal, convicted of the misdemeanor of soliciting business on behalf of an attorney, subjected to disciplinary proceedings, and censured by the court.*

If the profession has an obligation to "[Fulfill] Its Duty to Make Legal Counsel Available", strictures against advertising and soliciting are precisely the wrong way to go about it. Instead attorneys have a professional duty to stir up litigation when they are acting to advise people, who may be ignorant of their rights, to seek justice in the courts. As expressed by one authority:

> We must . . . discard . . . the assumption of Medieval Society, that a law suit is an evil in itself. It is hard to see how either the legal profession or our court machinery can justify its existence, if we go on the assumption that it is always better to suffer a wrong than to redress it by litigation. . . . If we have so little confidence in the process of law as to think otherwise, we shall do well to consider a fundamental overhauling of our system.[18]

---

* *In re Solomon Cohn,* N.Y.L.J., Feb. 19, 1974, at 1:6-7, 3:3. The opinion of the court notes that the attorney had an unblemished record and that before he undertook to represent people in court, he had worked as a volunteer for, and then as a staff member of, the Legal Aid Society. The last paragraph of the opinion reads: "We cannot, of course, condone respondent's unprofessional conduct. However, after giving due consideration to all the circumstances here involved, including respondent's expressions of self-reproach and the humiliation he has already suffered, we believe leniency to be warranted in this instance. Accordingly, the respondent should be censured. . . ."

Fortunately, there is authority, as well as notions of humanity, equal protection, freedom of speech, and the right to petition, in support of the view that the legal system exists to be used by people, and that people who need legal advice are entitled to have it. Indeed, the new ABA Code at one point makes such advice a matter of professional duty: "The legal profession should assist laymen to recognize legal problems because such problems may not be self-revealing and often are not timely noticed."[19] Advice regarding legal rights is therefore held proper when it is "motivated by a desire to protect one who does not recognize that he may have legal problems or who is ignorant of his legal rights or obligations".[20] At the same time, however, the Code properly condemns the instigation of litigation that is intended "merely to harass or injure another".[21]

The Code does suggest that an attorney should not solicit a client solely for the purpose of obtaining a fee.[22] However, when the lawyer's motives are mixed—that is, when the attorney acts with both a proper motive (to provide needed advice) and an "improper" motive (to earn a fee)—it is the proper motive that is determinative. For example, during the New Deal period, an organization was formed called the Liberty League, which was a group of lawyers opposed to such New Deal innovations as the National Labor Relations Act. The League published advertisements expressing its view that the Act was unconstitutional and offering to represent anyone who wanted to litigate against it. In Formal Opinion No. 148, the Committee on Professional Ethics of the American Bar Association held that the lawyers' activities were not only professionally proper but "wholesome and beneficial". Moreover, the Committee made it clear that the propriety of the advertisement would not be affected by a motive on the part of the lawyers to serve the interests of fee-paying clients:

> . . . We need not assume that these lawyers were actuated solely by altruistic motives. It would be extraordinary indeed if some of the lawyers in the list do not have some clients whose rights may be adversely affected by the legislation which the lawyers condemn, but their right to organize and declare their views cannot for that reason be denied, and no ethical principle is thereby violated.

It is clear, therefore, that even though an attorney may receive compensation, the solicitation of a client is not unethical if the client might otherwise have lost the opportunity to vindicate legal rights through ignorance of the law or of the availability of effective legal services.

As the foregoing discussion indicates, the Code of Professional Responsibility takes a schizophrenic position on solicitation and advertising. On one hand, it is good to advise people of their rights, even if a fee might result. On the other hand, there are some lawyers, for some clients, who had better not try to do it. One result of that inconsistency in the anti-solicitation rules has been that bar association disciplinary committees have been using it to harass public interest lawyers—even those working without fees from clients—who represent unpopular clients or causes.

In part because of that particular abuse of the rules, the Stern Community Law Firm in Washington, D.C. (of which I was then Director), decided to challenge the anti-solicitation rules as applied to non-fee cases. The test case related to child adoption. The District of Columbia then kept a larger proportion of its homeless children in public institutions than did any other American city. The District of Columbia institutions were notoriously overcrowded and understaffed. In the view of the Firm, the situation in the District of Columbia was in substantial part the result of arbitrary rules and bureaucratic policies and practices relating to adoption and foster care. For example, potential adoptive parents had been turned down or discouraged because they were single, because both parents were working, or because they were white and were seeking a black child.[23] Those parents did not meet the agencies' "text-book ideal" standards, but they were nevertheless able to provide healthy and loving homes that were far superior to the grossly inadequate institutions that were the sole actual alternative for the children.

The adoption agencies contended, on the other hand, that there were no such adoptive parents available, that no such arbitrary rules or practices existed, and that there was therefore no practical alternative to keeping the children in the institutions. It was therefore essential to the Firm's position that it demonstrate that potential adoptive parents were in fact available but were being arbitrarily rejected, despite the agencies' claims to the contrary. In order to produce such adoptive parents, the Firm published a Public Interest Legal Opinion in newspapers, magazines, and over radio and television to advise members of the community of the need for adoptive parents, the invalidity of the restrictive rules, and the availability of free legal services.

A second Public Service Legal Opinion published by the Firm related to our efforts to have the Food and Drug Administration declare certain toys to be hazardous to children and to provide that prior purchasers were entitled to return any such toys for a full refund. Despite having had such power through an act of Congress for nearly a year, and despite demands of consumer groups, the FDA had refused to act. Accordingly, Assistant Dean Harriet Rabb of Columbia Law School, then a staff attorney with the Firm, brought an action against the Secretary of HEW on behalf of the Consumers Union and the Children's Foundation to compel the FDA to take appropriate action. The agency at first opposed the litigation, but, while the case was on appeal, the FDA issued the requested ban on over three dozen named toys, declaring them to be capable of killing or maiming children. The FDA then failed, however, to act expeditiously to promulgate regulations providing for return of the toys for refund, so the Firm published a Public Service Legal Opinion setting forth the names and manufacturers of the toys found by the FDA to be hazardous, and expressing the legal opinion that purchasers were entitled immediately to return the toys for refund.

Predictably, some members of the bench and bar complained to the Committee on Legal Ethics and Grievances of the Bar Association of the District of Columbia. Although the Committee began with an attitude hostile to the idea of advertising, the members changed their views in the course of lengthy consideration of the merits of the issue. As a result, the Committee wrote the first Bar Association opinion in the country approving solicitation of clients by public interest lawyers serving without fees.[24] In its opinion, the Legal Ethics and Grievances Committee held that solicitation of clients by the Stern Firm was "consistent with the spirit and letter of the Code of Professional Responsibility" and "in keeping with the highest responsibilities of the legal profession". Fred Graham commented in *The New York Times*: "[F]or a profession that has forbidden lawyers to wear tie clasps bearing their state bar emblem or to send Christmas cards to prospective clients on the ground that such activities were unethical 'advertising,' the activities approved in the new ruling are unprecedented."

That appraisal, however, is somewhat exaggerated. In fact, the Supreme Court has held in a series of cases of major importance that rules of professional ethics must give way to constitutional rights. As the Stern Firm argued in its Memorandum to the Legal Ethics and Grievances Committee, the First Amendment protects solicitation as freedom of speech of the attorney and as an essential aspect of the client's right to petition for redress of grievances.[25] For example, the case of *NAACP v. Button* considered solicitation of clients in the context of efforts of the NAACP to recruit plaintiffs for school desegregation cases. The NAACP called a series of meetings, inviting not only its members and not only poor people, but all members of the community. At those meetings, the organization's paid staff attorneys took the platform to urge those present to authorize the lawyers to sue in their behalf.* The NAACP maintained the ensuing litigation by defraying all expenses, regardless of the financial means of a particular plaintiff.

Virginia contended that the NAACP's activities constituted improper solicitation under a state statute and fell within the traditional state power to regulate professional conduct. The Supreme Court held, however, that "the State's attempt to equate the activities of the NAACP and its lawyers with common-law barratry, maintenance and champerty, and to outlaw them accordingly, cannot obscure the serious encroachment . . . upon protected freedoms of expression". The Court concluded: "Thus it is no answer to the constitutional claims asserted by petitioner to say, as the Virginia Supreme Court of Appeals has said, that the purpose of these regulations was merely to insure high professional standards and not to curtail free expression. For a State may not, under the guise of prohibiting professional misconduct, ignore constitutional rights."[26]

Subsequently, in *Brotherhood of Railroad Trainmen v. Virginia ex rel. Virginia State Bar,* the Supreme Court considered the question of solicitation in a case in which a union's legal services plan resulted in channeling all or substantially all of the railroad workers' personal injury claims, on a private fee basis, to lawyers selected by the union and touted in its literature and at meetings. The Court again upheld the solicitation on constitutional grounds, despite the objection of the two dissenting Justices that by giving constitutional protection to the solicitation of personal injury claims, the Court "relegates the practice of law to the level of a commercial enterprise", "degrades the profession", and "contravenes both the accepted ethics of the profession and the statutory and judicial rules of acceptable conduct".[27]

In the *United Mine Workers* case the Supreme Court dealt with the argument that *Button* should be limited to litigation involving major political issues and not be extended to personal injury cases. The Court held that: "The litigation in question is, of course, not bound up with political matters of acute social moment, as in Button, but the First Amendment does not protect speech and assembly only to the extent it can be characterized as

---

* The Court has recognized the critical importance of solicitation to public interest litigation in noting that proscription of solicitation in *Button* would have "seriously crippled" the efforts of the NAACP. *United Mine Workers v. Illinois State Bar Ass'n, infra* note 25, at 223, 19 L. Ed. 2d at 431.

political. 'Great secular causes, with small ones are guarded. . . .' "[28] Finally, in the *United Transportation Union* case, the Court reversed a state injunction designed, in Justice Harlan's words, "to fend against 'ambulance chasing' ".[29] In that case a union paid investigators to keep track of accidents, to visit injured members, taking contingent fee contracts with them, and to urge the members to engage named private attorneys who were selected by the union and who had agreed to charge a fee set by prior agreement with the union. The investigators were also paid by the union for any time and expenses incurred in transporting potential clients to the designated lawyers' offices to enter retainer agreements.

In approving that arrangement, the Court reiterated that "collective activity undertaken to obtain meaningful access to the courts is a fundamental right within the protection of the First Amendment".[30] What is important to bear in mind, however, is that: (1) the attorneys in question were not in-house counsel for the union, but were private practitioners; (2) the attorneys earned substantial fees; (3) the cases were not "public interest" cases in the restricted sense, but were ordinary personal injury cases; and (4) the attorneys were retained as a result of the activities of "investigators", paid by the union, whose job it was to find out where accidents had occurred, to visit the victims as promptly as possible, to "tout" the particular lawyers and, if necessary, to take the victim to the lawyers' office to get a contingent fee contract signed.

The only question not decided by the Court was whether the investigators could properly have been paid directly by the lawyers. The dissenting Justices would have disapproved it, while the majority simply did not reach that issue, on the ground that it was not in the record before them. It is difficult, however, to see why a significant distinction should turn upon who pays the investigator. An unsophisticated person like Ms. Gunn needs information about the availability of legal services, regardless of whether she is a member of a union and regardless of who pays her informant. Furthermore, although the Court happened to be dealing in the union cases with group legal services, the people solicited in *Button* were not limited to members of NAACP.

We began with *Gunn v. Washek,* and it is an appropriate case with which to close. If lawyers are to take seriously the overriding rule expressed in Canon Two, the Bar must reverse the pattern illustrated by *Gunn.* First, we must vigorously discipline attorneys who abuse their training, skills, and status by misleading, overbearing, or overreaching unrepresented lay people. Second, we must encourage, rather than forbid, lawyers to seek out people like Ms. Gunn who have legal rights and who may, by ignorance, be deprived of access to the legal system.

In short, we should recognize that when Ernest Gene Gunn was injured by John J. Washek, the legal profession failed doubly in its duties when an insurance adjuster rather than a plaintiff's attorney was the first to call on Ms. Gunn.

Footnotes

[1] Gunn v. Washek, 405 Pa. 521, 176 A.2d 635 (1961); M. FREEDMAN, CONTRACTS 245 (1973).

[2] DR 7-101 (A) (1); EC 7-1, 7-4, 7-8.

[3] EC 7-9, 7-8.

[4] EC 2-26; DR 2-109, 2-110(C)(1)(e).

[5] DR 7-102 (A) (7); see also, DR 7-102 (A) (1).

[6] JAFFE, REPORT TO THE COMMITTEE OF CENSORS OF THE PHILADELPHIA BAR ASSOCIATION OF THE INVESTIGATION INTO UNETHICAL SOLICITATION BY PHILADELPHIA LAWYERS 41 (March 1, 1971). The Report also mentioned the possibility of remedial legislation, but no effort appears to have been made by the Bar Association toward that end.

[7] Id. at 40.

[8] DR 2-101—105.

[9] Jacksonville Bar Ass'n v. Wilson, 102 So. 2d 292 (Fla. S. Ct. 1958). See also, EC 2-9.

[10] Id. at 295.

[11] Kaufman, The Lawyers' New Code, 22 HARV. L. SCH'L BULL. 19 (1970).

[12] Shuchman, Ethics and Legal Ethics: The Propriety of the Canons as a Group Moral Code, 37 GEO. WASH. L. REV. 244 (1968); Cohen, Confronting Myth in the American Legal Profession: A Territorial Perspective, 22 ALA. L. REV. 513 (1970).

[13] EC 2-9.

[14] JAFFE, supra note 6, at 5.

[15] Campbell & Wilson, Public Attitudes to the Legal Profession in Scotland 69 (Mimeograph, 1973).

[16] Id. at 68.

[17] SPECIAL COMMITTEE ON LEGAL ETHICS, CANADIAN BAR ASSOCIATION, CODE OF PROFESSIONAL CONDUCT, RECOMMENDATION V, at vii (Preliminary Report, June, 1973). At the same time, the Committee expressed its opposition to "unregulated competitive advertising or professional touting or any other act or thing designed primarily to attract professional work". Id. at 88-89.

[18] Radin, Maintenance by Champerty, 24 CALIF. L. REV. 48, 72 (1935).

[19] EC 2-2.

[20] EC 2-3.

[21] Id.

[22] Id.

[23] Virtually all of the institutionalized children in the District were black.

[24] See, 41 D.C.B.J. 102 (1974). The opinion (which was issued in 1971) indicated that the advertisements could not include the name of an individual attorney and that the word "Law" could not be used in the Firm's name ("Stern Community Law Firm"). The Firm publicly rejected those limitations, which I consider to be unconstitutional. See, Freedman, Solicitation of Clients, JURIS DOCTOR, April, 1971.

[25] NAACP v. Button, 371 U.S. 415, 83 S. Ct. 328, 9 L. Ed. 2d 405 (1963); Brotherhood of R.R. Trainmen v. Virginia ex rel. Virginia State Bar, 377 U.S. 1, 84 S. Ct. 1113, 12 L. Ed. 2d 89 (1964); United Mine Workers v. Illinois State Bar Ass'n, 389 U.S. 217, 88 S. Ct. 353, 19 L. Ed. 2d 426 (1967); United Transp. Union v. State Bar, 401 U.S. 576, 91 S. Ct. 1076, 28 L. Ed. 2d 339 (1971).

[26] NAACP v. Button, supra note 25, at 438-39, 9 L. Ed. 2d at 421.

[27] *Brotherhood of R.R. Trainmen v. Virginia ex rel. Virginia State Bar,* *supra* note 25, at 9, 12 L. Ed. 2d at 95 (dissent by Justice Clark).

[28] *United Mine Workers v. Illinois Bar Ass'n, supra* note 25, at 223, 19 L. Ed. 2d at 431.

[29] *United Transp. Union v. State Bar, supra* note 25, at 597, 28 L. Ed. 2d at 353 (dissent by Justice Harlan).

[30] *Id.* at 585, 28 L. Ed. 2d at 347.

Appendix

This Appendix is in three parts. The first is a brief discussion of the three principal bodies of rules of professional responsibility that have been published by the American Bar Association: The Canons of Professional Ethics; the Code of Professional Responsibility; and the Standards Relating to the Prosecution Function and the Defense Function. The second part of this Appendix is the complete text of the new Code of Professional Responsibility.[1] The third part are my own annotations to the Code, including cross references to the text of this book. *The annotations are designated C1, C2, C3, etc., and are set forth in boldface type in the Code for convenient cross reference.*

A. THE CANONS, THE CODE, AND THE STANDARDS

The earliest effort to establish a body of rules of professional responsibility applicable to all lawyers in the United States was the Canons of Professional Ethics of the American Bar Association, which were adopted by the ABA in 1908. The Canons were based substantially upon the Code of Ethics adopted by the Alabama State Bar Association in 1887, which in turn were derived from a series of lectures by a Judge George Sharswood, which were published in 1854.

As amended over the years, the Canons came to consist of 47 relatively brief numbered provisions. The Canons tended to be general, vague, overlapping, and even inconsistent. The longest provisions relate to anti-competitive practices, such as minimum fee standards and restrictions on advertising. The Canons were interpreted in numerous Opinions of the Committee on Professional Ethics of the American Bar Association. However, the ABA itself has noted that those opinions "tend to support the Canons and are critical of them only in the most unusual case". Moreover, so many of those opinions deal with the "etiquette of law practice", such as advertising, partnership names and announcements, that "many lawyers came to assume that that is the exclusive field of interest of the Committee", and that the Committee "is not concerned with the more serious questions of professional standards and obligations".[2]

The new Code of Professional Responsibility, completed in 1969, is a significant departure from the old Canons. The Code

---

[1] The Code was drafted under the auspices of the American Bar Association, is copyrighted by the ABA, and is reproduced here by permission.
[2] ABA CODE OF PROFESSIONAL RESPONSIBILITY, PREFACE (1969).

is divided into nine general sections. Each section consists of a Canon, Ethical Considerations, and Disciplinary Rules. A Canon is a statement of an axiomatic norm, expressing a standard of professional conduct in general terms. Each Canon is in a single sentence. The Ethical Considerations are "aspirational in character". They are statements of principle intended to provide guidance, but their violation is not intended to result in disciplinary action. The Ethical Considerations are designated by the letters EC followed by the number of the particular Canon and the paragraph within the Canon. Thus, the first Ethical Consideration under Canon 1 is EC 1-1.

The Disciplinary Rules are "mandatory in character". They state the "minimum level of conduct below which no lawyer can fall without being subject to disciplinary action". The Disciplinary Rules are designated by the letters DR followed by the number of the particular Canon and section numbers beginning in each instance with 101. Thus, the First Disciplinary Rule under Canon 1 is DR 1-101.

The general concept of the Code is a sound one. The execution, however, is marred by considerable superficiality, avoidance of difficult issues, and a carry-over of the anti-competitive concerns of the old Canons of Ethics.

The Standards Relating to the Prosecution Function and the Defense Function were completed in 1971. They consist of two separate bodies of rules, one for the prosecution and one for the defense. The rules are set forth in numbered sections, followed by commentaries. The Standards refer throughout to what a prosecutor or defense attorney should or should not do. However, unless the phrase "unprofessional conduct" is used, a provision of the Standards is intended to be aspirational only. Although there are occasional flashes of candor in the Standards, taken all in all, they are disingenuous and wholly inadequate to the task that the drafters set out to perform.

B.   THE CODE OF PROFESSIONAL RESPONSIBILITY

Preface

On August 14, 1964, at the request of President Lewis F. Powell, Jr., the House of Delegates of the American Bar Association created the Special Committee on Evaluation of Ethical Standards to examine the current Canons of Professional Ethics and to make recommendations for changes. Your Committee has been at work since that time with the extremely competent assistance of its Reporter, Professor John F. Sutton, Jr., of the University of Texas School of Law. Since August of 1967 we have been aided by Mrs. Sarah Ragle Weddington, a member of the Texas Bar, who has served as Assistant to Mr. Sutton. The supporting research work was conducted under the supervision of Mr. Sutton in his capacity as Director of a research project for the American Bar Foundation. We also acknowledge with thanks the effective help of Frederick R. Franklin of the American Bar Association Division of Professional Service Activities, who served as Staff Assistant in the crowded latter months of our work.

After substantial study and a number of meetings, we concluded that the present Canons needed revision in four principal particulars: (1) There are important areas involving the conduct of lawyers that are either only partially covered in or totally omitted from the Canons; (2) Many Canons that are sound in substance are in need of editorial revision; (3) Most of the Canons do not lend themselves to practical sanctions for violations; and (4) Changed and changing conditions in our legal system and urbanized society require new statements of professional principles.

The original 32 Canons of Professional Ethics were adopted by the American Bar Association in 1908. They were based principally on the Code of Ethics adopted by the Alabama State Bar Association in 1887, which in turn had been borrowed largely from the lectures of Judge George Sharswood, published in 1854 under the title of *Professional Ethics*. Since then a limited number of amendments have been adopted on a piecemeal basis.

The thought of studying the Canons of Professional Ethics with a view of possible revision is not a new one. In 1928, 1933 and 1937 special committees of the American Bar Association, appointed for the purpose of investigating the subject, made reports recommending overall revisions, but nothing came of these efforts. In 1954 a distinguished committee of the American Bar Foundation made extensive studies of the Canons and recommended further work in the field, but the subject lay fallow for ten more years until the creation of our Committee.

As far back as 1934 Mr. Justice (later Chief Justice) Harlan Fiske Stone, in his memorable address entitled *The Public Influence of the Bar,* made this observation:

Before the Bar can function at all as a guardian of the public interests committed to its care, there must be appraisal and comprehension of the new conditions, and the changed relationship of the lawyer to his clients, to his professional brethren and to the public. That appraisal must pass beyond the petty details of form and manners which have been so largely the subject of our Codes of Ethics, to more fundamental consideration of the way in which our professional activities affect the welfare of society as a whole. Our canons of ethics for the most part are generalizations designed for an earlier era.

Our studies led us unanimously to the conclusion that the need for change in the statements of professional responsibility of lawyers could not be met by merely amending the present Canons. A new Code of Professional Responsibility could be the only answer.

While the opinions of the Committee on Professional Ethics of the American Bar Association have been published and given fairly wide distribution with resulting value to the bench and bar, they certainly are not conclusive as to the adequacy of the present Canons. Because the opinions are necessarily interpretations of the existing Canons, they tend to support the Canons and are critical of them only in the most unusual case. Since a large number of requests for opinions from the Committee on Professional Ethics deal with the etiquette of law practice, advertising, partnership names, announcements and the like, there has been a tendency for many lawyers to assume that this is the exclusive field of interest of the Committee and that it is not concerned with the more serious questions of professional standards and obligations.

The present Canons are not an effective teaching instrument and they fail to give guidance to young lawyers beyond the language of the Canons themselves. There is no organized interrelationship of the Canons and they often overlap. They are not cast in language designed for disciplinary enforcement and many abound with quaint expressions of the past. The present Canons, nevertheless, contain many provisions that are sound in substance, and all of these have been brought forward in the proposed Code.

In our studies and meetings we have relied heavily upon the monumental *Legal Ethics* (1953) of Henry S. Drinker, who served with great distinction for nine years as Chairman of the Committee on Professional Ethics (known in his day as the Committee on Professional Ethics and Grievances) of the American Bar Association.

We have had constant recourse to the opinions of the Committee on Professional Ethics. These opinions were collected and published in a single volume in 1967; since that time we have been favored with all opinions of the Committee in loose-leaf form.

Recent decisions of the Supreme Court of the United States have necessitated intensive studies of certain Canons. Among the landmark cases in this regard are *NAACP v. Button,* 371 U.S. 415, 83 S. Ct. 328, 9 L.Ed.2d 405 (1963), *Brotherhood of R. R. Trainmen v. Virginia,* 377 U.S. 1, 84 S. Ct. 1113, 12 L.Ed.2d 89 (1964), and *United Mine Workers v. Ill. State Bar Ass'n,* 389 U.S. 217, 88 S. Ct. 353, 19 L.Ed.2d 426 (1967). It is not here necessary to comment in detail on these far-reaching rulings since they are familiar to all lawyers.

Also, in recent years the Supreme Court of the United States has made important pronouncements in the areas of admission to the bar and discipline of lawyers. Without attempting an exhaustive catalogue in this regard, we refer to *Schware v. Bd. of Bar Examiners,* 353 U.S. 232, 77 S. Ct. 752, 1 L.Ed.2d 96 (1957), *Spevack v. Klein,* 385 U.S. 511, 87 S. Ct. 625, 17 L.Ed.2d 754 (1967), and *In re Ruffalo,* 390 U.S. 544, 88 S. Ct. 1222, 20 L.Ed.2d 117 (1968).

Our Committee has held meetings with 37 major units of the profession and has corresponded with more than 100 additional groups. The entire Committee has met a total of 71 days and the editorial subcommittee of three members has met 28 additional days. Geoffrey C. Hazard, Jr., of Chicago, Illinois, Director of the American Bar Foundation, John G. Bonomi, of New York, New York, a member of the A.B.A. Special Committee on Evaluation of Disciplinary Enforcement, and Paul Carrington, of Dallas, Texas, a member of the A.B.A. Special Committee on Availability of Legal Services, attended many of our meetings and each made invaluable suggestions in the course of our deliberations. Lawrence E. Walsh, of New York, New York, served as a member of our Committee in the first two years of its existence and rendered distinctive service in that period.

"The Code of Professional Responsibility was adopted by the House of Delegates of the American Bar Association on August 12, 1969 to become effective for American Bar Association members on January 1, 1970; as amended by the House of Delegates on February 24, 1970."

CODE OF PROFESSIONAL RESPONSIBILITY

Table of Contents

CODE OF PROFESSIONAL RESPONSIBILITY

Preamble and Preliminary Statement

Preamble[1]

The continued existence of a free and democratic society depends upon recognition of the concept that justice is based upon the rule of law grounded in respect for the dignity of the individual and his capacity through reason for enlightened self-government.[2] Law so grounded makes justice possible, for only through such law does the dignity of the individual attain respect and protection. Without it, individual rights become subject to unrestrained power, respect for law is destroyed, and rational self-government is impossible.

Lawyers, as guardians of the law, play a vital role in the preservation of society. The fulfillment of this role requires an understanding by lawyers of their relationship with and function in our legal system.[3] A consequent obligation of lawyers is to maintain the highest standards of ethical conduct.

In fulfilling his professional responsibilities, a lawyer necessarily assumes various roles that require the performance of many difficult tasks. Not every situation which he may encounter can be foreseen,[4] but fundamental ethical principles are always present to guide him. Within the framework of these principles, a lawyer must with courage and foresight be able and ready to shape the body of the law to the ever-changing relationships of society.[5]

---

[1] The footnotes are intended merely to enable the reader to relate the provisions of this Code to the ABA Canons of Professional Ethics adopted in 1908, as amended, the Opinions of the ABA Committee on Professional Ethics, and a limited number of other sources; they are not intended to be an annotation of the views taken by the ABA Special Committee on Evaluation of Ethical Standards. Footnotes citing ABA Canons refer to the ABA Canons of Professional Ethics, adopted in 1908, as amended.

[2] *Cf.* ABA Canons, Preamble.

[3] "[T]he lawyer stands today in special need of a clear understanding of his obligations and of the vital connection between those obligations and the role his profession plays in society." *Professional Responsibility: Report of the Joint Conference,* 44 A.B.A.J. 1159, 1160 (1958).

[4] "No general statement of the responsibilities of the legal profession can encompass all the situations in which the lawyer may be placed. Each position held by him makes its own peculiar demands. These demands the lawyer must clarify for himself in the light of the particular role in which he serves." *Professional Responsibility: Report of the Joint Conference,* 44 A.B.A.J. 1159, 1218 (1958).

[5] "The law and its institutions change as social conditions change. They must change if they are to preserve, much less advance, the political and social values from which they derive their purposes and their life. This is

The Code of Professional Responsibility points the way to the aspiring and provides standards by which to judge the transgressor. Each lawyer must find within his own conscience the touchstone against which to test the extent to which his actions should rise above minimum standards. But in the last analysis it is the desire for the respect and confidence of the members of his profession and of the society which he serves that should provide to a lawyer the incentive for the highest possible degree of ethical conduct. The possible loss of that respect and confidence is the ultimate sanction. So long as its practitioners are guided by these principles, the law will continue to be a noble profession. This is its greatness and its strength, which permit of no compromise.

Preliminary Statement

In furtherance of the principles stated in the Preamble, the American Bar Association has promulgated this Code of Professional Responsibility, consisting of three separate but interrelated parts: Canons, Ethical Considerations, and Disciplinary Rules.[6] The Code is designed to be adopted by appropriate agencies both as an inspirational guide to the members of the profession and as a basis for disciplinary action when the conduct of a lawyer falls below the required minimum standards stated in the Disciplinary Rules.

Obviously the Canons, Ethical Considerations, and Disciplinary Rules cannot apply to non-lawyers; however, they do define the type of ethical conduct that the public has a right to expect not only of lawyers but also of their non-professional employees and associates in all matters pertaining to professional employment. A lawyer should ultimately be responsible for the

---

true of the most important of legal institutions, the profession of law. The profession, too, must change when conditions change in order to preserve and advance the social values that are its reasons for being." Cheatham, *Availability of Legal Services: The Responsibility of the Individual Lawyer and the Organized Bar,* 12 U.C.L.A. L. REV. 438, 440 (1965).

[6] The Supreme Court of Wisconsin adopted a Code of Judicial Ethics in 1967. "The code is divided into standards and rules, the standards being statements of what the general desirable level of conduct should be, the rules being particular canons, the violation of which shall subject an individual judge to sanctions." In re Promulgation of a Code of Judicial Ethics, 36 Wis. 2d 252, 255, 153 N.W.2d 873, 874 (1967).

The portion of the Wisconsin Code of Judicial Ethics entitled "Standards" states that "[t]he following standards set forth the significant qualities of the ideal judge. . . ." *Id.,* 36 Wis. 2d at 256, 153 N.W.2d at 875. The portion entitled "Rules" states that "[t]he court promulgates the following rules because the requirements of judicial conduct embodied therein are of sufficient gravity to warrant sanctions if they are not obeyed. . . ." *Id.,* 36 Wis. 2d at 259, 153 N.W.2d at 876.

conduct of his employees and associates in the course of the professional representation of the client.

The Canons are statements of axiomatic norms, expressing in general terms the standards of professional conduct expected of lawyers in their relationships with the public, with the legal system, and with the legal profession. They embody the general concepts from which the Ethical Considerations and the Disciplinary Rules are derived.

The Ethical Considerations are aspirational in character and represent the objectives toward which every member of the profession should strive. They constitute a body of principles upon which the lawyer can rely for guidance in many specific situations.[7]

The Disciplinary Rules, unlike the Ethical Considerations, are mandatory in character. The Disciplinary Rules state the minimum level of conduct below which no lawyer can fall without being subject to disciplinary action. Within the framework of fair trial,[8] the Disciplinary Rules should be uniformly applied

---

[7] "Under the conditions of modern practice it is peculiarly necessary that the lawyer should understand, not merely the established standards of professional conduct, but the reasons underlying these standards. Today the lawyer plays a changing and increasingly varied role. In many developing fields the precise contribution of the legal profession is as yet undefined." *Professional Responsibility: Report of the Joint Conference*, 44 A.B.A.J. 1159 (1958).

"A true sense of professional responsibility must derive from an understanding of the reasons that lie back of specific restraints, such as those embodied in the Canons. The grounds for the lawyer's peculiar obligations are to be found in the nature of his calling. The lawyer who seeks a clear understanding of his duties will be led to reflect on the special services his profession renders to society and the services it might render if its full capacities were realized. When the lawyer fully understands the nature of his office, he will then discern what restraints are necessary to keep that office wholesome and effective." *Id.*

[8] "Disbarment, designed to protect the public, is a punishment or penalty imposed on the lawyer. . . . He is accordingly entitled to procedural due process, which includes fair notice of the charge." In re Ruffalo, 390 U.S. 544, 550, 20 L. Ed. 2d 117, 122, 88 S. Ct. 1222, 1226 (1968), *rehearing denied*, 391 U.S. 961, 20 L. Ed. 2d 874, 88 S. Ct. 1833 (1968).

"A State cannot exclude a person from the practice of law or from any other occupation in a manner or for reasons that contravene the Due Process or Equal Protection Clause of the Fourteenth Amendment. . . . A State can require high standards of qualification . . . but any qualification must have a rational connection with the applicant's fitness or capacity to practice law." Schware v. Bd. of Bar Examiners, 353 U.S. 232, 239, 1 L. Ed. 2d 796, 801-02, 77 S. Ct. 752, 756 (1957).

"[A]n accused lawyer may expect that he will not be condemned out of a capricious self-righteousness or denied the essentials of a fair hearing." Kingsland v. Dorsey, 338 U.S. 318, 320, 94 L. Ed. 123, 126, 70 S. Ct. 123, 124-25 (1949).

"The attorney and counsellor being, by the solemn judicial act of the court, clothed with his office, does not hold it as a matter of grace and favor.

to all lawyers,[9] regardless of the nature of their professional activities.[10] The Code makes no attempt to prescribe either disciplinary procedures or penalties[11] for violation of a Disciplinary Rule,[12] nor does it undertake to define standards for civil liability of lawyers for professional conduct. The severity of judgment against one found guilty of violating a Disciplinary Rule should be determined by the character of the offense and the attendant circumstances.[13] An enforcing agency, in applying the Disciplinary

---

The right which it confers upon him to appear for suitors, and to argue causes, is something more than a mere indulgence, revocable at the pleasure of the court, or at the command of the legislature. It is a right of which he can only be deprived by the judgment of the court, for moral or professional delinquency." Ex parte Garland, 71 U.S. (4 Wall.) 333, 378-79, 18 L. Ed. 366, 370 (1866).

See generally Comment, *Procedural Due Process and Character Hearings for Bar Applicants,* 15 STAN. L. REV. 500 (1963).

[9] "The canons of professional ethics must be enforced by the Courts and must be respected by members of the Bar if we are to maintain public confidence in the integrity and impartiality of the administration of justice." In re Meeker, 76 N.M. 354, 357, 414 P.2d 862, 864 (1966), *appeal dismissed,* 385 U.S. 449 (1967).

[10] *See* ABA CANON 45.

"The Canons of this Association govern all its members, irrespective of the nature of their practice, and the application of the Canons is not affected by statutes or regulations governing certain activities of lawyers which may prescribe less stringent standards." ABA COMM. ON PROFESSIONAL ETHICS. *OPINIONS,* No. 203 (1940) [hereinafter each Opinion is cited as *"ABA Opinion"*].

Cf. ABA Opinion 152 (1936).

[11] "There is generally no prescribed discipline for any particular type of improper conduct. The disciplinary measures taken are discretionary with the courts, which may disbar, suspend, or merely censure the attorney as the nature of the offense and past indicia of character may warrant." Note, 43 CORNELL L.Q. 489, 495 (1958).

[12] The Code seeks only to specify conduct for which a lawyer should be disciplined. Recommendations as to the procedures to be used in disciplinary actions and the gravity of disciplinary measures appropriate for violations of the Code are within the jurisdiction of the American Bar Association Special Committee on Evaluation of Disciplinary Enforcement.

[13] "The severity of the judgment of this court should be in proportion to the gravity of the offenses, the moral turpitude involved, and the extent that the defendant's acts and conduct affect his professional qualifications to practice law." Louisiana State Bar Ass'n v. Steiner, 204 La. 1073, 1092-93, 16 So. 2d 843, 850 (1944) (Higgins, J., concurring in decree).

"Certainly an erring lawyer who has been disciplined and who having paid the penalty has given satisfactory evidence of repentance and has been rehabilitated and restored to his place at the bar by the court which knows him best ought not to have what amounts to an order of permanent disbarment entered against him by a federal court solely on the basis of an earlier criminal record and without regard to his subsequent rehabilitation and present good character. . . . We think, therefore, that the district court should reconsider the appellant's application for admission and grant it unless the court finds it to be a fact that the appellant is not presently of good moral or professional character." In re Dreier, 258 F.2d 68, 69-70 (3d Cir. 1958).

Rules, may find interpretative guidance in the basic principles embodied in the Canons and in the objectives reflected in the Ethical Considerations.

CANON 1—A LAWYER SHOULD ASSIST IN MAINTAINING THE INTEGRITY AND COMPETENCE OF THE LEGAL PROFESSION.

Ethical Considerations

EC 1-1. A basic tenet of the professional responsibility of lawyers is that every person in our society should have ready access to the independent professional services of a lawyer of integrity and competence. Maintaining the integrity and improving the competence of the bar to meet the highest standards is the ethical responsibility of every lawyer.

EC 1-2. The public should be protected from those who are not qualified to be lawyers by reason of a deficiency in education[1] or moral standards[2] or of other relevant factors[3] but who never-

---

[1] "[W]e cannot conclude that all educational restrictions [on bar admission] are unlawful. We assume that few would deny that a grammar school education requirement, before taking the bar examination, was reasonable. Or that an applicant had to be able to read or write. Once we conclude that *some* restriction is proper, then it becomes a matter of degree —the problem of drawing the line.

. . . .

"We conclude the fundamental question here is whether Rule IV, Section 6 of the Rules Pertaining to Admission of Applicants to the State Bar of Arizona is 'arbitrary, capricious and unreasonable.' We conclude an educational requirement of graduation from an accredited law school is not." Hackin v. Lockwood, 361 F.2d 499, 503-4 (9th Cir. 1966), *cert. denied,* 385 U.S. 960, 17 L. Ed. 2d 305, 87 S. Ct. 396 (1966).

[2] "Every state in the United States, as a prerequisite for admission to the practice of law, requires that applicants possess 'good moral character.' Although the requirement is of judicial origin, it is now embodied in legislation in most states." Comment, *Procedural Due Process and Character Hearings for Bar Applicants,* 15 STAN. L. REV. 500 (1963).

"Good character in the members of the bar is essential to the preservation of the integrity of the courts. The duty and power of the court to guard its portals against intrusion by men and women who are mentally and morally dishonest, unfit because of bad character, evidenced by their course of conduct, to participate in the administrative law, would seem to be unquestioned in the matter of preservation of judicial dignity and integrity." In re Monaghan, 126 Vt. 53, 222 A.2d 665, 670 (1966).

"Fundamentally, the question involved in both situations [*i.e.* admission and disciplinary proceedings] is the same—is the applicant for admission or the attorney sought to be disciplined a fit and proper person to be permitted to practice law, and that usually turns upon whether he has committed or is likely to continue to commit acts of moral turpitude. At the time of oral argument the attorney for respondent frankly conceded that the test for admission and for discipline is and should be the same. We agree with this concession." Hallinan v. Comm. of Bar Examiners, 65 Cal. 2d 447, 453, 421 P.2d 76, 81, 55 Cal. Rptr. 228, 233 (1966).

[3] "Proceedings to gain admission to the bar are for the purpose of protecting the public and the courts from the ministrations of persons unfit

theless seek to practice law. To assure the maintenance of high moral and educational standards of the legal profession, lawyers should affirmatively assist courts and other appropriate bodies in promulgating, enforcing, and improving requirements for admission to the bar.[4] In like manner, the bar has a positive obligation to aid in the continued improvement of all phases of pre-admission and post-admission legal education.

EC 1-3. Before recommending an applicant for admission, a lawyer should satisfy himself that the applicant is of good moral character. Although a lawyer should not become a self-appointed investigator or judge of applicants for admission, he should report to proper officials all unfavorable information he possesses relating to the character or other qualifications of an applicant.[5]

EC 1-4. The integrity of the profession can be maintained only if conduct of lawyers in violation of the Disciplinary Rules is brought to the attention of the proper officials. A lawyer should reveal voluntarily to those officials all unprivileged knowledge of conduct of lawyers which he believes clearly to be in violation of the Disciplinary Rules.[6] A lawyer should, upon request serve on and assist committees and boards having responsibility for the administration of the Disciplinary Rules.[7]

EC 1-5. A lawyer should maintain high standards of professional conduct and should encourage fellow lawyers to do like-

---

to practice the profession. Attorneys are officers of the court appointed to assist the court in the administration of justice. Into their hands are committed the property, the liberty and sometimes the lives of their clients. This commitment demands a high degree of intelligence, knowledge of the law, respect for its function in society, sound and faithful judgment and, above all else, integrity of character in private and professional conduct." In re Monaghan, 126 Vt. 53, 222 A.2d 665, 676 (1966) (Holden, C.J., dissenting).

[4] "A bar composed of lawyers of good moral character is a worthy objective but it is unnecessary to sacrifice vital freedoms in order to obtain that goal. It is also important both to society and the bar itself that lawyers be unintimidated—free to think, speak, and act as members of an Independent Bar." Konigsberg v. State Bar, 353 U.S. 252, 273, 1 L. Ed. 2d 810, 825, 77 S. Ct. 722, 733 (1957).

[5] See ABA CANON 29.

[6] ABA CANON 28 designates certain conduct as unprofessional and then states that: "A duty to the public and to the profession devolves upon every member of the Bar having knowledge of such practices upon the part of any practitioner immediately to inform thereof, to the end that the offender may be disbarred." ABA CANON 29 states a broader admonition: "Lawyers should expose without fear or favor before the proper tribunals corrupt or dishonest conduct in the profession."

[7] "It is the obligation of the organized Bar and the individual lawyer to give unstinted cooperation and assistance to the highest court of the state in discharging its function and duty with respect to discipline and in purging the profession of the unworthy." *Report of the Special Committee on Disciplinary Procedures*, 80 A.B.A. REP. 463, 470 (1955).

wise. He should be temperate and dignified, and he should refrain from all illegal and morally reprehensible conduct.[8] Because of his position in society, even minor violations of law by a lawyer may tend to lessen public confidence in the legal profession. Obedience to law exemplifies respect for law. To lawyers especially, respect for the law should be more than a platitude.

EC 1-6. An applicant for admission to the bar or a lawyer may be unqualified, temporarily or permanently, for other than moral and educational reasons, such as mental or emotional instability. Lawyers should be diligent in taking steps to see that during a period of disqualification such person is not granted a license or, if licensed, is not permitted to practice.[9] In like manner, when the disqualification has terminated, members of the bar should assist such person in being licensed, or, if licensed, in being restored to his full right to practice.

Disciplinary Rules

DR 1-101. Maintaining Integrity and Competence of the Legal Profession.

(A)   A lawyer is subject to discipline if he has made a materially false statement in, or if he has deliberately failed to disclose a material fact requested in connection with, his application for admission to the bar.[10]

---

[8] *Cf.* ABA CANON 32.

[9] "We decline, on the present record, to disbar Mr. Sherman or to reprimand him—not because we condone his actions, but because, as heretofore indicated, we are concerned with whether he is mentally responsible for what he has done.

"The logic of the situation would seem to dictate the conclusion that, if he was mentally responsible for the conduct we have outlined, he should be disbarred; and, if he was not mentally responsible, he should not be permitted to practice law.

"However, the flaw in the logic is that he may have been mentally irresponsible [at the time of his offensive conduct] . . ., and, yet, have sufficiently improved in the almost two and one-half years intervening to be able to capably and competently represent his clients. . . .

. . . .

"We would make clear that we are satisfied that case has been made against Mr. Sherman, warranting a refusal to permit him to further practice law in this state unless he can establish his mental irresponsibility at the time of the offenses charged. The burden of proof is upon him.

"If he establishes such mental irresponsibility, the burden is then upon him to establish his present capability to practice law." In re Sherman, 58 Wash. 2d 1, 6-7, 354 P.2d 888, 890 (1960), *cert. denied*, 371 U.S. 951, 9 L. Ed. 2d 499, 83 S. Ct. 506 (1963).

[10] "This Court has the inherent power to revoke a license to practice law in this State where such license was issued by this Court, and its issuance was procured by the fraudulent concealment, or by the false and fraudulent representation by the applicant of a fact which was manifestly material to the issuance of the license." North Carolina ex rel. Attorney

(B)   A lawyer shall not further the application for admission to the bar of another person known by him to be unqualified in respect to character, education, or other relevant attribute.[11]

DR 1-102. [C1]   Misconduct.—(A)   A lawyer shall not:

(1) Violate a Disciplinary Rule.

(2) Circumvent a Disciplinary Rule through actions of another.[12]

(3) Engage in illegal conduct involving moral turpitude.[13]

General v. Gorson, 209 N.C. 320, 326, 183 S.E. 392, 395 (1936), *cert. denied*, 298 U.S. 662, 80 L. Ed. 1387, 56 S. Ct. 752 (1936).

See also Application of Patterson, 318 P.2d 907, 913 (Or. 1957), *cert. denied*, 356 U.S. 947, 2 L. Ed. 2d 822, 78 S. Ct. 795 (1958).

[11] *See* ABA CANON 29.

[12] In *ABA Opinion* 95 (1933), which held that a municipal attorney could not permit police officers to interview persons with claims against the municipality when the attorney knew the claimants to be represented by counsel, the Committee on Professional Ethics said:

"The law officer is, of course, responsible for the acts of those in his department who are under his supervision and control. *Opinion 85. In re Robinson*, 136 N.Y.S. 548 (affirmed 209 N.Y. 354-1912) held that it was a matter of disbarment for an attorney to adopt a general course of approving the unethical conduct of employees of his client, even though he did not actively participate therein.

" '. . . The attorney should not advise or sanction acts by his client which he himself should not do.' *Opinion 75*."

[13] "The most obvious non-professional ground for disbarment is conviction for a felony. Most states make conviction for a felony grounds for automatic disbarment. Some of these states, including New York, make disbarment manadatory upon conviction for *any* felony, while others require disbarment only for those felonies which involve moral turpitude. There are strong arguments that some felonies, such as involuntary manslaughter, reflect neither on an attorney's fitness, trustworthiness, nor competence and, therefore, should not be grounds for disbarment, but most states tend to disregard these arguments and, following the common law rule, make disbarment mandatory on conviction for any felony." Note, 43 CORNELL L.Q. 489, 490 (1958).

"Some states treat conviction for misdemeanors as grounds for automatic disbarment. . . . However, the vast majority, accepting the common law rule, require that the misdemeanor involve moral turpitude. While the definition of moral turpitude may prove difficult, it seems only proper that those minor offenses which do not affect the attorney's fitness to continue in the profession should not be grounds for disbarment. A good example is an assault and battery conviction which would not involve moral turpitude unless done with malice and deliberation." *Id.* at 491.

"The term 'moral turpitude' has been used in the law for centuries. It has been the subject of many decisions by the courts but has never been clearly defined because of the nature of the term. Perhaps the best general definition of the term 'moral turpitude' is that it imparts an act of baseness, vileness or depravity in the duties which one person owes to another or to society in general, which is contrary to the usual, accepted and customary rule of right and duty which a person should follow. 58 C.J.S. at page 1201. Although offenses against revenue laws have been held to be crimes of moral turpitude, it has also been held that the attempt to evade the payment of taxes due to the government or any subdivision thereof,

(4) Engage in conduct involving dishonesty, fraud, deceit, or misrepresentation.

(5) Engage in conduct that is prejudicial to the administration of justice.

(6) Engage in any other conduct that adversely reflects on his fitness to practice law.[14]

DR 1-103.   [C2]   Disclosure of Information to Authorities.

(A)   A lawyer possessing unprivileged knowledge of a violation of DR 1-102 shall report such knowledge to a tribunal or other authority empowered to investigate or act upon such violation.[15]

(B)   A lawyer possessing unprivileged knowledge or evidence concerning another lawyer or a judge shall reveal fully such knowledge or evidence upon proper request of a tribunal or other authority empowered to investigate or act upon the conduct of lawyers or judges.[16]

---

while wrong and unlawful, does not involve moral turpitude. 58 C.J.S. at page 1205." Comm. on Legal Ethics v. Scheer, 149 W. Va. 721, 726-27, 143 S.E.2d 141, 145 (1965).

"The right and power to discipline an attorney, as one of its officers, is inherent in the court. . . . This power is not limited to those instances of misconduct wherein he has been employed, or has acted, in a professional capacity; but, on the contrary, this power may be exercised where his misconduct outside the scope of his professional relations shows him to be an unfit person to practice law." In re Wilson, 391 S.W.2d 914, 917-18 (Mo. 1965).

[14] "It is a fair characterization of the lawyer's responsibility in our society that he stands 'as a shield,' to quote Devlin, J., in defense of right and to ward off wrong. From a profession charged with these responsibilities there must be exacted those qualities of truth-speaking, of a high sense of honor, of granite discretion, of the strictest observance of fiduciary responsibility, that have, throughout the centuries, been compendiously described as 'moral character.'" Schware v. Bd. of Bar Examiners, 353 U.S. 232, 247, 1 L. Ed. 2d 796, 806, 77 S. Ct. 752, 761 (1957) (Frankfurter, J., concurring).

"Particularly applicable here is Rule 4.47 providing that 'A lawyer should always maintain his integrity; and shall not willfully commit any act against the interest of the public; nor shall he violate his duty to the courts or his clients; *nor shall he, by any misconduct, commit any offense against the laws of Missouri or the United States of America, which amounts to a crime involving acts done by him contrary to justice, honesty, modesty or good morals;* nor shall he be guilty of any other misconduct whereby, for the protection of the public and those charged with the administration of justice, he should no longer be entrusted with the duties and responsibilities belonging to the office of an attorney.'" In re Wilson, 391 S.W.2d 914, 917 (Mo. 1965).

[15] *See* ABA CANON 29; *cf.* ABA CANON 28.

[16] *Cf.* ABA CANONS 28 and 29.

Canon 2 [C3]—A Lawyer Should Assist the Legal Profession in Fulfilling Its Duty to Make Legal Counsel Available.

Ethical Considerations

EC 2-1. The need of members of the public for legal services[1] is met only if they recognize their legal problems, appreciate the importance of seeking assistance,[2] and are able to obtain the services of acceptable legal counsel.[3] Hence, important functions of the legal profession are to educate laymen to recognize their problems, to facilitate the process of intelligent selection of lawyers, and to assist in making legal services fully available.[4]

---

[1] "Men have need for more than a system of law; they have need for a system of law which functions, and that means they have need for lawyers." Cheatham, *The Lawyer's Role and Surroundings,* 25 Rocky Mt. L. Rev. 405 (1953).

[2] "Law is not self-applying; men must apply and utilize it in concrete cases. But the ordinary man is incapable. He cannot know the principles of law or the rules guiding the machinery of law administration; he does not know how to formulate his desires with precision and to put them into writing; he is ineffective in the presentation of his claims." *Id.*

[3] "This need [to provide legal services] was recognized by . . . Mr. [Lewis F.] Powell [Jr., President, American Bar Association, 1963-64], who said: 'Looking at contemporary America realistically, we must admit that despite all our efforts to date (and these have not been insignificant), far too many persons are not able to obtain equal justice under law. This usually results because their poverty or their ignorance has prevented them from obtaining counsel.'" Address by E. Clinton Bamberger, Association of American Law Schools 1965 Annual Meeting, Dec. 28, 1965, in Proceedings, Part II, 1965, 61, 63-64 (1965).

"A wide gap separates the need for legal services and its satisfaction, as numerous studies reveal. Looked at from the side of the layman, one reason for the gap is poverty and the consequent inability to pay legal fees. Another set of reasons is ignorance of the need for and the value of legal services, and ignorance of where to find a dependable lawyer. There is fear of the mysterious processes and delays of the law, and there is fear of overreaching and overcharging by lawyers, a fear stimulated by the occasional exposure of shysters." Cheatham, *Availability of Legal Services: The Responsibility of the Individual Lawyer and of the Organized Bar,* 12 U.C.L.A. L. Rev. 438 (1965).

[4] "It is not only the right but the duty of the profession as a whole to utilize such methods as may be developed to bring the services of its members to those who need them, so long as this can be done ethically and with dignity." *ABA Opinion* 320 (1968).

"[T]here is a responsibility on the bar to make legal services available to those who need them. The maxim, 'privilege brings responsibilities,' can be expanded to read, exclusive privilege to render public service brings responsibility to assure that the service is available to those in need of it." Cheatham, *Availability of Legal Services: The Responsibility of the Individual Lawyer and of the Organized Bar,* 12 U.C.L.A. L. Rev. 438, 443 (1965).

"The obligation to provide legal services for those actually caught up in litigation carries with it the obligation to make preventive legal advice accessible to all. It is among those unaccustomed to business affairs and fearful of the ways of the law that such advice is often most needed. If

Recognition of Legal Problems

EC 2-2. The legal profession should assist laymen to recognize legal problems because such problems may not be self-revealing and often are not timely noticed.[5] Therefore, lawyers acting under proper auspices should encourage and participate in educational and public relations programs concerning our legal system with particular reference to legal problems that frequently arise. Such educational programs should be motivated by a desire to benefit the public rather than to obtain publicity or employment for particular lawyers.[6] Examples of permissible activities include preparation of institutional advertisements[7] and

---

it is not received in time, the most valiant and skillful representation in court may come too late." *Professional Responsibility: Report of the Joint Conference,* 44 A.B.A.J. 1159, 1216 (1958).

[5] "Over a period of years institutional advertising of programs for the benefit of the public have been approved by this and other Ethics Committees as well as by the courts. . . .

"To the same effect are opinions of this Committee: *Opinion 179* dealing with radio programs presenting a situation in which legal advice is suggested in connection with a drafting of a will; *Opinions 205* and *227* permitting institutional advertising of lawyer referral plans; *Opinion 191* holding that advertising by lawyer members of a non-bar associated sponsored plan violated *Canon 27.* The Illinois Ethics Committee, in its *Opinion 201,* sustained bar association institutional advertising of a check-up plan. . . .

"This Committee has passed squarely on the question of the propriety of institutional advertising in connection with a legal check-up plan. Informal Decision C-171 quotes with express approval the Michigan Ethics Committee as follows:

As a public service, the bar has in the past addressed the public as to the importance of making wills, consulting counsel in connection with real estate transactions, etc. In the same way, the bar, as such, may recommend this program, provided always that it does it in such a way that there is not suggestion of solicitation on behalf of any individual lawyer." *ABA Opinion* 307 (1962).

[6] "We recognize a distinction between teaching the lay public the importance of securing legal services preventive in character and the solicitation of professional employment by or for a particular lawyer. The former tends to promote the public interest and enhance the public estimation of the profession. The latter is calculated to injure the public and degrade the profession.

. . . .

"Advertising which is calculated to teach the layman the benefits and advantages of preventive legal services will benefit the lay public and enable the lawyer to render a more desirable and beneficial professional service. . . ." *ABA Opinion* 179 (1938).

[7] "[A bar association] may engage in a dignified institutional educational campaign so long as it does not involve the identification of a particular lawyer with the check-up program. Such educational material may point out the value of the annual check-up and may be printed in newspapers, magazines, pamphlets, and brochures, or produced by means of films, radio, television or other media. The printed materials may be distributed in a dignified way through the offices of persons having close dealings with lawyers as, for example, banks, real estate agents, insurance agents and others. They may be available in lawyers' offices. The bar association may prepare and

professional articles for lay publications[8] and participation in seminars, lectures, and civic programs. But a lawyer who participates in such activities should shun personal publicity.[9]

EC 2-3. Whether a lawyer acts properly in volunteering advice to a layman to seek legal services depends upon the circumstances.[10] The giving of advice that one should take legal action could well be in fulfillment of the duty of the legal profession to assist laymen in recognizing legal problems.[11] The

---

distribute to lawyers materials and forms for use in the annual legal check-up." *ABA Opinion* 307 (1962).

[8] "A lawyer may with propriety write articles for publications in which he gives information upon the law. . . ." ABA CANON 40.

"The newsletters, by means of which respondents are alleged to have advertised their wares, were sent to the officers of union clients represented by their firm. . . . They contain no reference to any cases handled by the respondents. Their contents are confined to rulings of boards, commissions and courts on problems of interest to labor union, together with proposed and completed legislation important to the Brotherhood, and other items which might affect unions and their members. The respondents cite Opinion 213 of the Committee on Professional Ethics and Grievances as permitting such practice. After studying this opinion, we agree that sending of newsletters of the above type to regular clients does not offend Canon 27." In re Ratner, 194 Kan. 362, 371, 399 P.2d 865, 872-73 (1965).

Cf. ABA Opinion 92 (1933).

[9] *Cf. ABA Opinions* 307 (1962) and 179 (1938).

"There is no ethical or other valid reason why an attorney may not write articles on legal subjects for magazines and newspapers. The fact that the publication is a trade journal or magazine, makes no difference as to the ethical question involved. On the other hand, it would be unethical and contrary to the precepts of the Canons for the attorney to allow his name to be carried in the magazine or other publication . . . as a free legal adviser for the subscribers to the publication. Such would be contrary to *Canons 27* and *35* and Opinions heretofore announced by the Committee on Professional Ethics and Grievances. (See *Opinions 31, 41, 42, and 56*)." *ABA Opinion* 162 (1936).

[10] *See* ABA CANON 28.

[11] This question can assume constitutional dimensions: "We meet at the outset the contention that 'solicitation' is wholly outside the area of freedoms protected by the First Amendment. To this contention there are two answers. The first is that a State cannot foreclose the exercise of constitutional rights by mere labels. The second is that abstract discussion is not the only species of communication which the Constitution protects; the First Amendment also protects vigorous advocacy, certainly of lawful ends, against governmental intrusion. . . .

. . . .

"However valid may be Virginia's interest in regulating the traditionally illegal practice of barratry, maintenance and champerty, that interest does not justify the prohibition of the NAACP activities disclosed by this record. Malicious intent was of the essence of the common-law offenses of fomenting or stirring up litigation. And whatever may be or may have been true of suits against governments in other countries, the exercise in our own, as in this case of First Amendment rights to enforce Constitutional rights through litigation, as a matter of law, cannot be deemed malicious." NAACP v. Button, 371 U.S. 415, 429, 439-40, 9 L. Ed. 2d 405, 415-16, 422, 83 S. Ct. 328, 336, 341 (1963).

advice is proper only if motivated by a desire to protect one who does not recognize that he may have legal problems or who is ignorant of his legal rights or obligations. Hence, the advice is improper if motivated by a desire to obtain personal benefit,[12] secure personal publicity, or cause litigation to be brought merely to harass or injure another. Obviously, a lawyer should not contact a non-client, directly or indirectly, for the purpose of being retained to represent him for compensation.

EC 2-4.   Since motivation is subjective and often difficult to judge, the motives of a lawyer who volunteers advice likely to produce legal controversy may well be suspect if he receives professional employment or other benefits as a result.[13] A lawyer who volunteers advice that one should obtain the services of a lawyer generally should not himself accept employment, compensation, or other benefit in connection with that matter. However, it is not improper for a lawyer to volunteer such advice and render resulting legal services to close friends, relatives, former clients (in regard to matters germane to former employment), and regular clients.[14]

EC 2-5.   A lawyer who writes or speaks for the purpose of educating members of the public to recognize their legal problems should carefully refrain from giving or appearing to give a general solution applicable to all apparently similar individual problems,[15] since slight changes in fact situations may require a

---

[12] *See* ABA CANON 27.

[13] "The Canons of Professional Ethics of the American Bar Association and the decisions of the courts quite generally prohibit the direct solicitation of business for gain by an attorney either through advertisement or personal communication; and also condemn the procuring of business by indirection through touters of any kind. It is disreputable for an attorney to breed litigation by seeking out those who have claims for personal injuries or other grounds of action in order to secure them as clients, or to employ agents or runners, or to reward those who bring or influence the bringing of business to his office. . . . Moreover, it tends quite easily to the institution of baseless litigation and the manufacture of perjured testimony. From early times, this danger has been recognized in the law by the condemnation of the crime of common barratry, or the stirring up of suits or quarrels between individuals at law or otherwise." In re Ades, 6 F. Supp. 467, 474-75 (D. Mary. 1934).

[14] *"Rule 2.*

"§a. . . .

"[A] member of the State Bar shall not solicit professional employment by

" (1) Volunteering counsel or advice except where ties of blood relationship or trust make it appropriate." CAL. BUSINESS AND PROFESSIONS CODE § 6076 (West 1962).

[15] *"Rule 18* . . . A member of the State Bar shall not advise inquirers or render opinions to them through or in connection with a newspaper, radio or other publicity medium of any kind in respect to their specific legal

material variance in the applicable advice; otherwise, the public may be misled and misadvised. Talks and writings by lawyers for laymen should caution them not to attempt to solve individual problems upon the basis of the information contained therein.[16]

Selection of a Lawyer: Generally

EC 2-6. Formerly a potential client usually knew the reputations of local lawyers for competency and integrity and therefore could select a practitioner in whom he had confidence. This traditional selection process worked well because it was initiated by the client and the choice was an informed one.

EC 2-7. Changed conditions, however, have seriously restricted the effectiveness of the traditional selection process. Often the reputations of lawyers are not sufficiently known to enable laymen to make intelligent choices.[17] The law has become increasingly complex and specialized. Few lawyers are willing and competent to deal with every kind of legal matter, and many laymen have difficulty in determining the competence of lawyers to render different types of legal services. The selection of legal counsel is particularly difficult for transients, persons moving into new areas, persons of limited education or means, and others who have little or no contact with lawyers.[18]

EC 2-8. Selection of a lawyer by a layman often is the result of the advice and recommendation of third parties—relatives, friends, acquaintances, business associates, or other lawyers. A layman is best served if the recommendation is disinterested and informed. In order that the recommendation be disinterested, a lawyer should not seek to influence another to recommend his employment.[19] A lawyer should not compensate another person

---

problems, whether or not such attorney shall be compensated for his services." CAL. BUSINESS AND PROFESSIONS CODE § 6076 (West 1962).

16 "In any case where a member might well apply the advice given in the opinion to his individual affairs, the lawyer rendering the opinion [concerning problems common to members of an association and distributed to the members through a periodic bulletin] should specifically state that this opinion should not be relied on by any member as a basis for handling his individual affairs, but that in every case he should consult his counsel. In the publication of the opinion the association should make a similar statement." *ABA Opinion* 273 (1946).

17 "A group of recent interrelated changes bears directly on the availability of legal services. . . . [One] change is the constantly accelerating urbanization of the country and the decline of personal and neighborhood knowledge of whom to retain as a professional man." Cheatham, *Availability of Legal Services: The Responsibility of the Individual Lawyer and of the Organized Bar*, 12 U.C.L.A. L. REV. 438, 440 (1965).

18 *Cf.* Cheatham, *A Lawyer When Needed: Legal Services for the Middle Classes*, 63 COLUM. L. REV. 973, 974 (1963).

19 *See* ABA CANON 27.

for recommending him, for influencing a prospective client to employ him, or to encourage future recommendations.[20]

Selection of a Lawyer: Professional Notices and Listings

EC 2-9. The traditional ban against advertising by lawyers, which is subject to certain limited exceptions, is rooted in the public interest. Competitive advertising would encourage extravagant, artful, self-laudatory[21] brashness in seeking business and thus could mislead the layman.[22] Furthermore, it would inevitably produce unrealistic expectations in particular cases and bring about distrust of the law and lawyers.[23] Thus, public confidence in our legal system would be impaired by such advertisements of professional services. The attorney-client relationship is personal and unique and should not be established as the result of pressures and deceptions.[24] History has demonstrated that public

---

[20] *See* ABA CANON 28.

[21] " 'Self-laudation' is a very flexible concept; Canon 27 does not define it, so what course of conduct would be said to constitute it under a given state of facts would no doubt vary as the opinions of men vary. As a famous English judge said, it would vary as the length of the chancellor's foot. It must be in words and tone that will 'offend the traditions and lower the tone of our profession.' When it does this, it is 'reprehensible.' This seems to be the test by which 'self-laudation' is measured." State v. Nichols, 151 So. 2d 257, 259 (Fla. 1963).

[22] "Were it not for the prohibitions of . . . [Canon 27] lawyers could, and no doubt would be forced to, engage competitively in advertising of all kinds in which each would seek to explain to the public why he could serve better and accomplish more than his brothers at the Bar.

"Susceptible as we are to advertising the public would then be encouraged to choose an attorney on the basis of which had the better, more attractive advertising program rather than on his reputation for professional ability.

"This would certainly maim, if not destroy, the dignity and professional status of the Bar of this State." State v. Nichols, 151 So. 2d 257, 268 (Fla. 1963) (O'Connell, J., concurring in part and dissenting in part).

[23] *Cf.* ABA CANON 8.

[24] "The prohibition of advertising by lawyers deserves some examination. All agree that advertising by an individual lawyer, if permitted, will detract from the dignity of the profession, but the matter goes deeper than this. Perhaps the most understandable and acceptable additional reasons we have found are stated by one commentator as follows:

" '1. That advertisements, unless kept within narrow limits, like any other form of solicitation, tend to stir up litigation, and such tendency is against the public interest.

" '2. That if there were no restrictions on advertisements, the least capable and least honorable lawyers would be apt to publish the most extravagant and alluring material about themselves, and that the harm which would result would, in large measure, fall on the ignorant and on those least able to afford it.

" '3. That the temptation would be strong to hold out as inducements for employment, assurances of success or of satisfaction to the client, which assurances could not be realized, and that the giving of such assurances would

confidence in the legal system is best preserved by strict, self-imposed controls over, rather than by unlimited, advertising.

EC 2-10. Methods of advertising that are subject to the objections stated above[25] should be and are prohibited.[26] However, the Disciplinary Rules recognize the value of giving assistance in the selection process through forms of advertising that furnish identification of a lawyer while avoiding such objections. For example, a lawyer may be identified in the classified section of the telephone directory,[27] in the office building directory, and on his letterhead and professional card.[28] But at all times the permitted notices should be dignified and accurate.

EC 2-11. The name under which a lawyer conducts his practice may be a factor in the selection process.[29] The use of a trade name or an assumed name could mislead laymen concerning the identity, responsibility, and status of those practicing thereunder.[30] Accordingly, a lawyer in private practice should practice only under his own name, the name of a lawyer employing him, a partnership name composed of the name of one or more of the lawyers practicing in a partnership, or, if permitted by law, in the name of a professional legal corporation, which should be clearly designated as such. For many years some law firms have used a firm name retaining one or more names of deceased or retired partners and such practice is not improper if the firm is a bona fide successor of a firm in which the deceased or retired person was a member, if the use of the name is authorized by law or by contract, and if the public is not misled thereby.[31]

---

materially increase the temptation to use ill means to secure the end desired by the client.

" 'In other words, the reasons for the rule, and for the conclusion that it is desirable to prohibit advertising entirely, or to limit it within such narrow bounds that it will not admit of abuse, are based on the possibility and probability that this means of publicity, if permitted, will be abused.' Harrison Hewitt in a comment at 15 A.B.A.J. 116 (1929) reproduced in CHEATHAM, CASES AND MATERIALS ON THE LEGAL PROFESSION (2d Ed., 1955), p. 525.

"Of course, competition is at the root of the abuses in advertising. If the individual lawyer were permitted to compete with his fellows in publicity through advertising, we have no doubt that Mr. Hewitt's three points, quoted above, would accurately forecast the result." Jacksonville Bar Ass'n v. Wilson, 102 So. 2d 292, 294-95 (Fla. 1958).

[25] *See* ABA CANON 27.
[26] *Cf. ABA Opinions* 309 (1963) and 284 (1951).
[27] *Cf. ABA Opinions* 313 (1964) and 284 (1951).
[28] *See* ABA CANON 27.
[29] *Cf. ABA Opinion* 303 (1961).
[30] *See* ABA CANON 33.
[31] *Id.*

"The continued use of a firm name by one or more surviving partners after the death of a member of the firm whose name is in the firm title is

However, the name of a partner who withdraws from a firm but continues to practice law should be omitted from the firm name in order to avoid misleading the public.

EC 2-12. A lawyer occupying a judicial, legislative, or public executive or administrative position who has the right to practice law concurrently may allow his name to remain in the name of the firm if he actively continues to practice law as a member thereof. Otherwise, his name should be removed from the firm name,[32] and he should not be identified as a past or present member of the firm; and he should not hold himself out as being a practicing lawyer.

EC 2-13. In order to avoid the possibility of misleading persons with whom he deals, a lawyer should be scrupulous in the representation of his professional status.[33] He should not hold himself out as being a partner or associate of a law firm if he is not one in fact,[34] and thus should not hold himself out as a partner or associate if he only shares offices with another lawyer.[35]

---

expressly permitted by the Canons of Ethics. The reason for this is that all of the partners have by their joint and several efforts over a period of years contributed to the good will attached to the firm name. In the case of a firm having widespread connections, this good will is disturbed by a change in firm name every time a name partner dies, and that reflects a loss in some degree of the good will to the building up of which the surviving partners have contributed their time, skill and labor through a period of years. To avoid this loss the firm name is continued, and to meet the requirements of the Canon the individuals constituting the firm from time to time are listed." *ABA Opinion* 267 (1945).

"Accepted local custom in New York recognizes that the name of a law firm does not necessarily identify the individual members of the firm, and hence the continued use of a firm name after the death of one or more partners is not a deception and is permissible. . . . The continued use of a deceased partner's name in the firm title is not affected by the fact that another partner withdraws from the firm and his name is dropped, or the name of the new partner is added to the firm name." *Opinion* No. 45, Committee on Professional Ethics, New York State Bar Ass'n, 39 N.Y.St.B.J. 455 (1967).

Cf. ABA Opinion 258 (1943).

[32] *Cf.* ABA CANON 33 and *ABA Opinion* 315 (1965).

[33] *Cf. ABA Opinions* 283 (1950) and 81 (1932).

[34] *See ABA Opinion* 316 (1967).

[35] "The word 'associates' has a variety of meanings. Principally through custom the word when used on the letterheads of law firms has come to be regarded as describing those who are employees of the firm. Because the word has acquired this special significance in connection with the practice of the law the use of the word to describe lawyer relationships other than employer-employee is likely to be misleading." In re Sussman and Tanner, 241 Ore. 246, 248, 405 P.2d 355, 356 (1965).

According to *ABA Opinion* 310 (1963), use of the term "associates" would be misleading in two situations: (1) where two lawyers are partners and they share both responsibility and liability for the partnership; and (2) where two lawyers practice separately, sharing no responsibility or liability, and only share a suite of offices and some costs.

EC 2-14. In some instances a lawyer confines his practice to a particular field of law.[36] In the absence of state controls to insure the existence of special competence, a lawyer should not be permitted to hold himself out as a specialist[37] or as having special training or ability, other than in the historically excepted fields of admiralty, trademark, and patent law.[38]

EC 2-15. The legal profession has developed lawyer referral systems designed to aid individuals who are able to pay fees but need assistance in locating lawyers competent to handle their particular problems. Use of a lawyer referral system enables a layman to avoid an uninformed selection of a lawyer because such a system makes possible the employment of competent lawyers who have indicated an interest in the subject matter involved. Lawyers should support the principle of lawyer referral systems and should encourage the evolution of other ethical plans which aid in the selection of qualified counsel.

Financial Ability to Employ Counsel: Generally

EC 2-16. The legal profession cannot remain a viable force in fulfilling its role in our society unless its members receive adequate compensation for services rendered, and reasonable fees[39] should be charged in appropriate cases to clients able to pay them. Nevertheless, persons unable to pay all or a portion of a reasonable fee should be able to obtain necessary legal services,[40] and lawyers should support and participate in ethical activities designed to achieve that objective.[41]

---

[36] "For a long time, many lawyers have, of necessity, limited their practice to certain branches of law. The increasing complexity of the law and the demand of the public for more expertness on the part of the lawyer has, in the past few years—particularly in the last ten years—brought about specialization on an increasing scale." *Report of the Special Committee on Specialization and Specialized Legal Services*, 79 A.B.A. REP. 582, 584 (1954).

[37] "In varying degrees specialization has become the *modus operandi* throughout the legal profession. . . . American society is specialization conscious. The present Canons, however, do not allow lawyers to make known to the lay public the fact that they engage in the practice of a specialty. . . ." Tucker, *The Large Law Firm: Considerations Concerning the Modernization of the Canons of Professional Ethics*, 1965 WIS. L. REV. 344, 348-49 (1965).

[38] *See* ABA CANON 27.

[39] *See* ABA CANON 12.

[40] *Cf.* ABA CANON 12.

[41] "If there is any fundamental proposition of government on which all would agree, it is that one of the highest goals of society must be to achieve and maintain equality before the law. Yet this ideal remains an empty form of words unless the legal profession is ready to provide adequate representation for those unable to pay the usual fees." *Professional Representation: Report of the Joint Conference*, 44 A.B.A.J. 1159, 1216 (1958).

Financial Ability to Employ Counsel: Persons Able to Pay Reasonable Fees

EC 2-17. The determination of a proper fee requires consideration of the interests of both client and lawyer.[42] A lawyer should not charge more than a reasonable fee,[43] for excessive cost of legal service would deter laymen from utilizing the legal system in protection of their rights. Furthermore, an excessive charge abuses the professional relationship between lawyer and client. On the other hand, adequate compensation is necessary in order to enable the lawyer to serve his client effectively and to preserve the integrity and independence of the profession.[44]

EC 2-18. The determination of the reasonableness of a fee requires consideration of all relevant circumstances,[45] including those stated in the Disciplinary Rules. The fees of a lawyer will vary according to many factors, including the time required, his experience, ability, and reputation, the nature of the employment, the responsibility involved, and the results obtained. [C4] Suggested fee schedules and economic reports of state and local bar associations provide some guidance on the subject of reasonable fees.[46] It is a commendable and long-standing tradition of the bar that special consideration is given in the fixing of any fee for services rendered a brother lawyer or a member of his immediate family.

EC 2-19. As soon as feasible after a lawyer has been employed, it is desirable that he reach a clear agreement with his client as to the basis of the fee charges to be made. Such a course will not only prevent later misunderstanding but will also work for good relations between the lawyer and the client. It is usually beneficial to reduce to writing the understanding of the parties regarding the fee, particularly when it is contingent. A lawyer should be mindful that many persons who desire to employ him may have had little or no experience with fee charges of lawyers,

---

[42] *See* ABA CANON 12.

[43] *Cf.* ABA CANON 12.

[44] "When members of the Bar are induced to render legal services for inadequate compensation, as a consequence the quality of the service rendered may be lowered, the welfare of the profession injured and the administration of justice made less efficient." *ABA Opinion* 302 (1961).

Cf. ABA Opinion 307 (1962).

[45] *See* ABA CANON 12.

[46] *Id.*

"[U]nder . . . [*Canon 12*], this Committee has consistently held that minimum fee schedules can only be suggested or recommended and cannot be made obligatory. . . ." *ABA Opinion* 302 (1961).

"[A] compulsory minimum fee schedule is contrary to *Canon 12* and repeated pronouncements of this committee." *ABA Opinion* 190 (1939).

Cf. ABA Opinions 171 (1937) and 28 (1930).

and for this reason he should explain fully to such persons the reasons for the particular fee arrangement he proposes.

EC 2-20.   Contingent fee arrangements[47] in civil cases have long been commonly accepted in the United States in proceedings to enforce claims. The historical bases of their acceptance are that (1) they often, and in a variety of circumstances, provide the only practical means by which one having a claim against another can economically afford, finance, and obtain the services of a competent lawyer to prosecute his claim, and (2) a successful prosecution of the claim produces a *res* out of which the fee can be paid.[48] Although a lawyer generally should decline to accept employment on a contingent fee basis by one who is able to pay a reasonable fixed fee, it is not necessarily improper for a lawyer, where justified by the particular circumstances of a case, to enter into a contingent fee contract in a civil case with any client who, after being fully informed of all relevant factors, desires that arrangement. Because of the human relationships involved and the unique character of the proceedings, contingent fee arrangements in domestic relation cases are rarely justified. In administrative agency proceedings contingent fee contracts should be governed by the same consideration as in other civil cases. Public policy properly condemns contingent fee arrangements in criminal cases, largely on the ground that legal services in criminal cases do not produce a *res* with which to pay the fee.

EC 2-21.   A lawyer should not accept compensation or any thing of value incident to his employment or services from one other than his client without the knowledge and consent of his client after full disclosure.[49]

EC 2-22.   Without the consent of his client, a lawyer should not associate in a particular matter another lawyer outside his

---

[47] *See* ABA CANON 13; *see also* MACKINNON, CONTINGENT FEES FOR LEGAL SERVICES (1964) (A report of the American Bar Foundation).

"A contract for a reasonable contingent fee where sanctioned by law is permitted by *Canon 13*, but the client must remain responsible to the lawyer for expenses advanced by the latter. 'There is to be no barter of the privilege of prosecuting a cause for gain in exchange for the promise of the attorney to prosecute at his own expense.' (Cardozo, C. J. in Matter of Gilman, 251 N.Y. 265, 270-271.)" *ABA Opinion* 246 (1942).

[48] *See* Comment, *Providing Legal Services for the Middle Class in Civil Matters: The Problem, the Duty and a Solution*, 26 U. PITT. L. REV. 811, 829 (1965).

[49] *See* ABA CANON 38.

"Of course, as . . . [Informal Opinion 679] points out, there must be full disclosure of the arrangement [that an entity other than the client pays the attorney's fee] by the attorney to the client. . . ." *ABA Opinion* 320 (1968).

firm. A fee may properly be divided between lawyers[50] properly associated if the division is in proportion to the services performed and the responsibility assumed by each lawyer[51] and if the total fee is reasonable.

EC 2-23. A lawyer should be zealous in his efforts to avoid controversies over fees with clients[52] and should attempt to resolve amicably any differences on the subject.[53] He should not sue a client for a fee unless necessary to prevent fraud or gross imposition by the client.[54]

Financial Ability to Employ Counsel: Persons Unable to Pay Reasonable Fees

EC 2-24. A layman whose financial ability is not sufficient to permit payment of any fee cannot obtain legal services, other than in cases where a contingent fee is appropriate, unless the services are provided for him. Even a person of moderate means may be unable to pay a reasonable fee which is large because of

---

[50] "Only lawyers may share in . . . a division of fees, but . . . it is not necessary that both lawyers be admitted to practice in the same state, so long as the division was based on the division of services or responsibility." *ABA Opinion* 316 (1967).

[51] *See* ABA CANON 34.

"We adhere to our previous rulings that where a lawyer merely brings about the employment of another lawyer *but renders no service and assumes no responsibility in the matter*, a division of the latter's fee is improper. *(Opinions 18 and 153.)*

"It is assumed that the bar, generally, understands what acts or conduct of a lawyer may constitute 'services' to a client within the intendment of *Canon 12*. Such acts or conduct invariably, if not always, involve 'responsibility' on the part of the lawyer, whether the word 'responsibility' be construed to denote the possible resultant legal or moral liability on the part of the lawyer to the client or to others, or the onus of deciding what should or should not be done in behalf of the client. The word 'services' in *Canon 12* must be construed in this broad sense and may apply to the selection and retainer of associate counsel as well as to other acts or conduct in the client's behalf." *ABA Opinion* 204 (1940).

[52] *See* ABA CANON 14.

[53] *Cf. ABA Opinion* 320 (1968).

[54] *See* ABA CANON 14.

"Ours is a learned profession, not a mere money-getting trade. . . . Suits to collect fees should be avoided. Only where the circumstances imperatively require, should resort be had to a suit to compel payment. And where a lawyer does resort to a suit to enforce payment of fees which involves a disclosure, he should carefully avoid any disclosure not clearly necessary to obtaining or defending his rights." *ABA Opinion* 250 (1943).

But cf. ABA Opinion 320 (1968).

the complexity, novelty, or difficulty of the problem or similar factors.[55]

EC 2-25. Historically, the need for legal services of those unable to pay reasonable fees has been met in part by lawyers who donated their services or accepted court appointments on behalf of such individuals. The basic responsibility for providing legal services for those unable to pay ultimately rests upon the individual lawyer, and personal involvement in the problems of the disadvantaged can be one of the most rewarding experiences in the life of a lawyer. Every lawyer, regardless of professional prominence or professional workload, should find time to participate in serving the disadvantaged. The rendition of free legal services to those unable to pay reasonable fees continues to be an obligation of each lawyer, but the efforts of individual lawyers are often not enough to meet the need.[56] Thus it has been necessary for the profession to institute additional programs to provide

---

[55] "As a society increases in size, sophistication and technology, the body of laws which is required to control that society also increases in size, scope and complexity. With this growth, the law directly affects more and more facets of individual behavior, creating an expanding need for legal services on the part of the individual members of the society. . . . As legal guidance in social and commercial behavior increasingly becomes necessary, there will come a concurrent demand from the layman that such guidance be made available to him. This demand will not come from those who are able to employ the best of legal talent, nor from those who can obtain legal assistance at little or no cost. It will come from the large 'forgotten middle income class,' who can neither afford to pay proportionately large fees nor qualify for ultra-low-cost services. The legal profession must recognize this inevitable demand and consider methods whereby it can be satisfied. If the profession fails to provide such methods, the laity will." Comment, *Providing Legal Services for the Middle Class in Civil Matters: The Problem, the Duty and a Solution,* 26 U. PITT. L. REV. 811, 811-12 (1965).

"The issue is not whether we shall do something or do nothing. The demand for ordinary everyday legal justice is so great and the moral nature of the demand is so strong that the issue has become whether we devise, maintain, and support suitable agencies able to satisfy the demand or, by our own default, force the government to take over the job, supplant us, and ultimately dominate us." Smith, *Legal Service Offices for Persons of Moderate Means,* 1949 WIS. L. REV. 416, 418 (1949).

[56] "Lawyers have peculiar responsibilities for the just administration of the law, and these responsibilities include providing advice and representation for needy persons. To a degree not always appreciated by the public at large, the bar has performed these obligations with zeal and devotion. The Committee is persuaded, however, that a system of justice that attempts, in mid-twentieth century America, to meet the needs of the financially incapacitated accused through primary or exclusive reliance on the uncompensated services of counsel will prove unsuccessful and inadequate. . . . A system of adequate representation, therefore, should be structured and financed in a manner reflecting its public importance. . . . We believe that fees for private appointed counsel should be set by the court within maximum limits established by the statute." REPORT OF THE ATT'Y GEN'S COMM. ON POVERTY AND THE ADMINISTRATION OF CRIMINAL JUSTICE 41-43 (1963).

legal services.[57] Accordingly, legal aid offices,[58] lawyer referral services,[59] and other related programs have been developed, and others will be developed, by the profession.[60] Every lawyer should support all proper efforts to meet this need for legal services.[61]

Acceptance and Retention of Employment

EC 2-26.   A lawyer is under no obligation to act as adviser or advocate for every person who may wish to become his client; but in furtherance of the objective of the bar to make legal services fully available, a lawyer should not lightly decline proffered employment. The fulfillment of this objective requires

---

[57] "At present this representation [of those unable to pay usual fees] is being supplied in some measure through the spontaneous generosity of individual lawyers, through legal aid societies, and—increasingly—through the organized efforts of the Bar. If those who stand in need of this service know of its availability and their need is in fact adequately met, the precise mechanism by which this service is provided becomes of secondary importance. It is of great importance, however, that both the impulse to render this service, and the plan for making that impulse effective, should arise within the legal profession itself." *Professional Responsibility: Report of the Joint Conference,* 44 A.B.A.J. 1159, 1216 (1958).

[58] "Free legal clinics carried on by the organized bar are not ethically objectionable. On the contrary, they serve a very worthwhile purpose and should be encouraged." *ABA Opinion* 191 (1939).

[59] "We are of the opinion that the [lawyer referral] plan here presented does not fall within the inhibition of the Canon. No solicitation for a particular lawyer is involved. The dominant purpose of the plan is to provide as an obligation of the profession competent legal services to persons in low-income groups at fees within their ability to pay. The plan is to be supervised and directed by the local Bar Association. There is to be no advertisement of the names of the lawyers constituting the panel. The general method and purpose of the plan only is to be advertised. Persons seeking the legal services will be directed to members of the panel by the Bar Association. Aside from the filing of the panel with the Bar Association, there is to be no advertisement of the names of the lawyers constituting the panel. If these limitations are observed, we think there is no solicitation of business by or for particular lawyers and no violation of the inhibition of *Canon 27.*" *ABA Opinion* 205 (1940).

[60] "Whereas the American Bar Association believes that it is a fundamental duty of the bar to see to it that all persons requiring legal advice be able to attain it, irrespective of their economic status. . . .

"Resolved, that the Association approves and sponsors the setting up by state and local bar associations of lawyer referral plans and low-cost legal service methods for the purpose of dealing with cases of persons who might not otherwise have the benefit of legal advice. . . ." *Proceedings of the House of Delegates of the American Bar Association,* Oct. 30, 1946, 71 A.B.A. REP. 103, 109-10 (1946).

[61] "The defense of indigent citizens, without compensation, is carried on throughout the country by lawyers representing legal aid societies, not only with the approval, but with the commendation of those acquainted with the work. Not infrequently services are rendered out of sympathy or for other philanthropic reasons, by individual lawyers who do not represent legal aid societies. There is nothing whatever in the Canons to prevent a lawyer from performing such an act, nor should there be." *ABA Opinion* 148 (1935).

acceptance by a lawyer of his share of tendered employment which may be unattractive both to him and the bar generally.[62]

EC 2-27. History is replete with instances of distinguished and sacrificial services by lawyers who have represented unpopular clients and causes. Regardless of his personal feelings, a lawyer should not decline representation because a client or a cause is unpopular or community reaction is adverse.[63]

EC 2-28. The personal preference of a lawyer to avoid adversary alignment against judges, other lawyers,[64] public officials, or influential members of the community does not justify his rejection of tendered employment.

EC 2-29. When a lawyer is appointed by a court or requested by a bar association to undertake representation of a person unable to obtain counsel, whether for financial or other reasons, he should not seek to be excused from undertaking the representation except for compelling reasons.[65] Compelling reasons do not include such factors as the repugnance of the subject matter of

---

[62] *But cf.* ABA CANON 31.

[63] "One of the highest services the lawyer can render to society is to appear in court on behalf of clients whose causes are in disfavor with the general public." *Professional Responsibility: Report of the Joint Conference,* 44 A.B.A.J. 1159, 1216 (1958).

One author proposes the following proposition to be included in "A Proper Oath for Advocates": "I recognize that it is sometimes difficult for clients with unpopular causes to obtain proper legal representation. I will do all that I can to assure that the client with the unpopular cause is properly represented, and that the lawyer representing such a client receives credit from and support of the bar for handling such a matter." Thode, *The Ethical Standard for the Advocate,* 39 TEXAS L. REV. 575, 592 (1961).

"§ 6068. . . . It is the duty of an attorney:

. . . .

"(h) Never to reject, for any consideration personal to himself, the cause of the defenseless or the oppressed." CAL. BUSINESS AND PROFESSIONS CODE § 6068 (West 1962). Virtually the same language is found in the Oregon statutes at ORE. REV. STATS. Ch. 9 § 9.460(8).

See Rostow, *The Lawyer and His Client,* 48 A.B.A.J. 25 and 146 (1962).

[64] *See* ABA CANONS 7 and 29.

"We are of the opinion that it is not professionally improper for a lawyer to accept employment to compel another lawyer to honor the just claim of a layman. On the contrary, it is highly proper that he do so. Unfortunately, there appears to be a widespread feeling among laymen that it is difficult, if not impossible, to obtain justice when they have claims against members of the Bar because other lawyers will not accept employment to proceed against them. The honor of the profession, whose members proudly style themselves officers of the court, must surely be sullied if its members bind themselves by custom to refrain from enforcing just claims of laymen against lawyers." *ABA Opinion* 144 (1935).

[65] ABA CANON 4 uses a slightly different test, saying, "A lawyer assigned as counsel for an indigent prisoner ought not to ask to be excused for any trivial reason. . . ."

the proceeding, the identity[66] or position of a person involved in the case, the belief of the lawyer that the defendant in a criminal proceeding is guilty,[67] or the belief of the lawyer regarding the merits of the civil case.[68]

EC 2-30.   Employment should not be accepted by a lawyer when he is unable to render competent service[69] or when he knows or it is obvious that the person seeking to employ him desires to institute or maintain an action merely for the purpose of harassing or maliciously injuring another.[70] Likewise, a lawyer should decline employment if the intensity of his personal feeling, as distinguished from a community attitude, may impair his effective representation of a prospective client. If a lawyer knows a client has previously obtained counsel, he should not accept employment in the matter unless the other counsel approves[71] or withdraws, or the client terminates the prior employment.[72]

EC 2-31.   Full availability of legal counsel requires both that persons be able to obtain counsel and that lawyers who undertake representation complete the work involved. Trial counsel for a convicted defendant should continue to represent his client by advising whether to take an appeal and, if the appeal is prosecuted, by representing him through the appeal unless new counsel is substituted or withdrawal is permitted by the appropriate court.

EC 2-32.   A decision by a lawyer to withdraw should be made only on the basis of compelling circumstances,[73] and in a matter

---

[66] *Cf.* ABA CANON 7.

[67] *See* ABA CANON 5.

[68] Dr. Johnson's reply to Boswell upon being asked what he thought of "supporting a cause which you know to be bad" was: "Sir, you do not know it to be good or bad till the Judge determines it. I have said that you are to state facts fairly; so that your thinking, or what you call knowing, a cause to be bad, must be from reasoning, must be from supposing your arguments to be weak and inconclusive. But, Sir, that is not enough. An argument which does not convince yourself, may convince the Judge to whom you urge it; and if it does convince him, why, then, Sir, you are wrong, and he is right." 2 BOSWELL, THE LIFE OF JOHNSON 47-48 (Hill ed. 1887).

[69] "The lawyer deciding whether to undertake a case must be able to judge objectively whether he is capable of handling it and whether he can assume its burdens without prejudice to previous commitments. . . ." *Professional Responsibility: Report of the Joint Conference,* 44 A.B.A.J. 1158, 1218 (1958).

[70] "The lawyer must decline to conduct a civil cause or to make a defense when convinced that it is intended merely to harass or to injure the opposite party or to work oppression or wrong." ABA CANON 30.

[71] *See* ABA CANON 7.

[72] *Id.*

"From the facts stated we assume that the client has discharged the first attorney and given notice of the discharge. Such being the case, the second attorney may properly accept employment. *Canon 7; Opinions 10, 130, 149." ABA Opinion* 209 (1941).

[73] *See* ABA CANON 44.

pending before a tribunal he must comply with the rules of the tribunal regarding withdrawal. A lawyer should not withdraw without considering carefully and endeavoring to minimize the possible adverse effect on the rights of his client and the possibility of prejudice to his client[74] as a result of his withdrawal. Even when he justifiably withdraws, a lawyer should protect the welfare of his client by giving due notice of his withdrawal,[75] suggesting employment of other counsel, delivering to the client all papers and property to which the client is entitled, cooperating with counsel subsequently employed, and otherwise endeavoring to minimize the possibility of harm. Further, he should refund to the client any compensation not earned during the employment.[76]

[C5]

Disciplinary Rules

DR 2-101. [C6] Publicity in General.[77]

(A) A lawyer shall not prepare, cause to be prepared, use, or participate in the use of, any form of public communication that contains professionally self-laudatory statements calculated to attract lay clients; as used herein, "public communication" includes, but is not limited to, communication by means of television, radio, motion picture, newspaper, magazine, or book.

(B) A lawyer shall not publicize himself, his partner, or associate as a lawyer through newspaper or magazine advertisements, radio or television announcements, display advertisements in city or telephone directories, or other means of commercial publicity,[78] nor shall he authorize or permit others to do so in his behalf[79] except as permitted under DR 2-103. This does not

---

"I will carefully consider, before taking a case, whether it appears that I can fully represent the client within the framework of law. If the decision is in the affirmative, then it will take extreme circumstances to cause me to decide later that I cannot so represent him." Thode, *The Ethical Standard for the Advocate*, 39 TEXAS L. REV. 575, 592 (1961) (from "A Proper Oath for Advocates").

[74] *ABA Opinion* 314 (1965) held that a lawyer should not disassociate himself from a cause when "it is obvious that the very act of disassociation would have the effect of violating *Canon 37.*"

[75] ABA CANON 44 enumerates instances in which ". . . the lawyer may be warranted in withdrawing on due notice to the client, allowing him time to employ another lawyer."

[76] *See* ABA CANON 44.

[77] *Cf.* ABA CANON 27; *see generally ABA Opinion* 293 (1957).

[78] *Cf.* ABA Opinions 133 (1935), 116 (1934), 107 (1934), 73 (1932), 59 (1931), and 43 (1931).

[79] "There can be no justification for the participation and acquiescence by an attorney in the development and publication of an article which, on its face, plainly amounts to a self-interest and unethical presentation of his

prohibit limited and dignified identification of a lawyer as a lawyer as well as by name:[80]

(1) In political advertisements when his professional status is germane to the political campaign or to a political issue.

(2) In public notices when the name and profession of a lawyer are required or authorized by law or are reasonably pertinent for a purpose other than the attraction of potential clients.[81]

(3) In routine reports and announcements of a bona fide business, civic, professional, or political organization in which he serves as a director or officer.

(4) In and on legal documents prepared by him.

(5) In and on legal textbooks, treatises, and other legal publications, and in dignified advertisements thereof.

(C) A lawyer shall not compensate or give any thing of value to representatives of the press, radio, television, or other communication medium in anticipation of or return for professional publicity in a news item.[82]

DR 2-102. Professional Notices, Letterheads, Offices, and Law Lists.

(A) A lawyer or law firm shall not use professional cards, professional announcement cards, office signs, letterheads, tele-

---

achievements and capabilities." Matter of Connelly, 18 App. Div. 2d 466, 478, 240 N.Y.S.2d 126, 138 (1963).

"An announcement of the fact that the lawyer had resigned and the name of the person to succeed him, or take over his work, would not be objectionable, either as an official communication to those employed by or connected with the administrative agency or instrumentality [that had employed him], or as a news release.

"But to include therein a statement of the lawyer's experience in and acquaintance with the various departments and agencies of the government, and a laudation of his legal ability, either generally or in a special branch of the law, is not only bad taste but ethically improper.

"It can have but one primary purpose or object: to aid the lawyer in securing professional employment in private practice by advertising his professional experience, attainments and ability." *ABA Opinion* 184 (1938).

Cf. *ABA Opinions* 285 (1951) and 140 (1935).

[80] "The question is always . . . whether under the circumstance the furtherance of the professional employment of the lawyer is the primary purpose of the advertisement, or is merely a necessary incident of a proper and legitimate objective of the client which does not have the effect of unduly advertising him." *ABA Opinion* 290 (1956).

See *ABA Opinion* 285 (1951).

[81] See *ABA Opinions* 299 (1961), 290 (1956), 158 (1936), and 100 (1933); cf. *ABA Opinion* 80 (1932).

[82] "Rule 2.

. . . .

"[A] member of the State Bar shall not solicit professional employment by. . . .

" (4) The making of gifts to representatives of the press, radio, television or any medium of communication in anticipation of or in return for publicity." CAL. BUSINESS AND PROFESSIONS CODE § 6076 (West 1962).

phone directory listings, law lists, legal directory listings, or similar professional notices or devices,[83] except that the following may be used if they are in dignified form:

(1) A professional card of a lawyer identifying him by name and as a lawyer, and giving his addresses, telephone numbers, the name of his law firm, and any information permitted under DR 2-105. A professional card of a law firm may also give the names of members and associates. Such cards may be used for identification[84] but may not be published in periodicals, magazines, newspapers,[85] or other media.[86]

(2) A brief professional announcement card stating new or changed associations or addresses, change of firm name, or similar matters pertaining to the professional office of a lawyer or law firm, which may be mailed to lawyers, clients, former clients, personal friends, and relatives.[87] It shall not state biographical data except to the extent reasonably necessary to identify the lawyer or to explain the change in his association, but it may state the immediate past position of the lawyer.[88] It may give the names and dates of predecessor firms in a continuing line of succession. It shall not state the nature of the practice except as permitted under DR 2-105.[89]

(3) A sign on or near the door of the office and in the building directory identifying the law office. The sign shall not state the nature of the practice, except as permitted under DR 2-105.

(4) A letterhead of a lawyer identifying him by name and as a lawyer, and giving his addresses, telephone numbers, the name of his law firm, associates and any information permitted under DR 2-105. A letterhead of a law firm may also give the names of members and associates,[90] and names and dates relating to deceased

---

[83] *Cf. ABA Opinions* 233 (1941) and 114 (1934).

[84] *See ABA Opinion* 175 (1938).

[85] *See ABA Opinions* 260 (1944) and 182 (1938).

[86] *But cf. ABA Opinions* 276 (1947) and 256 (1943).

[87] *See ABA Opinion* 301 (1961).

[88] "[I]t has become commonplace for many lawyers to participate in government service; to deny them the right, upon their return to private practice, to refer to their prior employment in a brief and dignified manner, would place an undue limitation upon a large element of our profession. It is entirely proper for a member of the profession to explain his absence from private practice, where such is the primary purpose of the announcement, by a brief and dignified reference to the prior employment.

". . . [A]ny such announcement should be limited to the immediate past connection of the lawyer with the government, made upon his leaving that position to enter private practice." *ABA Opinion* 301 (1961).

[89] *See ABA Opinion* 251 (1943).

[90] "Those lawyers who are working for an individual lawyer or a law firm may be designated on the letterhead and in other appropriate places as 'associates'." *ABA Opinion* 310 (1963).

and retired members.[91] A lawyer may be designated "Of Counsel" on a letterhead if he has a continuing relationship with a lawyer or law firm, other than as a partner or associate. A lawyer or law firm may be designated as "General Counsel" or by similar professional reference on stationery of a client if he or the firm devotes a substantial amount of professional time in the representation of that client.[92] The letterhead of a law firm may give the names and dates of predecessor firms in a continuing line of succession.

(5) A listing of the office of a lawyer or law firm in the alphabetical and classified sections of the telephone directory or directories for the geographical area or areas in which the lawyer resides or maintains offices or in which a significant part of his clientele resides[93] and in the city directory of the city in which his or the firm's office is located;[94] but the listing may give only the name of the lawyer or law firm, the fact he is a lawyer, addresses, and telephone numbers.[95] The listing shall not be in distinctive form[96] or type.[97] A law firm may have a listing in the firm name separate from that of its members and associates.[98] The listing in the classified section shall not be under a heading or classification other than "Attorneys" or "Lawyers,"[99] except that additional headings or classifications descriptive of the types of practice referred to in DR 2-105 are permitted.[100]

(6) A listing in a reputable law list[101] or legal directory giving brief biographical and other informative data. A law list or directory is not reputable if its management or contents are likely to

---

[91] See ABA CANON 33.

[92] But see ABA Opinion 285 (1951).

[93] See ABA Opinion 295 (1959).

[94] But see ABA Opinion 313 (1964) which says the Committee "approves a listing in the classified section of the city directory for lawyers only when the listing includes all lawyers residing in the community and when no charge is made therefor."

[95] "The listing should consist only of the lawyer's name, address and telephone number." ABA Opinion 313 (1964).

[96] "[A]dding to the regular classified listing a 'second line' in which a lawyer claims that he is engaged in a 'specialty' is an undue attempt to make his name distinctive." ABA Opinion 284 (1951).

[97] "[Opinion 284] held that a lawyer could not with propriety have his name listed in distinctive type in a telephone directory or city directory. We affirm that opinion." ABA Opinion 313 (1964).

See ABA Opinions 123 (1934) and 53 (1931).

[98] "[I]f a lawyer is a member of a law firm, both the firm, and the individual lawyer may be listed separately." ABA Opinion 313 (1964).

[99] See ABA Opinion 284 (1951).

[100] See Silverman v. State Bar of Texas, 405 F.2d 410, (5th Cir. 1968); but see ABA Opinion 286 (1952).

[101] Cf. ABA CANON 43.

be misleading or injurious to the public or to the profession.[102]
A law list is conclusively established to be reputable if it is certified by the American Bar Association as being in compliance with
its rules and standards. The published data may include only the
following: name, including name of law firm and names of professional associates; addresses[103] and telephone numbers; one or
more fields of law in which the lawyer or law firm concentrates;[104]
a statement that practice is limited to one or more fields of law;
a statement that the lawyer or law firm specializes in a particular
field of law or law practice but only if authorized under DR 2-105
(A) (4);[105] date and place of birth; date and place of admission to
the bar of state and federal courts; schools attended, with dates of
graduation, degrees, and other scholastic distinctions; public or
quasi-public offices; military service; posts of honor; legal authorships; legal teaching positions; memberships, offices, committee assignments, and section memberships in bar associations;
memberships and offices in legal fraternities and legal societies;
technical and professional licenses; memberships in scientific,
technical and professional associations and societies; foreign
language ability; names and addresses of references,[106] and, with
their consent, names of clients regularly represented.[107]

---

[102] *Cf. ABA Opinion* 255 (1943).

[103] "We are asked to define the word 'addresses' appearing in the second
paragraph of Canon 27. . . .
  "It is our opinion that an address (other than a cable address) within
the intendment of the canon is that of the lawyer's office or of his residence.
Neither address should be misleading. If, for example, an office address is
given, it must be that of a bona fide office. The residence address, if given,
should be identified as such if the city or other place of residence is not the
same as that in which the law office is located." *ABA Opinion* 249 (1942).

[104] "[T]oday in various parts of the country Committees on Professional
Ethics of local and state bar associations are authorizing lawyers to describe
themselves in announcements to the Bar and in notices in legal periodicals
and approved law lists as specialists in a great variety of things. Thus in
the approved law lists or professional announcements there appear, in
connection with the names of individual practitioners or firms, such designations as 'International Law, Public and Private'; 'Trial Preparation in
Personal Injury and Negligence Actions'; 'Philippine War Damage Claims';
'Anti-Trust'; 'Domestic Relations'; 'Tax Law'; 'Negligence Law'. It would
seem that the ABA has given at least its tacit approval to this sort of announcement.
  "It is important that this sort of description is not, in New York at least,
permitted on letterheads or shingles or elsewhere in communications to
laymen. This is subject to the single exception that such announcement to
laymen is permitted in the four traditional specialties, Admiralty, Patent,
Copyright and Trade-mark." *Report of the Special Committee on Specialization and Specialized Legal Education,* 79 A.B.A. REP. 582, 586 (1954).

[105] This provision is included to conform to action taken by the ABA
House of Delegates at the Mid-Winter Meeting, January, 1969.

[106] *See* ABA CANON 43 and *ABA Opinion* 119 (1934); *but see ABA
Opinion* 236 (1941).

[107] *See* ABA CANON 27.

(B) A lawyer in private practice shall not practice under a trade name, a name that is misleading as to the identity of the lawyer or lawyers practicing under such name, or a firm name containing names other than those of one or more of the lawyers in the firm, except that the name of a professional corporation or professional association may contain "P.C." or "P.A." or similar symbols indicating the nature of the organization, and if otherwise lawful a firm may use as, or continue to include in, its name the name or names of one or more deceased or retired members of the firm or of a predecessor firm in a continuing line of succession.[108] A lawyer who assumes a judicial, legislative, or public executive or administrative post or office shall not permit his name to remain in the name of a law firm or to be used in professional notices of the firm during any significant period in which he is not actively and regularly practicing law as a member of the firm,[109] and during such period other members of the firm shall not use his name in the firm name or in professional notices of the firm.[110]

(C) A lawyer shall not hold himself out as having a partnership with one or more other lawyers unless they are in fact partners.[111]

(D) A partnership shall not be formed or continued between or among lawyers licensed in different jurisdictions unless all enumerations of the members and associates of the firm on its letterhead and in other permissible listings make clear the jurisdictional limitations on those members and associates of the firm not licensed to practice in all listed jurisdictions;[112] however, the same firm name may be used in each jurisdiction.

---

[108] See ABA CANON 33; cf. ABA Opinions 318 (1967), 267 (1945), 219 (1941), 208 (1940), 192 (1939), 97 (1933), and 6 (1925).

[109] ABA Opinion 318 (1967) held, "anything to the contrary in Formal Opinion 315 or in the other opinions cited notwithstanding" that: "Where a partner whose name appears in the name of a law firm is elected or appointed to high local, state or federal office, which office he intends to occupy only temporarily, at the end of which time he intends to return to his position with the firm, and provided that he is not precluded by holding such office from engaging in the practice of law and does not in fact sever his relationship with the firm but only takes a leave of absence, and provided that there is no local law, statute or custom to the contrary, his name may be retained in the firm name during his term or terms of office, but only if proper precautions are taken not to mislead the public as to his degree of participation in the firm's affairs."

Cf. ABA Opinion 143 (1935), New York County Opinion 67, and New York City Opinions 36 and 798; but cf. ABA Opinion 192 (1939) and Michigan Opinion 164.

[110] Cf. ABA CANON 33.

[111] See ABA Opinion 277 (1948); cf. ABA CANON 33 and ABA Opinions 318 (1967), 126 (1935), 115 (1934), and 106 (1934).

[112] See ABA Opinions 318 (1967) and 316 (1967); cf. ABA CANON 33.

(E) A lawyer who is engaged both in the practice of law and another profession or business shall not so indicate on his letterhead, office sign, or professional card, nor shall he identify himself as a lawyer in any publication in connection with his other profession or business.

(F) Nothing contained herein shall prohibit a lawyer from using or permitting the use of, in connection with his name, an earned degree or title derived therefrom indicating his training in the law.

DR 2-103. Recommendation of Professional Employment.[113]

(A)   A lawyer shall not recommend employment, as a private practitioner,[114] of himself, his partner, or associate to a non-lawyer who has not sought his advice regarding employment of a lawyer.[115]

[C7] (B) Except as permitted under DR 2-103(C), a lawyer shall not compensate or give anything of value to a person or organization to recommend or secure his employment[116] by a client, or as a reward for having made a recommendation resulting in his employment[117] by a client.

[C7] (C) A lawyer shall not request a person or organization to recommend employment, as a private practitioner, of himself, his partner, or associate,[118] except that he may request referrals from a lawyer referral service operated, sponsored, or approved by a bar association representative of the general bar of the geographical area in which the association exists and may pay its fees incident thereto.[119]

---

[113] *Cf.* ABA Canons 27 and 28.

[114] "We think it clear that a lawyer's seeking employment in an ordinary law office, or appointment to a civil service position, is not prohibited by . . . [Canon 27]." *ABA Opinion* 197 (1939).

[115] "[A] lawyer may not seek from persons not his clients the opportunity to perform . . . a [legal] check-up." *ABA Opinion* 307 (1962).

[116] *Cf. ABA Opinion* 78 (1932).

[117] " 'No financial connection of any kind between the Brotherhood and any lawyer is permissible. No lawyer can properly pay any amount whatsoever to the Brotherhood or any of its departments, officers or members as compensation, reimbursement of expenses or gratuity in connection with the procurement of a case.' " In re Brotherhood of R.R. Trainmen, 13 Ill. 2d 391, 398, 150 N.E.2d 163, 167 (1958), *quoted in* In re Ratner, 194 Kan. 362, 372, 399 P.2d 865, 873 (1965).

See ABA Opinion 147 (1935).

[118] "This Court has condemned the practice of ambulance chasing through the media of runners and touters. In similar fashion we have with equal emphasis condemned the practice of direct solicitation by a lawyer. We have classified both offenses as serious breaches of the Canons of Ethics demanding severe treatment of the offending lawyer." State v. Dawson, 111 So. 2d 427, 431 (Fla. 1959).

[119] "Registrants [of a lawyer referral plan] may be required to contribute to the expense of operating it by a reasonable registration charge or by a reasonable percentage of fees collected by them." *ABA Opinion* 291 (1956).

Cf. ABA Opinion 227 (1941).

[C7] (D) A lawyer shall not knowingly assist a person or organization that recommends, furnishes, or pays for legal services to promote the use of his services or those of his partners or associates. However, he may cooperate in a dignified manner with the legal service activities of any of the following, provided that his independent professional judgment is exercised in behalf of his client without interference or control by any organization or other person:

(1) A legal aid office or public defender office:

(a) Operated or sponsored by a duly accredited law school.

(b) Operated or sponsored by a bona fide non-profit community organization.

(c) Operated or sponsored by a governmental agency.

(d) Operated, sponsored, or approved by a bar association representative of the general bar of the geographical area in which the association exists.[120]

(2) A military legal assistance office.

(3) A lawyer referral service operated, sponsored, or approved by a bar association representative of the general bar of the geographical area in which the association exists.[121]

(4) A bar association representative of the general bar of the geographical area in which the association exists.[122]

[C8] (5) Any other non-profit organization that recommends, furnishes, or pays for legal services to its members or beneficiaries, but only in those instances and to the extent that controlling constitutional interpretation at the time of the rendition of the services requires the allowance of such legal service activities,[123] and only if the following conditions, unless prohibited by such interpretation, are met:

(a) The primary purposes of such organization do not include the rendition of legal services.

(b) The recommending, furnishing, or paying for legal services to its members is incidental and reasonably related to the primary purposes of such organization.

---

[120] Cf. ABA Opinion 148 (1935).

[121] Cf. ABA Opinion 227 (1941).

[122] "If a bar association has embarked on a program of institutional advertising for an annual legal check-up and provides brochures and reprints, it is not improper to have these available in the lawyer's office for persons to read and take." ABA Opinion 307 (1962).

Cf. ABA Opinion 121 (1934).

[123] United Mine Workers v. Ill. State Bar Ass'n., 389 U.S. 217, 19 L. Ed. 2d 426, 88 S. Ct. 353 (1967); Brotherhood of R.R. Trainmen v. Virginia, 371 U.S. 1, 12 L. Ed. 2d 89, 84 S. Ct. 1113 (1964); NAACP v. Button, 371 U.S. 415, 9 L. Ed. 2d 405, 83 S. Ct. 328 (1963).

(c) Such organization does not derive a financial benefit from the rendition of legal services by the lawyer.

(d) The member or beneficiary for whom the legal services are rendered, and not such organization, is recognized as the client of the lawyer in that matter.

(E) A lawyer shall not accept employment when he knows or it is obvious that the person who seeks his services does so as a result of conduct prohibited under this Disciplinary Rule.

DR 2-104. Suggestion of Need of Legal Services.[124]

[C9] (A) A lawyer who has given unsolicited advice to a layman that he should obtain counsel or take legal action shall not accept employment resulting from that advice,[125] except that:

(1) A lawyer may accept employment by a close friend, relative, former client (if the advice is germane to the former employment), or one whom the lawyer reasonably believes to be a client.[126]

(2) A lawyer may accept employment that results from his participation in activities designed to educate laymen to recognize legal problems, to make intelligent selection of counsel, or to utilize available legal services if such activities are conducted or sponsored by any of the offices or organizations enumerated in DR 2-103(D)(1) through (5), to the extent and under the conditions prescribed therein.

(3) A lawyer who is furnished or paid by any of the offices or organizations enumerated in DR 2-103(D)(1), (2), or (5) may represent a member or beneficiary thereof, to the extent and under the conditions prescribed therein.

---

[124] ABA CANON 28.

[125] Cf. *ABA Opinions* 229 (1941) and 173 (1937).

[126] "It certainly is not improper for a lawyer to advise his regular clients of new statutes, court decisions, and administrative rulings, which may affect the client's interests, provided the communication is strictly limited to such information. . . .

"When such communications go to concerns or individuals other than regular clients of the lawyer, they are thinly disguised advertisements for professional employment, and are obviously improper." *ABA Opinion* 213 (1941).

"It is our opinion that where the lawyer has no reason to believe that he has been supplanted by another lawyer, it is not only his right, but it might even be his duty to advise his client of any change of fact or law which might defeat the client's testamentary purpose as expressed in the will.

"Periodic notices might be sent to the client for whom a lawyer has drawn a will, suggesting that it might be wise for the client to reexamine his will to determine whether or not there has been any change in his situation requiring a modification of his will." *ABA Opinion* 210 (1941).

Cf. ABA CANON 28.

(4) Without affecting his right to accept employment, a lawyer may speak publicly or write for publication on legal topics[127] so long as he does not emphasize his own professional experience or reputation and does not undertake to give individual advice.

(5) If success in asserting rights or defenses of his client in litigation in the nature of a class action is dependent upon the joinder of others, a lawyer may accept, but shall not seek, employment from those contacted for the purpose of obtaining their joinder.[128]

DR 2-105. Limitation of Practice.[129]

(A) A lawyer shall not hold himself out publicly as a specialist[130] or as limiting his practice,[131] except as permitted under DR 2-102(A)(6) or as follows:

(1) A lawyer admitted to practice before the United States Patent Office may use the designation "Patents," "Patent Attorney," or "Patent Lawyer," or any combination of those terms, on his letterhead and office sign. A lawyer engaged in the trademark practice may use the designation "Trademarks," "Trademark Attorney," or "Trademark Lawyer," or any combination of those terms, on his letterhead and office sign, and a lawyer engaged in the admiralty practice may use the designation "Admiralty," "Proctor in Admiralty," or "Admiralty Lawyer," or any combination of those terms, on his letterhead and office sign.[132]

(2) A lawyer may permit his name to be listed in lawyer referral service offices according to the fields of law in which he will accept referrals.

(3) A lawyer available to act as a consultant to or as an associate of other lawyers in a particular branch of law or legal service may distribute to other lawyers and publish in legal journals a dignified announcement of such availability,[133] but the announcement shall not contain a representation of special competence or experience.[134] The announcement shall not be distributed to lawyers more frequently than once in a calendar year, but it may be published periodically in legal journals.

(4) A lawyer who is certified as a specialist in a particular field of law or law practice by the authority having jurisdiction under state law over the subject of specialization by lawyers may

---

127 Cf. ABA Opinion 168 (1937).
128 But cf. ABA Opinion 111 (1934).
129 See ABA CANON 45; cf. ABA CANONS 27, 43, and 46.
130 Cf. ABA Opinions 228 (1941) and 194 (1939).
131 See ABA Opinions 251 (1943) and 175 (1938).
132 See ABA CANON 27; cf. ABA Opinion 286 (1952).
133 Cf. ABA Opinion 194 (1939).
134 See ABA CANON 46.

hold himself out as such specialist but only in accordance with the rules prescribed by that authority.[135]

DR 2-106.   Fees for Legal Services.[136]

(A)   A lawyer shall not enter into an agreement for, charge, or collect an illegal or clearly excessive fee.[137]

(B) A fee is clearly excessive when, after a review of the facts, a lawyer of ordinary prudence would be left with a definite and firm conviction that the fee is in excess of a reasonable fee. Factors to be considered as guides in determining the reasonableness of a fee include the following:

(1) The time and labor required, the novelty and difficulty of the questions involved, and the skill requisite to perform the legal service properly.

(2) The likelihood, if apparent to the client, that the acceptance of the particular employment will preclude other employment by the lawyer.

(3) The fee customarily charged in the locality for similar legal services.

(4) The amount involved and the results obtained.

(5) The time limitations imposed by the client or by the circumstances.

(6) The nature and length of the professional relationship with the client.

(7) The experience, reputation, and ability of the lawyer or lawyers performing the services.

(8) Whether the fee is fixed or contingent.[138]

(C) A lawyer shall not enter into an arrangement for, charge, or collect a contingent fee for representing a defendant in a criminal case.[139]

---

[135] This provision is included to conform to action taken by the ABA House of Delegates at the Mid-Winter Meeting, January, 1969.

[136] *See* ABA CANON 12.

[137] The charging of a "clearly excessive fee" is a ground for discipline. State ex rel. Nebraska State Bar Ass'n. v. Richards, 165 Neb. 80, 90, 84 N.W. 2d 136, 143 (1957).

"An attorney has the right to contract for any fee he chooses so long as it is not excessive (see Opinion 190), and this Committee is not concerned with the amount of such fees unless so excessive as to constitute a misappropriation of the client's funds (see Opinion 27)." *ABA Opinion* 320 (1968).

Cf. ABA Opinions 209 (1940), 190 (1939), and 27 (1930) and State ex rel. Lee v. Buchanan, 191 So. 2d 33 (Fla. 1966).

[138] *Cf.* ABA CANON 13; *see generally* MacKINNON, CONTINGENT FEES FOR LEGAL SERVICES (1964) (A Report of the American Bar Foundation).

[139] "Contingent fees, whether in civil or criminal cases, are a special concern of the law. . . .

DR 2-107. Division of Fees Among Lawyers.

(A) A lawyer shall not divide a fee for legal services with another lawyer who is not a partner in or associate of his law firm or law office, unless:

(1) The client consents to employment of the other lawyer after a full disclosure that a division of fees will be made.

(2) The division is made in proportion to the services performed and responsibility assumed by each.[140]

(3) The total fee of the lawyers does not clearly exceed reasonable compensation for all legal services they rendered the client.[141]

(B) This Disciplinary Rule does not prohibit payment to a former partner or associate pursuant to a separation or retirement agreement.

DR 2-108. Agreements Restricting the Practice of a Lawyer.

(A) A lawyer shall not be a party to or participate in a partnership or employment agreement with another lawyer that restricts the right of a lawyer to practice law after the termination of a relationship created by the agreement, except as a condition to payment of retirement benefits.[142]

(B) In connection with the settlement of a controversy or suit, a lawyer shall not enter into an agreement that restricts his right to practice law.

"In criminal cases, the rule is stricter because of the danger of corrupting justice. The second part of Section 542 of the Restatement [of Contracts] reads: 'A bargain to conduct a criminal case . . . in consideration of a promise of a fee contingent on success is illegal. . . .'" Peyton v. Margiotti, 398 Pa. 86, 156 A.2d 865, 967 (1959).

"The third area of practice in which the use of the contingent fee is generally considered to be prohibited is the prosecution and defense of criminal cases. However, there are so few cases, and these are predominantly old, that it is doubtful that there can be said to be any current law on the subject. . . . In the absence of cases on the validity of contingent fees for defense attorneys, it is necessary to rely on the consensus among commentators that such a fee is void as against public policy. The nature of criminal practice itself makes unlikely the use of contingent fee contracts." MacKinnon, Contingent Fees for Legal Services 52 (1964) (A Report of the American Bar Foundation).

[140] See ABA Canon 34 and ABA Opinions 316 (1967) and 294 (1958); see generally ABA Opinions 265 (1945), 204 (1940), 190 (1939), 171 (1937), 153 (1936), 97 (1933), 63 (1932), 28 (1930), 27 (1930), and 18 (1930).

[141] "Canon 12 contemplates that a lawyer's fee should not exceed the value of the services rendered. . . .

"Canon 12 applies, whether joint or separate fees are charged [by associate attorneys]. . . ." ABA Opinion 204 (1940).

[142] "[A] general covenant restricting an employed lawyer, after leaving the employment, from practicing in the community for a stated period, appears to this Committee to be an unwarranted restriction on the right of a lawyer to choose where he will practice and inconsistent with our professional status. Accordingly, the Committee is of the opinion it would be

DR 2-109.   Acceptance of Employment.

(A) A lawyer shall not accept employment on behalf of a person if he knows or it is obvious that such person wishes to:

(1) Bring a legal action, conduct a defense, or assert a position in litigation, or otherwise have steps taken for him, merely for the purpose of harassing or maliciously injuring any person.[143]

(2) Present a claim or defense in litigation that is not warranted under existing law, unless it can be supported by good faith argument for an extension, modification, or reversal of existing law.

DR 2-110.   Withdrawal from Employment.[144]

(A)   In general.

(1) If permission for withdrawal from employment is required by the rules of a tribunal, a lawyer shall not withdraw from employment in a proceeding before that tribunal without its permission.

(2) In any event, a lawyer shall not withdraw from employment until he has taken reasonable steps to avoid foreseeable prejudice to the rights of his client, including giving due notice to his client, allowing time for employment of other counsel, delivering to the client all papers and property to which the client is entitled, and complying with applicable laws and rules.

(3) A lawyer who withdraws from employment shall refund promptly any part of a fee paid in advance that has not been earned.

(B) Mandatory withdrawal.—A lawyer representing a client before a tribunal, with its permission if required by its rules, shall withdraw from employment, and a lawyer representing a client in other matters shall withdraw from employment, if:

(1) He knows or it is obvious that his client is bringing the legal action, conducting the defense, or asserting a position in the litigation, or is otherwise having steps taken for him, merely for the purpose of harassing or maliciously injuring any person.

(2) He knows or it is obvious that his continued employment will result in violation of a Disciplinary Rule.[145]

---

improper for the employing lawyer to require the covenant and likewise for the employed lawyer to agree to it." *ABA Opinion* 300 (1961).

[143] *See* ABA CANON 30.

"*Rule 13.* . . . A member of the State Bar shall not accept employment to prosecute or defend a case solely out of spite, or solely for the purpose of harassing or delaying another. . . ." CAL. BUSINESS AND PROFESSIONS CODE § 6067 (West 1962).

[144] *Cf.* ABA CANON 44.

[145] *See also* Code of Professional Responsibility, DR 5-102 and DR 5-105.

(3) His mental or physical condition renders it unreasonably difficult for him to carry out the employment effectively.

(4) He is discharged by his client.

(C) Permissive withdrawal.[146]—If DR 2-110(B) is not applicable, a lawyer may not request permission to withdraw in matters pending before a tribunal, and may not withdraw in other matters, unless such request or such withdrawal is because:

(1) His client:

(a) Insists upon presenting a claim or defense that is not warranted under existing law and cannot be supported by good faith argument for an extension, modification, or reversal of existing law.[147]

(b) Personally seeks to pursue an illegal course of conduct.

(c) Insists that the lawyer pursue a course of conduct that is illegal or that is prohibited under the Disciplinary Rules.

(d) By other conduct renders it unreasonably difficult for the lawyer to carry out his employment effectively.

(e) Insists, in a matter not pending before a tribunal, that the lawyer engage in conduct that is contrary to the judgment and advice of the lawyer but not prohibited under the Disciplinary Rules.

(f) Deliberately disregards an agreement or obligation to the lawyer as to expenses or fees.

(2) His continued employment is likely to result in a violation of a Disciplinary Rule.

(3) His inability to work with co-counsel indicates that the best interests of the client likely will be served by withdrawal.

(4) His mental or physical condition renders it difficult for him to carry out the employment effectively.

(5) His client knowingly and freely assents to termination of his employment.

(6) He believes in good faith, in a proceeding pending before a tribunal, that the tribunal will find the existence of other good cause for withdrawal.

---

[146] *Cf.* ABA Canon 4.

[147] *Cf.* Anders v. California, 386 U.S. 738, 18 L. Ed. 2d 493, 87 S. Ct. 1396 (1967), *rehearing denied,* 388 U.S. 924, 18 L. Ed. 2d 1377, 87 S. Ct. 2094 (1967).

Canon 3—A Lawyer Should Assist in Preventing the Unauthorized Practice of Law.

Ethical Considerations

EC 3-1. The prohibition against the practice of law by a layman is grounded in the need of the public for integrity and competence of those who undertake to render legal services. Because of the fiduciary and personal character of the lawyer-client relationship and the inherently complex nature of our legal system, the public can better be assured of the requisite responsibility and competence if the practice of law is confined to those who are subject to the requirements and regulations imposed upon members of the legal profession.

EC 3-2. The sensitive variations in the considerations that bear on legal determinations often make it difficult even for a lawyer to exercise appropriate professional judgment, and it is therefore essential that the personal nature of the relationship of client and lawyer be preserved. Competent professional judgment is the product of a trained familiarity with law and legal processes, a disciplined, analytical approach to legal problems, and a firm ethical commitment.

EC 3-3. A non-lawyer who undertakes to handle legal matters is not governed as to integrity or legal competence by the same rules that govern the conduct of a lawyer. A lawyer is not only subject to that regulation but also is committed to high standards of ethical conduct. The public interest is best served in legal matters by a regulated profession committed to such standards.[1] The Disciplinary Rules protect the public in that they prohibit a lawyer from seeking employment by improper overtures, from acting in cases of divided loyalties, and from submitting to the control of others in the exercise of his judgment. Moreover, a person who entrusts legal matters to a lawyer is protected by the attorney-client privilege and by the duty of the lawyer to hold inviolate the confidences and secrets of his client.

EC 3-4. A layman who seeks legal services often is not in a position to judge whether he will receive proper professional attention. The entrustment of a legal matter may well involve

---

[1] "The condemnation of the unauthorized practice of law is designed to protect the public from legal services by persons unskilled in the law. The prohibition of lay intermediaries is intended to insure the loyalty of the lawyer to the client unimpaired by intervening and possibly conflicting interests." Cheatham, *Availability of Legal Services: The Responsibility of the Individual Lawyer and of the Organized Bar,* 12 U.C.L.A. L. Rev. 438, 439 (1965).

the confidences, the reputation, the property, the freedom, or even the life of the client. Proper protection of members of the public demands that no person be permitted to act in the confidential and demanding capacity of a lawyer unless he is subject to the regulations of the legal profession.

EC 3-5.   It is neither necessary nor desirable to attempt the formulation of a single, specific definition of what constitutes the practice of law.[2] Functionally, the practice of law relates to the rendition of services for others that call for the professional judgment of a lawyer. The essence of the professional judgment of the lawyer is his educated ability to relate the general body and philosophy of law to a specific legal problem of a client; and thus, the public interest will be better served if only lawyers are permitted to act in matters involving professional judgment. Where this professional judgment is not involved, non-lawyers, such as court clerks, police officers, abstracters, and many governmental employees, may engage in occupations that require a special knowledge of law in certain areas. But the services of a lawyer are essential in the public interest whenever the exercise of professional legal judgment is required.

EC 3-6.   A lawyer often delegates tasks to clerks, secretaries, and other lay persons. Such delegation is proper if the lawyer maintains a direct relationship with his client, supervises the delegated work, and has complete professional responsibility for the work product.[3] This delegation enables a lawyer to render legal service more economically and efficiently.

---

[2] "What constitutes unauthorized practice of the law in a particular jurisdiction is a matter for determination by the courts of that jurisdiction." *ABA Opinion* 198 (1939).

"In the light of the historical development of the lawyer's functions, it is impossible to lay down an exhaustive definition of 'the practice of law' by attempting to enumerate every conceivable act performed by lawyers in the normal course of their work." State Bar of Arizona v. Arizona Land Title & Trust Co., 90 Ariz. 76, 87, 366 P.2d 1, 8-9 (1961), *modified,* 91 Ariz. 293, 371 P.2d 1020 (1962).

[3] "A lawyer can employ lay secretaries, lay investigators, lay detectives, lay researchers, accountants, lay scriveners, nonlawyer draftsmen or nonlawyer researchers. In fact, he may employ nonlawyers to do any task for him except counsel clients about law matters, engage directly in the practice of law, appear in court or appear in formal proceedings a part of the judicial process, so long as it is he who takes the work and vouches for it to the client and becomes responsible to the client." *ABA Opinion* 316 (1967).

ABA Opinion 316 (1967) also stated that if a lawyer practices law as part of a law firm which includes lawyers from several states, he may delegate tasks to firm members in other states so long as he "is the person who, on behalf of the firm, vouched for the work of all of the others and, with the client and in the courts, did the legal acts defined by that state as the practice of law."

EC 3-7. The prohibition against a non-lawyer practicing law does not prevent a layman from representing himself, for then he is ordinarily exposing only himself to possible injury. The purpose of the legal profession is to make educated legal representation available to the public; but anyone who does not wish to avail himself of such representation is not required to do so. Even so, the legal profession should help members of the public to recognize legal problems and to understand why it may be unwise for them to act for themselves in matters having legal consequences.

EC 3-8. Since a lawyer should not aid or encourage a layman to practice law, he should not practice law in association with a layman or otherwise share legal fees with a layman.[4] This does not mean, however, that the pecuniary value of the interest of a deceased lawyer in his firm or practice may not be paid to his estate or specified persons such as his widow or heirs.[5] In like

---

"A lawyer cannot delegate his professional responsibility to a law student employed in his office. He may avail himself of the assistance of the student in many of the fields of the lawyer's work, such as examination of case law, finding and interviewing witnesses, making collections of claims, examining court records, delivering papers, conveying important messages, and other similar matters. But the student is not permitted, until he is admitted to the Bar, to perform the professional functions of a lawyer, such as conducting court trials, giving professional advice to clients or drawing legal documents for them. The student in all his work must act as agent for the lawyer employing him, who must supervise his work and be responsible for his good conduct." *ABA Opinion* 85 (1932).

[4] "No division of fees for legal services is proper, except with another lawyer. . . ." ABA CANON 34. Otherwise, according to *ABA Opinion* 316 (1967), "[t]he Canons of Ethics do not examine into the method by which such persons are remunerated by the lawyer. . . . They may be paid a salary, a per diem charge, a flat fee, a contract price, etc."

See ABA CANONS 33 and 47.

[5] "Many partnership agreements provide that the active partners, on the death of any one of them, are to make payments to the estate or to the nominee of a deceased partner on a pre-determined formula. It is only where the effect of such an arrangement is to make the estate or nominee a member of the partnership along with the surviving partners that it is prohibited by *Canon* 34. Where the payments are made in accordance with a pre-existing agreement entered into by the deceased partner during his lifetime and providing for a fixed method for determining their amount based upon the value of services rendered during the partner's lifetime and providing for a fixed period over which the payments are to be made, this is not the case. Under these circumstances, whether the payments are considered to be delayed payment of compensation earned but withheld during the partner's lifetime, or whether they are considered to be an approximation of his interest in matters pending at the time of his death, is immaterial. In either event, as Henry S. Drinker says in his book, LEGAL ETHICS, at page 189: 'It would seem, however, that a reasonable agreement to pay the estate a proportion of the receipts for a reasonable period is a proper practical settlement for the lawyer's services to his retirement or death.' " *ABA Opinion* 308 (1963).

manner, profit-sharing retirement plans of a lawyer or law firm which include non-lawyer office employees are not improper.[6] These limited exceptions to the rule against sharing legal fees with laymen are permissible since they do not aid or encourage laymen to practice law.

EC 3-9. Regulation of the practice of law is accomplished principally by the respective states.[7] Authority to engage in the practice of law conferred in any jurisdiction is not per se a grant of the right to practice elsewhere, and it is improper for a lawyer to engage in practice where he is not permitted by law or by court order to do so. However, the demands of business and the mobility of our society pose distinct problems in the regulation of the practice of law by the states.[8] In furtherance of the public interest, the legal profession should discourage regulation that unreasonably imposes territorial limitations upon the right of a lawyer to handle the legal affairs of his client or upon the opportunity of a client to obtain the services of a lawyer of his choice in all matters including the presentation of a contested matter in a tribunal before which the lawyer is not permanently admitted to practice.[9]

Disciplinary Rules

DR 3-101. Aiding Unauthorized Practice of Law.[10]

(A) A lawyer shall not aid a non-lawyer in the unauthorized practice of law.[11]

---

[6] *Cf. ABA Opinion* 311 (1964).

[7] "That the States have broad power to regulate the practice of law is, of course, beyond question." United Mine Workers v. Ill. State Bar Ass'n, 389 U.S. 217, 222 (1967).

"It is a matter of law, not of ethics, as to where an individual may practice law. Each state has its own rules." *ABA Opinion* 316 (1967).

[8] "Much of clients' business crosses state lines. People are mobile, moving from state to state. Many metropolitan areas cross state lines. It is common today to have a single economic and social community involving more than one state. The business of a single client may involve legal problems in several states." *ABA Opinion* 316 (1967).

[9] "[W]e reaffirmed the general principle that legal services to New Jersey residents with respect to New Jersey matters may ordinarily be furnished only by New Jersey counsel; but we pointed out that there may be multistate transactions where strict adherence to this thesis would not be in the public interest and that, under the circumstances, it would have been not only more costly to the client but also 'grossly impractical and inefficient' to have had the settlement negotiations conducted by separate lawyers from different states." In re Estate of Waring, 47 N.J. 367, 376, 221 A.2d 193, 197 (1966).

Cf. ABA Opinion 316 (1967).

[10] Conduct permitted by the Disciplinary Rules of Canons 2 and 5 does not violate DR 3-101.

[11] *See* ABA CANON 47.

(B) A lawyer shall not practice law in a jurisdiction where to do so would be in violation of regulations of the profession in that jurisdiction.[12]

DR 3-102. Dividing Legal Fees with a Non-Lawyer.

(A) A lawyer or law firm shall not share legal fees with a non-lawyer,[13] except that:

(1) An agreement by a waiver with his firm, partner, or associate may provide for the payment of money, over a reasonable period of time after his death, to his estate or to one or more specified persons.[14]

(2) A lawyer who undertakes to complete unfinished legal business of a deceased lawyer may pay to the estate of the deceased lawyer that proportion of the total compensation which fairly represents the services rendered by the deceased lawyer.

(3) A lawyer or law firm may include non-lawyer employees in a retirement plan, even though the plan is based in whole or in part on a profit-sharing arrangement.[15]

DR 3-103. Forming a Partnership with a Non-Lawyer.

(A) A lawyer shall not form a partnership with a non-lawyer if any of the activities of the partnership consist of the practice of law.[16]

CANON 4 [C10]—A LAWYER SHOULD PRESERVE THE CONFIDENCES AND SECRETS OF A CLIENT.

Ethical Considerations

EC 4-1. Both the fiduciary relationship existing between lawyer and client and the proper functioning of the legal system

---

[12] It should be noted, however, that a lawyer may engage in conduct, otherwise prohibited by this Disciplinary Rule, where such conduct is authorized by preemptive federal legislation. *See* Sperry v. Florida, 373 U.S. 379, 10 L. Ed. 2d 428, 83 S. Ct. 1322 (1963).

[13] *See* ABA CANON 34 and *ABA Opinions* 316 (1967), 180 (1938), and 48 (1931).

"The receiving attorney shall not under any guise or form share his fee for legal services with a lay agency, personal or corporate, without prejudice, however, to the right of the lay forwarder to charge and collect from the creditor proper compensation for non-legal services rendered by the law [*sic*] forwarder which are separate and apart from the services performed by the receiving attorney." *ABA Opinion* 294 (1958).

[14] *See ABA Opinions* 309 (1963) and 266 (1945).

[15] *Cf. ABA Opinion* 311 (1964).

[16] *See* ABA CANON 33; *cf. ABA Opinions* 239 (1942) and 201 (1940).

ABA Opinion 316 (1967) states that lawyers licensed in different jurisdictions may, under certain conditions, enter "into an arrangement for the practice of law" and that a lawyer licensed in State A is not, for such purpose, a layman in State B.

require the preservation by the lawyer of confidences and secrets of one who has employed or sought to employ him.[1] A client must feel free to discuss whatever he wishes with his lawyer and a lawyer must be equally free to obtain information beyond that volunteered by his client.[2] A lawyer should be fully informed of all the facts of the matter he is handling in order for his client to obtain the full advantage of our legal system. It is for the lawyer in the exercise of his independent professional judgment to separate the relevant and important from the irrelevant and unimportant. The observance of the ethical obligation of a lawyer to hold inviolate the confidences and secrets of his client not only facilitates the full development of facts essential to proper representation of the client but also encourages laymen to seek early legal assistance.

EC 4-2. The obligation to protect confidences and secrets obviously does not preclude a lawyer from revealing information

---

[1] *See* ABA Canons 6 and 37 and *ABA Opinion* 287 (1953).

"The reason underlying the rule with respect to confidential communications between attorney and client is well stated in Mecham on Agency, 2d Ed., Vol. 2, § 2297, as follows: 'The purposes and necessities of the relation between a client and his attorney require, in many cases, on the part of the client, the fullest and freest disclosures to the attorney of the client's objects, motives and acts. This disclosure is made in the strictest confidence, relying upon the attorney's honor and fidelity. To permit the attorney to reveal to others what is so disclosed, would be not only a gross violation of a sacred trust upon his part, but it would utterly destroy and prevent the usefulness and benefits to be derived from professional assistance. Based upon considerations of public policy, therefore, the law wisely declares that all confidential communications and disclosures, made by a client to his legal adviser for the purpose of obtaining his professional aid or advice, shall be strictly privileged;—that the attorney shall not be permitted, without the consent of his client,—and much less will he be compelled—to reveal or disclose communications made to him under such circumstances.' " *ABA Opinion* 250 (1943).

"While it is true that complete revelation of relevant facts should be encouraged for trial purposes, nevertheless an attorney's dealings with his client, if both are sincere, and if the dealings involve more than mere technical matters, should be immune to discovery proceedings. There must be freedom from fear of revealment of matters disclosed to an attorney because of the peculiarly intimate relationship existing." Ellis-Foster Co. v. Union Carbide & Carbon Corp., 159 F. Supp. 917, 919 (D.N.J. 1958).

Cf. ABA Opinions 314 (1965), 274 (1946) and 268 (1945).

[2] "While it is the great purpose of law to ascertain the truth, there is the countervailing necessity of insuring the right of every person to freely and fully confer and confide in one having knowledge of the law, and skilled in its practice, in order that the former may have adequate advice and a proper defense. This assistance can be made safely and readily available only when the client is free from the consequences of apprehension of disclosure by reason of the subsequent statements of the skilled lawyer. Baird v. Koerner, 279 F.2d 623, 629-30 (9th Cir. 1960).

Cf. ABA Opinion 150 (1936).

when his client consents after full disclosure,[3] when necessary to perform his professional employment, when permitted by a Disciplinary Rule, or when required by law. Unless the client otherwise directs, a lawyer may disclose the affairs of his client to partners or associates of his firm. It is a matter of common knowledge that the normal operation of a law office exposes confidential professional information to non-lawyer employees of the office, particularly secretaries and those having access to the files; and this obligates a lawyer to exercise care in selecting and training his employees so that the sanctity of all confidences and secrets of his clients may be preserved. If the obligation extends to two or more clients as to the same information, a lawyer should obtain the permission of all before revealing the information. A lawyer must always be sensitive to the rights and wishes of his client and act scrupulously in the making of decisions which may involve the disclosure of information obtained in his professional relationship.[4] Thus, in the absence of consent of his client after full disclosure, a lawyer should not associate another lawyer in the handling of a matter; nor should he, in the absence of consent, seek counsel from another lawyer if there is a reasonable possibility that the identity of the client or his confidences or secrets would be revealed to such lawyer. Both social amenities and professional duty should cause a lawyer to shun indiscreet conversations concerning his clients.

EC 4-3. Unless the client otherwise directs, it is not improper for a lawyer to give limited information from his files to an outside agency necessary for statistical, bookkeeping, accounting, data processing, banking, printing, or other legitimate purposes, provided he exercises due care in the selection of the agency and warns the agency that the information must be kept confidential.

EC 4-4. The attorney-client privilege is more limited than the ethical obligation of a lawyer to guard the confidence and secrets of his client. This ethical precept, unlike the evidentiary privilege, exists without regard to the nature or source of information or the fact that others share the knowledge. A lawyer

---

[3] "Where . . . [a client] knowingly and after full disclosure participates in a [legal fee] financing plan which requires the furnishing of certain information to the bank, clearly by his conduct he has waived any privilege as to that information." *ABA Opinion* 320 (1968).

[4] "The lawyer must decide when he takes a case whether it is a suitable one for him to undertake and after this decision is made, he is not justified in turning against his client by exposing injurious evidence entrusted to him. . . . [D]oing something intrinsically regrettable, because the only alternative involves worse consequences, is a necessity in every profession." WILLISTON, LIFE AND LAW 271 (1940).

Cf. ABA Opinions 177 (1938) and 83 (1932).

should endeavor to act in a manner which preserves the evidentiary privilege; for example, he should avoid professional discussions in the presence of persons to whom the privilege does not extend. A lawyer owes an obligation to advise the client of the attorney-client privilege and timely to assert the privilege unless it is waived by the client.

EC 4-5. A lawyer should not use information acquired in the course of the representation of a client to the disadvantage of the client and a lawyer should not use, except with the consent of his client after full disclosure, such information for his own purposes.[5] Likewise, a lawyer should be diligent in his efforts to prevent the misuse of such information by his employees and associates.[6] Care should be exercised by a lawyer to prevent the disclosure of the confidences and secrets of one client to another,[7] and no employment should be accepted that might require such disclosure.

EC 4-6. The obligation of a lawyer to preserve the confidences and secrets of his client continues after the termination of his employment.[8] Thus a lawyer should not attempt to sell a law practice as a going business because, among other reasons, to do so would involve the disclosure of confidences and secrets.[9] A lawyer should also provide for the protection of the confidences and secrets of his client following the termination of the practice of the lawyer, whether termination is due to death, disability, or retirement. For example, a lawyer might provide for the personal papers of the client to be returned to him and for the papers of the lawyer to be delivered to another lawyer or to be destroyed. In determining the method of disposition, the instructions and wishes of the client should be a dominant consideration.

---

[5] *See* ABA CANON 11.

[6] *See* ABA CANON 37.

[7] *See* ABA CANONS 6 and 37.

"[A]n attorney must not accept professional employment against a client or a former client which will, or even *may* require him to use confidential information obtained by the attorney in the course of his professional relations with such client regarding the subject matter of the employment. . . ." *ABA Opinion* 165 (1936).

[8] *See* ABA CANON 37.

"Confidential communications between an attorney and his client, made because of the relationship and concerning the subject-matter of the attorney's employment, are generally privileged from disclosure without the consent of the client, and this privilege outlasts the attorney's employment. *Canon 37." ABA Opinion* 154 (1936).

[9] *Cf. ABA Opinion* 266 (1945).

Disciplinary Rules

DR 4-101. Preservation of Confidences and Secrets of a Client.[10]

(A) "Confidence" refers to information protected by the attorney-client privilege under applicable law, and "secret" refers to other information gained in the professional relationship that the client has requested be held inviolate or the disclosure of which would be embarrassing or would be likely to be detrimental to the client.

(B) Except when permitted under DR 4-101(C), a lawyer shall not knowingly:

(1) Reveal a confidence or secret of his client.[11]

(2) Use a confidence or secret of his client to the disadvantage of the client.

(3) Use a confidence or secret of his client for the advantage of himself[12] or of a third person,[13] unless the client consents after full disclosure.

(C) A lawyer may reveal:

(1) Confidences or secrets with the consent of the client or clients affected, but only after a full disclosure to them.[14]

---

[10] *See* ABA CANON 37; *cf.* ABA CANON 6.

[11] "§ 6068 . . . It is the duty of an attorney:

. . . .

" (e) To maintain inviolate the confidence, and at every peril to himself to preserve the secrets, of his client." CAL. BUSINESS AND PROFESSIONS CODE § 6068 (West 1962). Virtually the same provision is found in the Oregon statutes. ORE. REV. STATS. ch. 9 § 9.460 (5).

"Communications between lawyer and client are privileged (WIGMORE ON EVIDENCE, 3d Ed., Vol. 8, §§ 2290-2329). The modern theory underlying the privilege is subjective and is to give the client freedom of apprehension in consulting his legal adviser (*ibid.*, § 2290, p. 548). The privilege applies to communications made in seeking legal advice for any purpose (*ibid.*, § 2294, p. 563). The mere circumstance that the advice is given without charge therefor does not nullify the privilege (*ibid.*, § 2303)." *ABA Opinion* 216 (1941).

"It is the duty of an attorney to maintain the confidence and preserve inviolate the secrets of his client. . . ." *ABA Opinion* 155 (1936).

[12] *See* ABA CANON 11.

"The provision respecting employment is in accord with the general rule announced in the adjudicated cases that a lawyer may not make use of knowledge or information acquired by him through his professional relations with his client, or in the conduct of his client's business, to his own advantage or profit (7 C.J.S., § 125, p. 958; Healy v. Gray, 184 Iowa 111, 168 N.W. 222; Baumgardner v. Hudson, D.C. App., 277 F. 552; Goodrum v. Clement, D.C. App., 277 F. 586)." *ABA Opinion* 250 (1943).

[13] *See ABA Opinion* 177 (1938).

[14] "[A lawyer] may not divulge confidential communications, information, and secrets imparted to him by the client or acquired during their professional relations, unless he is authorized to do so by the client (People v. Gerold, 265 Ill. 448, 107 N.E. 165, 178; Murphy v. Riggs, 238 Mich. 151,

(2) Confidences or secrets when permitted under Disciplinary Rules or required by law or court order.[15]

(3) The intention of his client to commit a crime[16] and the information necessary to prevent the crime.[17]

(4) Confidences or secrets necessary to establish or collect his fee[18] or to defend himself or his employees or associates against an accusation of wrongful conduct.[19]

---

213 N.W. 110, 112; Opinion of this Committee, No. 91)." *ABA Opinion* 202 (1940).

    Cf. ABA Opinion 91 (1933).

[15] "A defendant in a criminal case when admitted to bail is not only regarded as in the custody of his bail, but he is also in the custody of the law, and admission to bail does not deprive the court of its inherent power to deal with the person of the prisoner. Being in lawful custody, the defendant is guilty of an escape when he gains his liberty before he is delivered in due process of law, and is guilty of a separate offense for which he may be punished. In failing to disclose his client's whereabouts as a fugitive under these circumstances the attorney would not only be aiding his client to escape trial on the charge for which he was indicted; but would likewise be aiding him in evading prosecution for the additional offense of escape.

    "It is the opinion of the committee that under such circumstances the attorney's knowledge of his client's whereabouts is not privileged, and that he may be disciplined for failing to disclose that information to the proper authorities. . . ." *ABA Opinion* 155 (1936).

    "We held in *Opinion* 155 that a communication by a client to his attorney in respect to the future commission of an unlawful act or to a continuing wrong is not privileged from disclosure. Public policy forbids that the relation of attorney and client should be used to conceal wrongdoing on the part of the client.

    . . . .

    "When an attorney representing a defendant in a criminal case applies on his behalf for probation or suspension of sentence, he represents to the court, by implication at least, that his client will abide by the terms and conditions of the court's order. When that attorney is later advised of a violation of that order, it is his duty to advise his client of the consequences of his act, and endeavor to prevent a continuance of the wrongdoing. If his client thereafter persists in violating the terms and conditions of his probation, it is the duty of the attorney as an officer of the court to advise the proper authorities concerning his client's conduct. Such information, even though coming to the attorney from the client in the course of his professional relations with respect to other matters in which he represents the defendant, is not privileged from disclosure. . . ." *ABA Opinion* 156 (1936).

[16] *ABA Opinion* 314 (1965) indicates that a lawyer must disclose even the confidences of his clients if "the facts in the attorney's possession indicate beyond reasonable doubt that a crime will be committed."

    See ABA Opinion 155 (1936).

[17] *See* ABA CANON 37 and *ABA Opinion* 202 (1940).

[18] *Cf. ABA Opinion* 250 (1943).

[19] *See* ABA CANON 37 and *ABA Opinions* 202 (1940) and 19 (1930).

    "[T]he adjudicated cases recognize an exception to the rule [that a lawyer shall not reveal the confidences of his client], where disclosure is necessary to protect the attorney's interests arising out of the relation of attorney and client in which disclosure was made.

    "The exception is stated in MECHAM ON AGENCY, 2d Ed., Vol. 2, § 2313, as follows: 'But the attorney may disclose information received from the client when it becomes necessary for his own protection, as if the

(D) A lawyer shall exercise reasonable care to prevent his employees, associates, and others whose services are utilized by him from disclosing or using confidences or secrets of a client, except that a lawyer may reveal the information allowed by DR 4-101(C) through an employee.

CANON 5—A LAWYER SHOULD EXERCISE INDEPENDENT PROFESSIONAL JUDGMENT ON BEHALF OF A CLIENT.

Ethical Considerations

EC 5-1. The professional judgment of a lawyer should be exercised, within the bounds of the law, solely for the benefit of his client and free of compromising influences and loyalties.[1]

---

client should bring an action against the attorney for negligence or misconduct, and it became necessary for the attorney to show what his instructions were, or what was the nature of the duty which the client expected him to perform. So if it became necessary for the attorney to bring an action against the client, the client's privilege could not prevent the attorney from disclosing what was essential as a means of obtaining or defending his own rights.'

"Mr. Jones, in his COMMENTARIES ON EVIDENCE, 2d Ed., Vol. 5, § 2165, states the exception thus: 'It has frequently been held that the rule as to privileged communications does not apply when litigation arises between attorney and client to the extent that their communications are relevant to the issue. In such cases, if the disclosure of privileged communications becomes necessary to protect the attorney's rights, he is released from those obligations of secrecy which the law places upon him. He should not, however, disclose more than is necessary for his own protection. It would be a manifest injustice to allow the client to take advantage of the rule of exclusion as to professional confidence to the prejudice of his attorney, or that it should be carried to the extent of depriving the attorney of the means of obtaining or defending his own rights. In such cases the attorney is exempted from the obligations of secrecy.' " *ABA Opinion* 250 (1943).

[1] *Cf.* ABA CANON 35.

"[A lawyer's] fiduciary duty is of the highest order and he must not represent interests adverse to those of the client. It is true that because of his professional responsibility and the confidence and trust which his client may legitimately repose in him, he must adhere to a high standard of honesty, integrity and good faith in dealing with his client. He is not permitted to take advantage of his position or superior knowledge to impose upon the client; nor to conceal facts or law, nor in any way deceive him without being held responsible therefor." Smoot v. Lund, 13 Utah 2d 168, 172, 369 P.2d 933, 936 (1962).

"When a client engages the services of a lawyer in a given piece of business he is entitled to feel that, until that business is finally disposed of in some manner, he has the undivided loyalty of the one upon whom he looks as his advocate and champion. If, as in this case, he is sued and his home attached by his own attorney, who is representing him in another matter, all feeling of loyalty is necessarily destroyed, and the profession is exposed to the charge that it is interested only in money." Grievance Comm. v. Rattner, 152 Conn. 59, 65, 203 A.2d 82, 84 (1964).

"One of the cardinal principles confronting every attorney in the representation of a client is the requirement of complete loyalty and service in good faith to the best of his ability. In a criminal case the client is en-

Neither his personal interests, the interests of other clients, nor the desires of third persons should be permitted to dilute his loyalty to his client.

Interests of a Lawyer That May Affect His Judgment

EC 5-2. A lawyer should not accept proffered employment if his personal interests or desires will, or there is a reasonable probability that they will, affect adversely the advice to be given or services to be rendered the prospective client.[2] After accepting employment, a lawyer carefully should refrain from acquiring a property right or assuming a position that would tend to make his judgment less protective of the interests of his client.

EC 5-3. The self-interest of a lawyer resulting from his ownership of property in which his client also has an interest or which may affect property of his client may interfere with the exercise of free judgment on behalf of his client. If such interference would occur with respect to a prospective client, a lawyer should decline employment proffered by him. After accepting employment, a lawyer should not acquire property rights that would adversely affect his professional judgment in the representation of his client. Even if the property interests of a lawyer do not presently interfere with the exercise of his independent judgment, but the likelihood of interference can reasonably be foreseen by him, a lawyer should explain the situation to his client

---

titled to a fair trial, but not a perfect one. These are fundamental requirements of due process under the Fourteenth Amendment. . . . The same principles are applicable in Sixth Amendment cases (not pertinent herein) and suggest that an attorney should have no conflict of interest and that he must devote his full and faithful efforts toward the defense of his client." Johns v. Smyth, 176 F. Supp. 949, 952 (E.D. Va. 1959), *modified,* United States ex rel. Wilkins v. Banmiller, 205 F. Supp. 123, 128 n. 5 (E.D. Pa. 1962), *aff'd,* 325 F.2d 514 (3d Cir. 1963), *cert. denied,* 379 U.S. 847, 13 L. Ed. 2d 51, 85 S. Ct. 87 (1964).

[2] "Attorneys must not allow their private interests to conflict with those of their clients. . . . They owe their entire devotion to the interests of their clients." United States v. Anonymous, 215 F. Supp. 111, 113 (E.D. Tenn. 1963).

"[T]he court [below] concluded that a firm may not accept any action against a person whom they are presently representing even though there is no relationship between the two cases. In arriving at this conclusion, the court cited an opinion of the Committee on Professional Ethics of the New York County Lawyers' Association which stated in part: 'While under the circumstances . . . there may be no actual conflict of interest . . . "maintenance of public confidence in the Bar requires an attorney who has accepted representation of a client to decline, while representing such client, any employment from an adverse party in any matter even though wholly unrelated to the original retainer." See Question and Answer No. 350, N. Y. County L. Ass'n, Questions and Answer No. 450 (June 21, 1956).' " Grievance Comm. v. Rattner, 152 Conn. 59, 65, 203 A.2d 82, 84 (1964).

and should decline employment or withdraw unless the client consents to the continuance of the relationship after full disclosure. A lawyer should not seek to persuade his client to permit him to invest in an undertaking of his client nor make improper use of his professional relationship to influence his client to invest in an enterprise in which the lawyer is interested.

EC 5-4. If, in the course of his representation of a client, a lawyer is permitted to receive from his client a beneficial ownership in publication rights relating to the subject matter of the employment, he may be tempted to subordinate the interests of his client to his own anticipated pecuniary gain. For example, a lawyer in a criminal case who obtains from his client television, radio, motion picture, newspaper, magazine, book, or other publication rights with respect to the case may be influenced, consciously or unconsciously, to a course of conduct that will enhance the value of his publication rights to the prejudice of his client. To prevent these potentially differing interests, such arrangements should be scrupulously avoided prior to the termination of all aspects of the matter giving rise to the employment, even though his employment has previously ended.

EC 5-5. A lawyer should not suggest to his client that a gift be made to himself or for his benefit. If a lawyer accepts a gift from his client, he is peculiarly susceptible to the charge that he unduly influenced or over-reached the client. If a client voluntarily offers to make a gift to his lawyer, the lawyer may accept the gift, but before doing so, he should urge that his client secure disinterested advice from an independent, competent person who is cognizant of all the circumstances.[3] Other than in exceptional circumstances, a lawyer should insist that an instrument in which

---

[3] "Courts of equity will scrutinize with jealous vigilance transactions between parties occupying fiduciary relations toward each other. . . . A deed will not be held invalid, however, if made by the grantor with full knowledge of its nature and effect, and because of the deliberate, voluntary and intelligent desire of the grantor. . . . Where a fiduciary relation exists, the burden of proof is on the grantee or beneficiary of an instrument executed during the existence of such relationship to show the fairness of the transaction, that it was equitable and just and that it did not proceed from undue influence. . . . The same rule has application where an attorney engages in a transaction with a client during the existence of the relation and is benefited thereby. . . . Conversely, an attorney is not prohibited from dealing with his client or buying his property, and such contracts, if open, fair and honest, when deliberately made, are as valid as contracts between other parties. . . . [I]mportant factors in determining whether a transaction is fair include a showing by the fiduciary (1) that he made a full and frank disclosure of all the relevant information that he had; (2) that the consideration was adequate; and (3) that the principal had independent advice before completing the transaction." McFail v. Braden, 19 Ill. 2d 108, 117-18, 166 N.E.2d 46, 52 (1960).

his client desires to name him beneficially be prepared by another lawyer selected by the client.[4]

EC 5-6. A lawyer should not consciously influence a client to name him as executor, trustee, or lawyer in an instrument. In those cases where a client wishes to name his lawyer as such, care should be taken by the lawyer to avoid even the appearance of impropriety.[5]

EC 5-7. The possibility of an adverse effect upon the exercise of free judgment by a lawyer on behalf of his client during litigation generally makes it undesirable for the lawyer to acquire a proprietary interest in the cause of his client or otherwise to become financially interested in the outcome of the litigation.[6] However, it is not improper for a lawyer to protect his right to collect a fee for his services by the assertion of legally permissible liens, even though by doing so he may acquire an interest in the outcome of litigation. Although a contingent fee arrangement[7] gives a lawyer a financial interest in the outcome of litigation, a reasonable contingent fee is permissible in civil cases because it may be the only means by which a layman can obtain the services of a lawyer of his choice. But a lawyer, because he is in a better position to evaluate a cause of action, should enter into a contingent fee arrangement only in those instances where the arrangement will be beneficial to the client.

EC 5-8. A financial interest in the outcome of litigation also results if monetary advances are made by the lawyer to his client.[8] Although this assistance generally is not encouraged, there are instances when it is not improper to make loans to a client. For example, the advancing or guaranteeing of payment of the costs and expenses of litigation by a lawyer may be the only way a client can enforce his cause of action,[9] but the ultimate liability for such costs and expenses must be that of the client.

---

[4] See State ex rel. Nebraska State Bar Ass'n v. Richards, 165 Neb. 80, 94-95, 84 N.W.2d 136, 146 (1957).

[5] *See* ABA CANON 9.

[6] *See* ABA CANON 10.

[7] *See* CODE OF PROFESSIONAL RESPONSIBILITY, EC 2-20.

[8] *See* ABA CANON 42.

[9] *"Rule 3a.* . . . A member of the State Bar shall not directly or indirectly pay or agree to pay, or represent or sanction the representation that he will pay, medical, hospital or nursing bills or other personal expenses incurred by or for a client, prospective or existing; provided this rule shall not prohibit a member:

" (1) with the consent of the client, from paying or agreeing to pay to third persons such expenses from funds collected or to be collected for the client; or

(2) after he has been employed, from lending money to his client upon the client's promise in writing to repay such loan; or

EC 5-9.   Occasionally a lawyer is called upon to decide in a particular case whether he will be a witness or an advocate. If a lawyer is both counsel and witness, he becomes more easily impeachable for interest and thus may be a less effective witness. Conversely, the opposing counsel may be handicapped in challenging the credibility of the lawyer when the lawyer also appears as an advocate in the case. An advocate who becomes a witness is in the unseemly and ineffective position of arguing his own credibility. The roles of an advocate and of a witness are inconsistent; the function of an advocate is to advance or argue the cause of another, while that of a witness is to state facts objectively.

EC 5-10.   Problems incident to the lawyer-witness relationship arise at different stages; they relate either to whether a lawyer should accept employment or should withdraw from employment.[10] Regardless of when the problem arises, his decision is to be governed by the same basic considerations. It is not objectionable for a lawyer who is a potential witness to be an advocate if it is unlikely that he will be called as a witness because his testimony would be merely cumulative or if his testimony will relate only to an uncontested issue.[11] In the exceptional situation where it will be manifestly unfair to the client for the lawyer to refuse employment or to withdraw when he will likely be a witness on a contested issue, he may serve as advocate even though he may be a witness.[12] In making such decision, he should determine the personal or financial sacrifice of the client that may result from his refusal of employment or withdrawal therefrom,

---

(3) from advancing the costs of prosecuting or defending a claim or action. Such costs within the meaning of this subparagraph (3) include all taxable costs or disbursements, costs of investigation and costs of obtaining and presenting evidence." CAL. BUSINESS AND PROFESSIONS CODE § 6076 (West. Supp. 1967).

[10] "When a lawyer knows, prior to trial, that he will be a necessary witness, except as to merely formal matters such as identification or custody of a document or the like, neither he nor his firm or associates should conduct the trial. If, during the trial, he discovers that the ends of justice require his testimony, he should, from that point on, if feasible and not prejudicial to his client's case, leave further conduct of the trial to other counsel. If circumstances do not permit withdrawal from the conduct of the trial, the lawyer should not argue the credibility of his own testimony." *A Code of Trial Conduct: Promulgated by the American College of Trial Lawyers*, 43 A.B.A.J. 223, 224-25 (1957).

[11] *Cf.* CANON 19: "When a lawyer is a witness for his client, except as to merely formal matters, such as the attestation or custody of an instrument and the like, he should leave the trial of the case to other counsel."

[12] "It is the general rule that a lawyer may not testify in litigation in which he is an advocate unless circumstances arise which could not be anticipated and it is necessary to prevent a miscarriage of justice. In those rare cases where the testimony of an attorney is needed to protect his client's interests, it is not only proper but mandatory that it be forthcoming." Schwartz v. Wenger, 267 Minn. 40, 43-44, 124 N.W.2d 489, 492 (1963).

the materiality of his testimony, and the effectiveness of his representation in view of his personal involvement. In weighing these factors, it should be clear that refusal or withdrawal will impose an unreasonable hardship upon the client before the lawyer accepts or continues the employment.[13] Where the question arises, doubts should be resolved in favor of the lawyer testifying and against his becoming or continuing as an advocate.[14]

EC 5-11. A lawyer should not permit his personal interests to influence his advice relative to a suggestion by his client that additional counsel be employed.[15] In like manner, his personal interests should not deter him from suggesting that additional counsel be employed; on the contrary, he should be alert to the desirability of recommending additional counsel when, in his judgment, the proper representation of his client requires it. However, a lawyer should advise his client not to employ additional counsel suggested by the client if the lawyer believes that such employment would be a disservice to the client, and he should disclose the reasons for his belief.

EC 5-12. Inability of co-counsel to agree on a matter vital to the representation of their client requires that their disagreement be submitted by them jointly to their client for his resolution, and the decision of the client shall control the action to be taken.[16]

EC 5-13. A lawyer should not maintain membership in or be influenced by any organization of employees that undertakes to prescribe, direct, or suggest when or how he should fulfill his professional obligations to a person or organization that employs him as a lawyer. Although it is not necessarily improper for a lawyer employed by a corporation or similar entity to be a

---

[13] "The great weight of authority in this country holds that the attorney who acts as counsel and witness, in behalf of his client, in the same cause on a material matter, not of a merely formal character, and not in an emergency, but having knowledge that he would be required to be a witness in ample time to have secured other counsel and given up his service in the case, violates a highly important provision of the Code of Ethics and a rule of professional conduct, but does not commit a legal error in so testifying, as a result of which a new trial will be granted." Erwin M. Jennings Co. v. DiGenova, 107 Conn. 491, 499, 141 A. 866, 869 (1928).

[14] "[C]ases may arise, and in practice often do arise, in which there would be a failure of justice should the attorney withhold his testimony. In such a case it would be a vicious professional sentiment which would deprive the client of the benefit of his attorney's testimony." Connolly v. Straw, 53 Wis. 645, 649, 11 N.W. 17, 19 (1881).

But see CANON 19: "Except when essential to the ends of justice, a lawyer should avoid testifying in court in behalf of his client."

[15] *Cf.* ABA CANON 7.

[16] *See* ABA CANON 7.

member of an organization of employees, he should be vigilant to safeguard his fidelity as a lawyer to his employer, free from outside influences.

Interests of Multiple Clients [C11]

EC 5-14. Maintaining the independence of professional judgment required of a lawyer precludes his acceptance or continuation of employment that will adversely affect his judgment on behalf of or dilute his loyalty to a client.[17] This problem arises whenever a lawyer is asked to represent two or more clients who may have differing interests, whether such interests be conflicting, inconsistent, diverse, or otherwise discordant.[18]

EC 5-15. If a lawyer is requested to undertake or to continue representation of multiple clients having potentially differing interests, he must weigh carefully the possibility that his judgment may be impaired or his loyalty divided if he accepts or continues the employment. He should resolve all doubts against the propriety of the representation. A lawyer should never represent in litigation multiple clients with differing interests;[19] and there are few situations in which he would be justified in representing in litigation multiple clients with potentially differing interests. If a lawyer accepted such employment and the interests did become actually differing, he would have to with-

---

[17] *See* ABA CANON 6; *cf. ABA Opinions* 261 (1944), 242 (1942), 142 (1935), and 30 (1931).

[18] The ABA Canons speak of "conflicting interests" rather than "differing interests" but make no attempt to define such other than the statement in Canon 6: "Within the meaning of this canon, a lawyer represents conflicting interests when, in behalf of one client, it is his duty to contend for that which duty to another client requires him to oppose."

[19] "Canon 6 of the Canons of Professional Ethics, adopted by the American Bar Association on September 30, 1937, and by the Pennsylvania Bar Association on January 7, 1938, provides in part that 'It is unprofessional to represent conflicting interests, except by express consent of all concerned given after a full disclosure of the facts. Within the meaning of this Canon, a lawyer represents conflicting interests when, in behalf of one client, it is his duty to contend for that which duty to another client requires him to oppose.' The full disclosure required by this canon contemplates that the possibly adverse effect of the conflict be fully explained by the attorney to the client to be affected and by him thoroughly understood. . . .

"The foregoing canon applies to cases where the circumstances are such that possibly conflicting interests may permissibly be represented by the same attorney. But manifestly, there are instances where the conflicts of interest are so critically adverse as not to admit of one attorney's representing both sides. Such is the situation which this record presents. No one could conscionably contend that the same attorney may represent both the plaintiff and defendant in an adversary action. Yet, that is what is being done in this case." Jedwabny v. Philadelphia Transportation Co., 390 Pa. 231, 235, 135 A.2d 252, 254 (1957), *cert. denied,* 355 U.S. 966, 2 L. Ed. 2d 541, 78 S. Ct. 557 (1958).

draw from employment with likelihood of resulting hardship on the clients; and for this reason it is preferable that he refuse the employment initially. On the other hand, there are many instances in which a lawyer may properly serve multiple clients having potentially differing interests in matters not involving litigation. If the interests vary only slightly, it is generally likely that the lawyer will not be subjected to an adverse influence and that he can retain his independent judgment on behalf of each client; and if the interests become differing, withdrawal is less likely to have a disruptive effect upon the causes of his clients.

EC 5-16. In those instances in which a lawyer is justified in representing two or more clients having differing interests, it is nevertheless essential that each client be given the opportunity to evaluate his need for representation free of any potential conflict and to obtain other counsel if he so desires.[20] Thus before a lawyer may represent multiple clients, he should explain fully to each client the implications of the common representation and should accept or continue employment only if the clients consent.[21] If there are present other circumstances that might cause any of the multiple clients to question the undivided loyalty of the lawyer, he should also advise all of the clients of those circumstances.[22]

EC 5-17. Typically recurring situations involving potentially differing interests are those in which a lawyer is asked to represent co-defendants in a criminal case, co-plaintiffs in a personal injury case, an insured and his insurer,[23] and beneficiaries of the estate

---

[20] "Glasser wished the benefit of the undivided assistance of counsel of his own choice. We think that such a desire on the part of an accused should be respected. Irrespective of any conflict of interest, the additional burden of representing another party may conceivably impair counsel's effectiveness.

"To determine the precise degree of prejudice sustained by Glasser as a result of the court's appointment of Stewart as counsel for Kretske is at once difficult and unnecessary. The right to have the assistance of counsel is too fundamental and absolute to allow courts to indulge in nice calculations as to the amount of prejudice arising from its denial." Glasser v. United States, 315 U.S. 60, 75-76, 86 L. Ed. 680, 702 S. Ct. 457, 467 (1942).

[21] *See* ABA CANON 6.

[22] *Id.*

[23] *Cf. ABA Opinion* 282 (1950).

"When counsel, although paid by the casualty company, undertakes to represent the policyholder and files his notice of appearance, he owes to his client, the assured, an undeviating and single allegiance. His fealty embraces the requirement to produce in court all witnesses, fact and expert, who are available and necessary for the proper protection of the rights of his client.

. . .

". . . The Canons of Professional Ethics make it pellucid that there are not two standards, one applying to counsel privately retained by a client, and the other to counsel paid by an insurance carrier." American Employers Ins. Co. v. Goble Aircraft Specialties, 205 Misc. 1066, 1075, 131 N.Y.S.2d

of a decedent. Whether a lawyer can fairly and adequately protect the interests of multiple clients in these and similar situations depends upon an analysis of each case. In certain circumstances, there may exist little chance of the judgment of the lawyer being adversely affected by the slight possibility that the interests will become actually differing; in other circumstances, the chance of adverse effect upon his judgment is not unlikely.

EC 5-18. A lawyer employed or retained by a corporation or similar entity owes his allegiance to the entity and not to a stockholder, director, officer, employee, representative, or other person connected with the entity. In advising the entity, a lawyer should keep paramount its interests and his professional judgment should not be influenced by the personal desires of any person or organization. Occasionally a lawyer for an entity is requested by a stockholder, director, officer, employee, representative, or other person connected with the entity to represent him in an individual capacity; in such case the lawyer may serve the individual only if the lawyer is convinced that differing interests are not present.

EC 5-19. A lawyer may represent several clients whose interests are not actually or potentially differing. Nevertheless, he should explain any circumstances that might cause a client to question his undivided loyalty.[24] Regardless of the belief of a lawyer that he may properly represent multiple clients, he must defer to a client who holds the contrary belief and withdraw from representation of that client.

EC 5-20. A lawyer is often asked to serve as an impartial arbitrator or mediator in matters which involve present or former clients. He may serve in either capacity if he first discloses such present or former relationships. After a lawyer has undertaken

---

393, 401 (1954), *motion to withdraw appeal granted,* 1 App. Div. 2d 1008, 154 N.Y.S.2d 835 (1956).

"[C]ounsel, selected by State Farm to defend Dorothy Walker's suit for $50,000 damages, was apprised by Walker that his earlier version of the accident was untrue and that actually the accident occurred because he lost control of his car in passing a Cadillac just ahead. At that point, Walker's counsel should have refused to participate further in view of the conflict of interest between Walker and State Farm. . . . Instead he participated in the ensuing deposition of the Walkers, even took an *ex parte* sworn statement from Mr. Walker in order to advise State Farm what action it should take, and later used the statement against Walker in the District Court. This action appears to contravene an Indiana attorney's duty 'at every peril to himself, to preserve the secrets of his client'. . . ." State Farm Mut. Auto Ins. Co. v. Walker, 382 F.2d 548, 552 (1967), *cert. denied,* 389 U.S. 1045, 19 L. Ed. 2d 837, 88 S. Ct. 789 (1968).

[24] *See* ABA CANON 6.

to act as an impartial arbitrator or mediator, he should not thereafter represent in the dispute any of the parties involved.

Desires of Third Persons

EC 5-21.   The obligation of a lawyer to exercise professional
judgment solely on behalf of his client requires that he disregard
the desires of others that might impair his free judgment.[25] The
desires of a third person will seldom adversely affect a lawyer
unless that person is in a position to exert strong economic, political, or social pressures upon the lawyer. These influences are
often subtle, and a lawyer must be alert to their existence. A
lawyer subjected to outside pressures should make full disclosure
of them to his client;[26] and if he or his client believes that the
effectiveness of his representation has been or will be impaired
thereby, the lawyer should take proper steps to withdraw from
representation of his client.

EC 5-22.   Economic, political, or social pressures by third
persons are less likely to impinge upon the independent judgment of a lawyer in a matter in which he is compensated directly
by his client and his professional work is exclusively with his
client. On the other hand, if a lawyer is compensated from a
source other than his client, he may feel a sense of responsibility
to someone other than his client.

EC 5-23.   A person or organization that pays or furnishes
lawyers to represent others possesses a potential power to exert
strong pressures against the independent judgment of those lawyers. Some employers may be interested in furthering their own
economic, political, or social goals without regard to the professional responsibility of the lawyer to his individual client. Others
may be far more concerned with establishment or extension of
legal principles than in the immediate protection of the rights of
the lawyer's individual client. On some occasions, decisions on

---

[25] *See* ABA CANON 35.

"Objection to the intervention of a lay intermediary, who may control
litigation or otherwise interfere with the rendering of legal services in a
confidential relationship, . . . derives from the element of pecuniary gain.
Fearful of dangers thought to arise from that element, the courts of several
States have sustained regulations aimed at these activities. We intimate no
view one way or the other as to the merits of those decisions with respect
to the particular arrangements against which they are directed. It is enough
that the superficial resemblance in form between those arrangements and that
at bar cannot obscure the vital fact that here the entire arrangement employs
constitutionally privileged means of expression to secure constitutionally
guaranteed civil rights." NAACP v. Button, 371 U.S. 415, 441-42, 9 L. Ed. 2d
405, 423-24, 83 S. Ct. 328, 342-43 (1963).

[26] *Cf.* ABA CANON 38.

priority of work may be made by the employer rather than the lawyer with the result that prosecution of work already undertaken for clients is postponed to their detriment. Similarly, an employer may seek, consciously or unconsciously, to further its own economic interests through the actions of the lawyers employed by it. Since a lawyer must always be free to exercise his professional judgment without regard to the interests or motives of a third person, the lawyer who is employed by one to represent another must constantly guard against erosion of his professional freedom.[27]

EC 5-24. To assist a lawyer in preserving his professional independence, a number of courses are available to him. For example, a lawyer should not practice with or in the form of a professional legal corporation, even though the corporate form is permitted by law,[28] if any director, officer, or stockholder of it is a non-lawyer. Although a lawyer may be employed by a business corporation with non-lawyers serving as directors or officers, and they necessarily have the right to make decisions of business policy, a lawyer must decline to accept direction of his professional judgment from any layman. Various types of legal aid offices are administered by boards of directors composed of lawyers and laymen. A lawyer should not accept employment from such an organization unless the board sets only broad policies and there is no interference in the relationship of the lawyer and the individual client he serves. Where a lawyer is employed by an organization, a written agreement that defines the relationship between him and the organization and provides for his independence is desirable since it may serve to prevent misunderstanding as to their respective roles. Although other innovations in the means of supplying legal counsel may develop, the responsibility of the lawyer to maintain his professional independence

---

[27] "Certainly it is true that 'the professional relationship between an attorney and his client is highly personal, involving an intimate appreciation of each individual client's particular problem.' And this Committee does not condone practices which interfere with that relationship. However, the mere fact the lawyer is actually paid by some entity other than the client does not affect that relationship, so long as the lawyer is selected by and is directly responsible to the client. See Informal Opinions 469 and 679. Of course, as the latter decision points out, there must be full disclosure of the arrangement by the attorney to the client. . . ." *ABA Opinion* 320 (1968).

"[A] third party may pay the cost of legal services as long as control remains in the client and the responsibility of the lawyer is solely to the client. Informal Opinions 469 ad [*sic*] 679. *See also Opinion* 237." *Id.*

[28] *ABA Opinion* 303 (1961) recognized that "[s]tatutory provisions now exist in several states which are designed to make [the practice of law in a form that will be classified as a corporation for federal income tax purposes] legally possible, either as a result of lawyers incorporating or forming associations with various corporate characteristics."

remains constant, and the legal profession must insure that changing circumstances do not result in loss of the professional independence of the lawyer.

Disciplinary Rules

DR 5-101. Refusing Employment When the Interests of the Lawyer May Impair His Independent Professional Judgment.

(A) Except with the consent of his client after full disclosure, a lawyer shall not accept employment if the exercise of his professional judgment on behalf of his client will be or reasonably may be affected by his own financial, business, property, or personal interests.[29]

(B) A lawyer shall not accept employment in contemplated or pending litigation if he knows or it is obvious that he or a lawyer in his firm ought to be called as a witness, except that he may undertake the employment and he or a lawyer in his firm may testify:

(1) If the testimony will relate solely to an uncontested matter.

(2) If the testimony will relate solely to a matter of formality and there is no reason to believe that substantial evidence will be offered in opposition to the testimony.

(3) If the testimony will relate solely to the nature and value of legal services rendered in the case by the lawyer or his firm to the client.

(4) As to any matter, if refusal would work a substantial hardship on the client because of the distinctive value of the lawyer or his firm as counsel in the particular case.

---

[29] *Cf.* ABA CANON 6 and *ABA Opinions* 181 (1938), 104 (1934), 103 (1933), 72 (1932), 50 (1931), 49 (1931), and 33 (1931).

"New York County [Opinion] 203. . . . [A lawyer] should not advise a client to employ an investment company in which he is interested, without informing him of this." DRINKER, LEGAL ETHICS 956 (1953).

"In *Opinions* 72 and 49 this Committee held: The relations of partners in a law firm are such that neither the firm nor any member or associate thereof, may accept any professional employment which any member of the firm cannot properly accept.

"In *Opinion* 16 this Committee held that a member of a law firm could not represent a defendant in a criminal case which was being prosecuted by another member of the firm who was public prosecuting attorney. The Opinion stated that it was clearly unethical for one member of the firm to oppose the interest of the state while another member represented those interests. . . . Since the prosecutor himself could not represent both the public and the defendant, no member of his law firm could either." *ABA Opinion* 296 (1959).

DR 5-102. Withdrawal as Counsel When the Lawyer Becomes a Witness.[30]

(A) If, after undertaking employment in contemplated or pending litigation, a lawyer learns or it is obvious that he or a lawyer in his firm ought to be called as a witness on behalf of his client, he shall withdraw from the conduct of the trial and his firm, if any, shall not continue representation in the trial, except that he may continue the representation and he or a lawyer in his firm may testify in the circumstances enumerated in DR 5-101(B)(1) through (4).

(B) If, after undertaking employment in contemplated or pending litigation, a lawyer learns or it is obvious that he or a lawyer in his firm may be called as a witness other than on behalf of his client, he may continue the representation until it is apparent that his testimony is or may be prejudicial to his client.[31]

DR 5-103. Avoiding Acquisition of Interest in Litigation.

(A) A lawyer shall not acquire a proprietary interest in the cause of action or subject matter of litigation he is conducting for a client,[32] except that he may:

(1) Acquire a lien granted by law to secure his fee or expenses.

(2) Contract with a client for a reasonable contingent fee in a civil case.[33]

(B) While representing a client in connection with contemplated or pending litigation, a lawyer shall not advance or guarantee financial assistance to his client,[34] except that a lawyer may advance or guarantee the expenses of litigation, including court costs, expenses of investigation, expenses of medical examination, and costs of obtaining and presenting evidence, provided the client remains ultimately liable for such expenses.

---

[30] *Cf.* ABA Canon 19 and *ABA Opinions* 220 (1941), 185 (1938), 50 (1931), and 33 (1931); *but cf.* Erwin M. Jennings Co. v. DiGenova, 107 Conn. 491, 498-99, 141 A. 866, 868 (1928).

[31] This *Canon* [19] *of Ethics* needs no elaboration to be applied to the facts here. Apparently, the object of this precept is to avoid putting a lawyer in the obviously embarrassing predicament of testifying and then having to argue the credibility and effect of his own testimony. It was not designed to permit a lawyer to call opposing counsel as a witness and thereby disqualify him as counsel." Galarowicz v. Ward, 119 Utah 611, 620, 230 P.2d 576, 580 (1951).

[32] ABA Canon 10 and *ABA Opinions* 279 (1949), 246 (1942), and 176 (1938).

[33] *See* Code of Professional Responsibility, DR 2-106(C).

[34] *See* ABA Canon 42; *cf. ABA Opinion* 288 (1954).

DR 5-104. Limiting Business Relations with a Client.

(A) A lawyer shall not enter into a business transaction with a client if they have differing interests therein and if the client expects the lawyer to exercise his professional judgment therein for the protection of the client, unless the client has consented after full disclosure.

(B) Prior to conclusion of all aspects of the matter giving rise to his employment, a lawyer shall not enter into any arrangement or understanding with a client or a prospective client by which he acquires an interest in publication rights with respect to the subject matter of his employment or proposed employment.

DR 5-105. Refusing to Accept or Continue Employment if the Interests of Another Client May Impair the Independent Professional Judgment of the Lawyer.

[C12] (A) A lawyer shall decline proffered employment if the exercise of his independent professional judgment in behalf of a client will be or is likely to be adversely affected by the acceptance of the proffered employment,[35] except to the extent permitted under DR 5-105(C).[36]

[C13] (B) A lawyer shall not continue multiple employment if the exercise of his independent professional judgment in behalf of a client will be or is likely to be adversely affected by his representation of another client, except to the extent permitted under DR 5-105(C).[37]

(C) In the situations covered by DR 5-105(A) and (B), a lawyer may represent multiple clients if it is obvious that he can adequately represent the interest of each and if each consents to the representation after full disclosure of the possible effect of such representation on the exercise of his independent professional judgment on behalf of each.

[C14] (D) If a lawyer is required to decline employment or to withdraw from employment under DR 5-105, no partner

---

[35] See ABA CANON 6; cf. ABA Opinions 167 (1937), 60 (1931), and 40 (1931).

[36] ABA Opinion 247 (1942) held that an attorney could not investigate a night club shooting on behalf of one of the owner's liability insurers, obtaining the cooperation of the owner, and later represent the injured patron in an action against the owner and a different insurance company unless the attorney obtain the "express consent of all concerned given after a full disclosure of the facts," since to do so would be to represent conflicting interests.
See ABA Opinions 247 (1942), 224 (1941), 222 (1941), 218 (1941), 112 (1934), 83 (1932), and 86 (1932).

[37] Cf. ABA Opinions 231 (1941) and 160 (1936).

or associate of his or his firm may accept or continue such employment.

DR 5-106.   Settling Similar Claims of Clients.[38]

(A)   A lawyer who represents two or more clients shall not make or participate in the making of an aggregate settlement of the claims of or against his clients, unless each client has consented to the settlement after being advised of the existence and nature of all the claims involved in the proposed settlement, of the total amount of the settlement, and of the participation of each person in the settlement.

DR 5-107.   Avoiding Influence by Others Than the Client.

(A)   Except with the consent of his client after full disclosure, a lawyer shall not:

(1)   Accept compensation for his legal services from one other than his client.

(2)   Accept from one other than his client any thing of value related to his representation of or his employment by his client.[39]

(B)   A lawyer shall not permit a person who recommends, employs, or pays him to render legal services for another to direct or regulate his professional judgment in rendering such legal services.[40]

(C)   A lawyer shall not practice with or in the form of a professional corporation or association authorized to practice law for a profit, if:

(1)   A non-lawyer owns any interest therein,[41] except that a fiduciary representative of the estate of a lawyer may hold the stock or interest of the lawyer for a reasonable time during administration;

---

[38] Cf. ABA Opinions 243 (1942) and 235 (1941).

[39] See ABA CANON 38.

"A lawyer who receives a commission (whether delayed or not) from a title insurance company or guaranty fund for recommending or selling the insurance to his client, or for work done for the client or the company, without either fully disclosing to the client his financial interest in the transaction, or crediting the client's bill with the amount thus received, is guilty of unethical conduct." ABA Opinion 304 (1962).

[40] See ABA CANON 35; cf. ABA Opinion 237 (1941).

"When the lay forwarder, as agent for the creditor, forwards a claim to an attorney, the direct relationship of attorney and client shall then exist between the attorney and the creditor, and the forwarder shall not interpose itself as an intermediary to control the activities of the attorney." ABA Opinion 294 (1958).

[41] "Permanent beneficial and voting rights in the organization set up to practice law, whatever its form, must be restricted to lawyers while the organization is engaged in the practice of law." ABA Opinion 303 (1961).

(2)   A non-lawyer is a corporate director or officer thereof;[42] or

(3)   A non-lawyer has the right to direct or control the professional judgment of a lawyer.[43]

CANON 6—A LAWYER SHOULD REPRESENT A CLIENT COMPETENTLY.

Ethical Considerations

EC 6-1.   Because of his vital role in the legal process, a lawyer should act with competence and proper care in representing clients. He should strive to become and remain proficient in his practice[1] and should accept employment only in matters which he is or intends to become competent to handle.

EC 6-2.   A lawyer is aided in attaining and maintaining his competence by keeping abreast of current legal literature and developments, participating in continuing legal education pro-

---

[42] "*Canon 33* . . . promulgates underlying principles that must be observed no matter in what form of organization lawyers practice law. Its requirement that no person shall be admitted or held out as a practitioner or member who is not a member of the legal profession duly authorized to practice, and amenable to professional discipline, makes it clear that any centralized management must be in lawyers to avoid a violation of this Canon." *ABA Opinion* 303 (1961).

[43] "There is no intervention of any lay agency between lawyer and client when centralized management provided only by lawyers may give guidance or direction to the services being rendered by a lawyer-member of the organization to a client. The language in *Canon 35* that a lawyer should avoid all relations which direct the performance of his duties by or in the interest of an intermediary refers to lay intermediaries and not lawyer intermediaries with whom he is associated in the practice of law." *ABA Opinion* 303 (1961).

[1] "[W]hen a citizen is faced with the need for a lawyer, he wants, and is entitled to, the best informed counsel he can obtain. Changing times produce changes in our laws and legal procedures. The natural complexities of law require continuing intensive study by a lawyer if he is to render his clients a maximum of efficient service. And, in so doing, he maintains the high standards of the legal profession; and he also increases respect and confidence by the general public." Rochelle & Payne, *The Struggle for Public Understanding*, 25 TEXAS B.J. 109, 160 (1962).

"We have undergone enormous changes in the last fifty years within the lives of most of the adults living today who may be seeking advice. Most of these changes have been accompanied by changes and developments in the law. . . . Every practicing lawyer encounters these problems and is often perplexed with his own inability to keep up, not only with changes in the law, but also with changes in the lives of his clients and their legal problems.

"To be sure, no client has a right to expect that his lawyer will have all of the answers at the end of his tongue or even in the back of his head at all times. But the client does have the right to expect that the lawyer will have devoted his time and energies to maintaining and improving his competence to know where to look for the answers, to know how to deal with the problems, and to know how to advise to the best of his legal talents and abilities." Levy & Sprague, *Accounting and Law: Is Dual Practice in the Public Interest?*, 52 A.B.A.J. 1110, 1112 (1966).

grams,[2] concentrating in particular areas of the law, and by utilizing other available means. He has the additional ethical obligation to assist in improving the legal profession, and he may do so by participating in bar activities intended to advance the quality and standards of members of the profession. Of particular importance is the careful training of his younger associates and the giving of sound guidance to all lawyers who consult him. In short, a lawyer should strive at all levels to aid the legal profession in advancing the highest possible standards of integrity and competence and to meet those standards himself.

EC 6-3.   While the licensing of a lawyer is evidence that he has met the standards then prevailing for admission to the bar, a lawyer generally should not accept employment in any area of the law in which he is not qualified.[3] However, he may accept such employment if in good faith he expects to become qualified through study and investigation, as long as such preparation would not result in unreasonable delay or expense to his client. Proper preparation and representation may require the association by the lawyer of professionals in other disciplines. A lawyer offered employment in a matter in which he is not and does not expect to become so qualified should either decline the employment or, with the consent of his client, accept the employment and associate a lawyer who is competent in the matter.[4]

EC 6-4.   Having undertaken representation, a lawyer should use proper care to safeguard the interests of his client. If a lawyer has accepted employment in a matter beyond his competence but in which he expected to become competent, he should diligently undertake the work and study necessary to qualify himself. In addition to being qualified to handle a particular matter, his obligation to his client requires him to prepare adequately for and give appropriate attention to his legal work.

---

[2] "The whole purpose of continuing legal education, so enthusiastically supported by the ABA, is to make it possible for lawyers to make themselves better lawyers. But there are no nostrums for proficiency in the law; it must come through the hard work of the lawyer himself. To the extent that that work, whether it be in attending institutes or lecture courses, in studying after hours or in the actual day in and day out practice of his profession, can be concentrated within a limited field, the greater the proficiency and expertness that can be developed." *Report of the Special Committee on Specialization and Specialized Legal Education,* 79 A.B.A. REP. 582, 588 (1954).

[3] "If the attorney is not competent to skillfully and properly perform the work, he should not undertake the service." Degen v. Steinbrink, 202 App. Div. 477, 481, 195 N.Y.S. 810, 814 (1922), *aff'd mem.,* 236 N.Y. 669, 142 N.E. 328 (1923).

[4] *Cf. ABA Opinion* 232 (1941).

EC 6-5. A lawyer should have pride in his professional endeavors. His obligation to act competently calls for higher motivation than that arising from fear of civil liability or disciplinary penalty.

EC 6-6. A lawyer should not seek, by contract or other means, to limit his individual liability to his client for his malpractice. A lawyer who handles the affairs of his client properly has no need to attempt to limit his liability for his professional activities and one who does not handle the affairs of his client properly should not be permitted to do so. A lawyer who is a stockholder in or is associated with a professional legal corporation may, however, limit his liability for malpractice of his associates in the corporation, but only to the extent permitted by law.[5]

Disciplinary Rules

DR 6-101. Failing to Act Competently.

(A) A lawyer shall not:

(1) Handle a legal matter which he knows or should know that he is not competent to handle, without associating with him a lawyer who is competent to handle it.

(2) Handle a legal matter without preparation adequate in the circumstances.

(3) Neglect a legal matter entrusted to him.[6]

DR 6-102. Limiting Liability to Client.

(A) A lawyer shall not attempt to exonerate himself from or limit his liability to his client for his personal malpractice.

CANON 7 [C15]—A LAWYER SHOULD REPRESENT A CLIENT ZEALOUSLY WITHIN THE BOUNDS OF THE LAW.

Ethical Considerations

EC 7-1. The duty of a lawyer, both to his client[1] and to

---

[5] *See ABA Opinion* 303 (1961); *cf.* CODE OF PROFESSIONAL RESPONSIBILITY, EC 2-11.

[6] The annual report for 1967-1968 of the Committee on Grievances of the Association of the Bar of the City of New York showed a receipt of 2,232 complaints; of the 828 offenses against clients, 76 involved conversion, 49 involved "overreaching," and 452, or more than half of all such offenses, involved neglect. *Annual Report of the Committee on Grievances of the Association of the Bar of the City of New York,* N.Y.L.J., Sept. 12, 1968, at 4, col. 5.

[1] "The right to be heard would be, in many cases, of little avail if it did not comprehend the right to be heard by counsel. Even the intelligent and educated layman has small and sometimes no skill in the science of

the legal system, is to represent his client zealously[2] within the
bounds of the law,[3] which includes Disciplinary Rules and enforce-

---

law." Powell v. Alabama, 287 U.S. 45, 68-69, 77 L. Ed. 158, 170, 53 S. Ct. 55,
64 (1932).

[2] *Cf.* ABA CANON 4.

"At times . . . [the tax lawyer] will be wise to discard some arguments
and he should exercise discretion to emphasize the arguments which in his
judgment are most likely to be persuasive. But this process involves legal
judgment rather than moral attitudes. The tax lawyer should put aside
private disagreements with Congressional and Treasury policies. His own
notions of policy, and his personal view of what the law should be, are
irrelevant. The job entrusted to him by his client is to use all his learning
and ability to protect his client's rights, not to help in the process of pro-
moting a better tax system. The tax lawyer need not accept his client's
economic and social opinions, but the client is paying for technical attention
and undivided concentration upon his affairs. He is equally entitled to performance unfettered by his attorney's economic and social predilections."
Paul, *The Lawyer as a Tax Adviser*, 25 ROCKY MT. L. REV. 412, 418 (1953).

[3] *See* ABA CANONS 15 and 32.

ABA Canon 5, although only speaking of one accused of crime, imposes
a similar obligation on the lawyer: "[T]he lawyer is bound, by all fair and
honorable means, to present every defense that the law of the land permits,
to the end that no person may be deprived of life or liberty, but by due
process of law."

"Any persuasion or pressure on the advocate which deters him from
planning and carrying out the litigation on the basis of 'what, within the
framework of the law, is best for my client's interest?' interferes with the
obligation to represent the client fully within the law.

"This obligation, in its fullest sense, is the heart of the adversary
process. Each attorney, as an advocate, acts for and seeks that which in his
judgment is best for his client, within the bounds authoritatively established.
The advocate does not *decide* what is just in this case—he would be usurping
the function of the judge and jury—he acts for and seeks for his client that
which he is entitled to under the law. He can do no less and properly
represent the client." Thode, *The Ethical Standard for the Advocate*, 39
TEXAS L. REV. 575, 584 (1961).

"The [Texas public opinion] survey indicates that distrust of the lawyer
can be traced directly to certain factors. Foremost of these is a basic misunderstanding of the function of the lawyer as an advocate in an adversary
system.

"Lawyers are accused of taking advantage of 'loopholes' and 'technical-
ities' to win. Persons who make this charge are unaware, or do not understand, that the lawyer is hired to win, and if he does not exercise every
legitimate effort in his client's behalf, then he is betraying a sacred trust."
Rochelle & Payne, *The Struggle for Public Understanding*, 25 TEXAS B.J. 109,
159 (1962).

"The importance of the attorney's undivided allegiance and faithful
service to one accused of crime, irrespective of the attorney's personal opinion
as to the guilt of his client, lies in Canon 5 of the American Bar Association
Canon of Ethics.

"The difficulty lies, of course, in ascertaining whether the attorney has
been guilty of an error of judgment, such as an election with respect to trial
tactics, or has otherwise been actuated by his conscience or belief that his
client should be convicted in any event. All too frequently courts are called
upon to review actions of defense counsel which are, at the most, errors of
judgment, not properly reviewable on habeas corpus unless the trial is a
farce and a mockery of justice which requires the court to intervene. . . .
But when defense counsel, in a truly adverse proceeding, admits that his

able professional regulations.[4] The professional responsibility of a lawyer derives from his membership in a profession which has the duty of assisting members of the public to secure and protect available legal rights and benefits. In our government of laws and not of men, each member of our society is entitled to have his conduct judged and regulated in accordance with the law;[5] to seek any lawful objective[6] through legally permissible means;[7] and to present for adjudication any lawful claim, issue, or defense.

---

conscience would not permit him to adopt certain customary trial procedures, this extends beyond the realm of judgment and strongly suggests an invasion of constitutional rights." Johns v. Smyth, 176 F. Supp. 949, 952 (E.D. Va. 1959), modified, United States ex rel. Wilkins v. Banmiller, 205 F. Supp. 123, 128, n. 5 (E.D. Pa. 1962), aff'd, 325 F.2d 514 (3d Cir. 1963), cert. denied, 379 U.S. 847, 13 L. Ed. 2d 51, 85 S. Ct. 87 (1964).

"The adversary system in law administration bears a striking resemblance to the competitive economic system. In each we assume that the individual through partisanship or through self-interest will strive mightily for his side, and that kind of striving we must have. But neither system would be tolerable without restraints and modifications, and at times without outright departures from the system itself. Since the legal profession is entrusted with the system of law administration, a part of its task is to develop in its members appropriate restraints without impairing the values of partisan striving. An accompanying task is to aid in the modification of the adversary system or departure from it in areas to which the system is unsuited." Cheatham, The Lawyer's Role and Surroundings, 25 ROCKY MT. L. REV. 405, 410 (1953).

[4] "Rule 4.15 prohibits, in the pursuit of a client's cause, 'any manner of fraud or chicane'; Rule 4.22 requires 'candor and fairness' in the conduct of the lawyer, and forbids the making of knowing misquotations; Rule 4.47 provides that a lawyer 'should always maintain his integrity,' and generally forbids all misconduct injurious to the interests of the public, the courts, or his clients, and acts contrary to 'justice, honesty, modesty or good morals.' Our Commissioner has accurately paraphrased these rules as follows; 'An attorney does not have the duty to do all and whatever he can that may enable him to win his client's cause or to further his client's interest. His duty and efforts in these respects, although they should be prompted by his "entire devotion" to the interest of his client, must be within and not without the bounds of the law.'" In re Wines, 370 S.W.2d 328, 333 (Mo. 1963).

See Note, 38 TEXAS L. REV. 107, 110 (1959).

[5] "Under our system of government the process of adjudication is surrounded by safeguards evolved from centuries of experience. These safeguards are not designed merely to lend formality and decorum to the trial of causes. They are predicated on the assumption that to secure for any controversy a truly informed and dispassionate decision is a difficult thing, requiring for its achievement a special summoning and organization of human effort and the adoption of measures to exclude the biases and prejudgments that have free play outside the courtroom. All of this goes for naught if the man with an unpopular cause is unable to find a competent lawyer courageous enough to represent him. His chance to have his day in court loses much of its meaning if his case is handicapped from the outset by the very kind of prejudgment our rules of evidence and procedure are intended to prevent." Professional Responsibility: Report of the Joint Conference, 44 A.B.A.J. 1159, 1216 (1958).

[6] "[I]t is . . . [the tax lawyer's] positive duty to show the client how to avail himself to the full of what the law permits. He is not the keeper of

EC 7-2. The bounds of the law in a given case are often difficult to ascertain.[8] The language of legislative enactments and judicial opinions may be uncertain as applied to varying factual situations. The limits and specific meaning of apparently relevant law may be made doubtful by changing or developing constitutional interpretations, inadequately expressed statutes or judicial opinions, and changing public and judicial attitudes. Certainty of law ranges from well-settled rules through areas of conflicting authority to areas without precedent.

EC 7-3. Where the bounds of law are uncertain, the action of a lawyer may depend on whether he is serving as advocate or adviser. A lawyer may serve simultaneously as both advocate and adviser, but the two roles are essentially different.[9] In asserting a position on behalf of his client, an advocate for the most

---

the Congressional conscience." Paul, *The Lawyer as a Tax Adviser*, 25 ROCKY MT. L. REV. 412, 418 (1953).

[7] *See* ABA CANONS 15 and 30.

[8] "The fact that it desired to evade the law, as it is called, is immaterial, because the very meaning of a line in the law is that you intentionally may go as close to it as you can if you do not pass it. . . . It is a matter of proximity and degree as to which minds will differ. . . ." Justice Holmes, in Superior Oil Co. v. Mississippi, 280 U.S. 390, 395-96, 74 L. Ed. 504, 508, 50 S. Ct. 169, 170 (1930).

[9] "Today's lawyers perform two distinct types of functions, and our ethical standards should, but in the main do not, recognize these two functions. Judge Philbrick McCoy recently reported to the American Bar Association the need for a reappraisal of the Canons in light of the new and distinct function of counselor, as distinguished from advocate, which today predominates in the legal profession. . . .

". . . In the first place, any revision of the canons must take into account and speak to this new and now predominant function of the lawyer. . . . It is beyond the scope of this paper to discuss the ethical standards to be applied to the counselor except to state that in my opinion such standards should require a greater recognition and protection for the interest of the public generally than is presently expressed in the canons. Also, the counselor's obligation should extend to requiring him to inform and to impress upon the client a just solution of the problem, considering all interests involved." Thode, *The Ethical Standard for the Advocate*, 39 TEXAS L. REV. 575, 578-79 (1961).

"The man who has been called into court to answer for his own actions is entitled to fair hearing. Partisan advocacy plays its essential part in such a hearing, and the lawyer pleading his client's case may properly present it in the most favorable light. A similar resolution of doubts in one direction becomes inappropriate when the lawyer acts as counselor. The reasons that justify and even require partisan advocacy in the trial of a cause do not grant any license to the lawyer to participate as legal advisor in a line of conduct that is immoral, unfair, or of doubtful legality. In saving himself from this unworthy involvement, the lawyer cannot be guided solely by an unreflective inner sense of good faith; he must be at pains to preserve a sufficient detachment from his client's interests so that he remains capable of a sound and objective appraisal of the propriety of what his client proposes to do." *Professional Responsibility: Report of the Joint Conference*, 44 A.B.A.J. 1159, 1161 (1958).

part deals with past conduct and must take the facts as he finds them. By contrast, a lawyer serving as adviser primarily assists his client in determining the course of future conduct and relationships. While serving as advocate, a lawyer should resolve in favor of his client doubts as to the bounds of the law.[10] In serving a client as adviser, a lawyer in appropriate circumstances should give his professional opinion as to what the ultimate decisions of the courts would likely be as to the applicable law.

Duty of the Lawyer to a Client

EC 7-4.   The advocate may urge any permissible construction of the law favorable to his client, without regard to his professional opinion as to the likelihood that the construction will ultimately prevail.[11] His conduct is within the bounds of the law, and therefore permissible, if the position taken is supported by the law or is supportable by a good faith argument for an extension, modification, or reversal of the law. However, a lawyer is not justified in asserting a position in litigation that is frivolous.[12]

---

[10] "[A] lawyer who is asked to advise his client . . . may freely urge the statement of positions most favorable to the client just as long as there is reasonable basis for those positions." *ABA Opinion* 314 (1965).

[11] "The lawyer . . . is not an umpire, but an advocate. He is under no duty to refrain from making every proper argument in support of any legal point because he is not convinced of its inherent soundness. . . . His personal belief in the soundness of his cause or of the authorities supporting it, is irrelevant." *ABA Opinion* 280 (1949).

"Counsel apparently misconceived his role. It was his duty to honorably present his client's contentions in the light most favorable to his client. Instead he presumed to advise the court as to the validity and sufficiency of prisoner's motion, by letter. We therefore conclude that prisoner had no effective assistance of counsel and remand this case to the District Court with instructions to set aside the Judgment, appoint new counsel to represent the prisoner if he makes no objection thereto, and proceed anew." McCartney v. United States, 343 F.2d 471, 472 (9th Cir. 1965).

[12] "Here the court-appointed counsel had the transcript but refused to proceed with the appeal because he found no merit in it. . . . We cannot say that there was a finding of frivolity by either of the California courts or that counsel acted in any greater capacity than merely as *amicus curiae* which was condemned in *Ellis, supra.* Hence California's procedure did not furnish petitioner with counsel acting in the role of an advocate nor did it provide that full consideration and resolution of the matter as is obtained when counsel is acting in that capacity. . . .

"The constitutional requirement of substantial equality and fair process can only be attained where counsel acts in the role of an active advocate in behalf of his client, as opposed to that of *amicus curiae.* The no-merit letter and the procedure it triggers do not reach that dignity. Counsel should, and can with honor and without conflict, be of more assistance to his client and to the court. His role as advocate requires that he support his client's appeal to the best of his ability. Of course, if counsel finds his case to be wholly frivolous, after a conscientious examination of it, he should so advise the court and request permission to withdraw. That request must, however,

EC 7-5. A lawyer as adviser furthers the interest of his client by giving his professional opinion as to what he believes would likely be the ultimate decision of the courts on the matter at hand and by informing his client of the practical effect of such decision.[13] He may continue in the representation of his client even though his client has elected to pursue a course of conduct contrary to the advice of the lawyer so long as he does not thereby knowingly assist the client to engage in illegal conduct or to take a frivolous legal position. A lawyer should never encourage or aid his client to commit criminal acts or counsel his client on how to violate the law and avoid punishment therefor.[14]

EC 7-6. Whether the proposed action of a lawyer is within the bounds of the law may be a perplexing question when his client is contemplating a course of conduct having legal consequences that vary according to the client's intent, motive, or desires at the time of the action. Often a lawyer is asked to assist his client in developing evidence relevant to the state of mind of the client at a particular time. He may properly assist his client in the development and preservation of evidence of existing motive, intent, or desire; obviously, he may not do anything furthering the creation or preservation of false evidence. In many cases a lawyer may not be certain as to the state of mind of his

---

be accompanied by a brief referring to anything in the record that might arguably support the appeal. A copy of counsel's brief should be furnished the indigent and time allowed him to raise any points that he chooses; the court—not counsel—then proceeds, after a full examination of all the proceedings, to decide whether the case is wholly frivolous. If it so finds it may grant counsel's request to withdraw and dismiss the appeal insofar as federal requirements are concerned, or proceed to a decision on the merits, if state law so requires. On the other hand, if it finds any of the legal points arguable on their merits (and therefore not frivolous) it must, prior to decision, afford the indigent the assistance of counsel to argue the appeal." Anders v. California, 386 U.S. 738, 744, 18 L. Ed. 2d 493, 498, 87 S. Ct. 1396, 1399-1400 (1967), *rehearing denied*, 388 U.S. 924, 18 L. Ed. 2d 1377, 87 S. Ct. 2094 (1967).

     See Paul, *The Lawyer As a Tax Adviser*, 25 ROCKY MT. L. REV. 412, 432 (1953).

[13] *See* ABA CANON 32.

[14] "For a lawyer to represent a syndicate notoriously engaged in the violation of the law for the purpose of advising the members how to break the law and at the same time escape it, is manifestly improper. While a lawyer may see to it that anyone accused of crime, no matter how serious and flagrant, has a fair trial, and present all available defenses, he may not cooperate in planning violations of the law. There is a sharp distinction, of course, between advising what can lawfully be done and advising how unlawful acts can be done in a way to avoid conviction. Where a lawyer accepts a retainer from an organization, known to be unlawful, and agrees in advance to defend its members when from time to time they are accused of crime arising out of its unlawful activities, this is equally improper." "See also *Opinion 155*." *ABA Opinion* 281 (1952).

client, and in those situations he should resolve reasonable doubts in favor of his client.

EC 7-7. In certain areas of legal representation not affecting the merits of the cause or substantially prejudicing the rights of a client, a lawyer is entitled to make decisions on his own. But otherwise the authority to make decisions is exclusively that of the client and, if made within the framework of the law, such decisions are binding on his lawyer. As typical examples in civil cases, it is for the client to decide whether he will accept a settlement offer or whether he will waive his right to plead an affirmative defense. A defense lawyer in a criminal case has the duty to advise his client fully on whether a particular plea to a charge appears to be desirable and as to the prospects of success on appeal, but it is for the client to decide what plea should be entered and whether an appeal should be taken.[15]

EC 7-8. A lawyer should exert his best efforts to insure that decisions of his client are made only after the client has been informed of relevant considerations. A lawyer ought to initiate this decision-making process if the client does not do so. Advice of a lawyer to his client need not be confined to purely legal considerations.[16] A lawyer should advise his client of the possible effect of each legal alternative.[17] A lawyer should bring to bear upon this decision-making process the fullness of his experience as well as his objective viewpoint.[18] In assisting his client to reach a proper decision, it is often desirable for a lawyer to point out those factors which may lead to a decision that is morally just as well as legally permissible.[19] He may emphasize the possibility

---

[15] *See* ABA Special Committee on Minimum Standards for the Administration of Criminal Justice, *Standards Relating to Pleas of Guilty* pp. 69-70 (1968).

[16] "First of all, a truly great lawyer is a wise counselor to all manner of men in the varied crises of their lives when they most need distinterested advice. Effective counseling necessarily involves a thoroughgoing knowledge of the principles of the law not merely as they appear in the books but as they actually operate in action." Vanderbilt, *The Five Functions of the Lawyer: Service to Clients and the Public,* 40 A.B.A.J. 31 (1954).

[17] "A lawyer should endeavor to obtain full knowledge of his client's cause before advising thereon. . . ." ABA CANON 8.

[18] "[I]n devising charters of collaborative effort the lawyer often acts where all of the affected parties are present as participants. But the lawyer also performs a similar function in situations where this is not so, as, for example, in planning estates and drafting wills. Here the instrument defining the terms of collaboration may affect persons not present and often not born. Yet here, too, the good lawyer does not serve merely as a legal conduit for his client's desires, but as a wise counselor, experienced in the art of devising arrangements that will put in workable order the entangled affairs and interests of human beings." *Professional Responsibility: Report of the Joint Conference,* 44 A.B.A.J. 1159, 1162 (1958).

[19] *See* ABA CANON 8.

of harsh consequences that might result from assertion of legally permissible positions. In the final analysis, however, the lawyer should always remember that the decision whether to forego legally available objectives or methods because of non-legal factors is ultimately for the client and not for himself. In the event that the client in a non-adjudicatory matter insists upon a course of conduct that is contrary to the judgment and advice of the lawyer but not prohibited by Disciplinary Rules, the lawyer may withdraw from the employment.[20]

EC 7-9. In the exercise of his professional judgment on those decisions which are for his determination in the handling of a legal matter,[21] a lawyer should always act in a manner consistent with the best interests of his client.[22] However, when an action in the best interest of his client seems to him to be unjust, he may ask his client for permission to forego such action.[23]

EC 7-10. The duty of a lawyer to represent his client with zeal does not militate against his concurrent obligation to treat with consideration all persons involved in the legal process and to avoid the infliction of needless harm.

EC 7-11. The responsibilities of a lawyer may vary according to the intelligence, experience, mental condition or age of a client, the obligation of a public officer, or the nature of a particular proceeding. Examples include the representation of an illiterate or an incompetent, service as a public prosecutor or

---

"Vital as is the lawyer's role in adjudication, it should not be thought that it is only as an advocate pleading in open court that he contributes to the administration of the law. The most effective realization of the law's aims often takes place in the attorney's office, where litigation is forestalled by anticipating its outcome, where the lawyer's quiet counsel takes the place of public force. Contrary to popular belief, the compliance with the law thus brought about is not generally lip-serving and narrow, for by reminding him of its long-run costs the lawyer often deters his client from a course of conduct technically permissible under existing law, though inconsistent with its underlying spirit and purpose." *Professional Responsibility: Report of the Joint Conference*, 44 A.B.A.J. 1159, 1161 (1958).

[20] "My summation of Judge Sharswood's view of the advocate's duty to the client is that he owes to the client the duty to use all legal means in support of the client's case. However, at the same time Judge Sharswood recognized that many advocates would find this obligation unbearable if applicable without exception. Therefore, the individual lawyer is given the choice of representing his client fully within the bounds set by the law or of *telling his client that he cannot do so,* so that the client may obtain another attorney if he wishes." Thode, *The Ethical Standard for the Advocate,* 39 TEXAS L. REV. 575, 582 (1961).
Cf. CODE OF PROFESSIONAL RESPONSIBILITY, DR 2-110 (C).
[21] *See* ABA CANON 24.
[22] Thode, *The Ethical Standard for the Advocate,* 39 TEXAS L. REV. 575, 592 (1961).
[23] *Cf. ABA Opinions* 253 (1946) and 178 (1938).

other government lawyer, and appearances before administrative and legislative bodies.

EC 7-12. Any mental or physical condition of a client that renders him incapable of making a considered judgment on his own behalf casts additional responsibilities upon his lawyer. Where an incompetent is acting through a guardian or other legal representative, a lawyer must look to such representative for those decisions which are normally the prerogative of the client to make. If a client under disability has no legal representative, his lawyer may be compelled in court proceedings to make decisions on behalf of the client. If the client is capable of understanding the matter in question or of contributing to the advancement of his interests, regardless of whether he is legally disqualified from performing certain acts, the lawyer should obtain from him all possible aid. If the disability of a client and the lack of a legal representative compel the lawyer to make decisions for his client, the lawyer should consider all circumstances then prevailing and act with care to safeguard and advance the interests of his client. But obviously a lawyer cannot perform any act or make any decision which the law requires his client to perform or make, either acting for himself if competent, or by a duly constituted representative if legally incompetent.

[C16] EC 7-13. The responsibility of a public prosecutor differs from that of the usual advocate; his duty is to seek justice, not merely to convict.[24] This special duty exists because: (1) the prosecutor represents the sovereign and therefore should use restraint in the discretionary exercise of governmental powers, such as in the selection of cases to prosecute; (2) during trial the prosecutor is not only an advocate but he also may make decisions normally made by an individual client, and those affect-

---

[24] *See* ABA CANON 5 and Berger v. United States, 295 U.S. 78, 79 L. Ed. 1314, 55 S. Ct. 629 (1935).

"The public prosecutor cannot take as a guide for the conduct of his office the standards of an attorney appearing on behalf of an individual client. The freedom elsewhere wisely granted to a partisan advocate must be severely curtailed if the prosecutor's duties are to be properly discharged. The public prosecutor must recall that he occupies a dual role, being obligated, on the one hand, to furnish that adversary element essential to the informed decision of any controversy, but being possessed, on the other, of important governmental powers that are pledged to the accomplishment of one objective only, that of impartial justice. Where the prosecutor is recreant to the truth implicit in his office, he undermines confidence, not only in his profession, but in government and the very ideal of justice itself." *Professional Responsibility: Report of the Joint Conference,* 44 A.B.A.J. 1159, 1218 (1958).

"The prosecuting attorney is the attorney for the state, and it is his primary duty not to convict but to see that justice is done." *ABA Opinion* 150 (1936).

ing the public interest should be fair to all; and (3) in our system of criminal justice the accused is to be given the benefit of all reasonable doubts. With respect to evidence and witnesses, the prosecutor has responsibilities different from those of a lawyer in private practice: the prosecutor should make timely disclosure to the defense of available evidence, known to him, that tends to negate the guilt of the accused, mitigate the degree of the offense, or reduce the punishment. Further, a prosecutor should not intentionally avoid pursuit of evidence merely because he believes it will damage the prosecutor's case or aid the accused.

[C17] EC 7-14.   A government lawyer who has discretionary power relative to litigation should refrain from instituting or continuing litigation that is obviously unfair. A government lawyer not having such discretionary power who believes there is lack of merit in a controversy submitted to him should so advise his superiors and recommend the avoidance of unfair litigation. A government lawyer in a civil action or administrative proceeding has the responsibility to seek justice and to develop a full and fair record, and he should not use his position or the economic power of the government to harass parties or to bring about unjust settlements or results.

EC 7-15.   The nature and purpose of proceedings before administrative agencies vary widely. The proceedings may be legislative or quasi-judicial, or a combination of both. They may be *ex parte* in character, in which event they may originate either at the instance of the agency or upon motion of an interested party. The scope of an inquiry may be purely investigative or it may be truly adversary looking toward the adjudication of specific rights of a party or of classes of parties. The foregoing are but examples of some of the types of proceedings conducted by administrative agencies. A lawyer appearing before an administrative agency,[25] regardless of the nature of the proceeding it is conducting, has the continuing duty to advance the cause of his client within the bounds of the law.[26] Where the applicable rules of the agency impose specific obligations upon a lawyer, it is his duty to comply therewith, unless the lawyer has a legitimate basis for challenging the validity thereof. In all appearances before

---

[25] As to appearances before a department of government, Canon 26 provides: "A lawyer openly . . . may render professional services . . . in advocacy of claims before departments of government, upon the same principles of ethics which justify his appearance before the Courts. . . ."

[26] "But as an advocate before a service which itself represents the adversary point of view, where his client's case is fairly arguable, a lawyer is under no duty to disclose its weaknesses, any more than he would be to make such a disclosure to a brother lawyer. The limitations within which he must operate are best expressed in Canon 22. . . ." *ABA Opinion* 314 (1965).

administrative agencies, a lawyer should identify himself, his client if identity of his client is not privileged,[27] and the representative nature of his appearance. It is not improper, however, for a lawyer to seek from an agency information available to the public without identifying his client.

EC 7-16. The primary business of a legislative body is to enact laws rather than to adjudicate controversies, although on occasion the activities of a legislative body may take on the characteristics of an adversary proceeding, particularly in investigative and impeachment matters. The role of a lawyer supporting or opposing proposed legislation normally is quite different from his role in representing a person under investigation or on trial by a legislative body. When a lawyer appears in connection with proposed legislation, he seeks to affect the lawmaking process, but when he appears on behalf of a client in investigatory or impeachment proceedings, he is concerned with the protection of the rights of his client. In either event, he should identify himself and his client, if identity of his client is not privileged, and should comply with applicable laws and legislative rules.[28]

EC 7-17. The obligation of loyalty to his client applies only to a lawyer in the discharge of his professional duties and implies no obligation to adopt a personal viewpoint favorable to the interests or desires of his client.[29] While a lawyer must act always with circumspection in order that his conduct will not adversely affect the rights of a client in a matter he is then handling, he may take positions on public issues and espouse legal reforms he favors without regard to the individual views of any client.

EC 7-18. The legal system in its broadest sense functions best when persons in need of legal advice or assistance are repre-

---

[27] See Baird v. Koerner, 279 F.2d 623 (9th Cir. 1960).

[28] *See* ABA CANON 26.

[29] "Law should be so practiced that the lawyer remains free to make up his own mind how he will vote, what causes he will support, what economic and political philosophy he will espouse. It is one of the glories of the profession that it admits of this freedom. Distinguished examples can be cited of lawyers whose views were at variance from those of their clients, lawyers whose skill and wisdom make them valued advisers to those who had little sympathy with their views as citizens." *Professional Responsibility: Report of the Joint Conference,* 44 A.B.A.J. 1159, 1217 (1958).

"No doubt some tax lawyers feel constrained to abstain from activities on behalf of a better tax system because they think that their clients may object. Clients have no right to object if the tax adviser handles their affairs competently and faithfully and independently of his private views as to tax policy. They buy his expert services, not his private opinions or his silence on issues that gravely affect the public interest." Paul, *The Lawyer as a Tax Adviser,* 25 ROCKY MT. L. REV. 412, 434 (1953).

sented by their own counsel. For this reason a lawyer should not communicate on the subject matter of the representation of his client with a person he knows to be represented in the matter by a lawyer, unless pursuant to law or rule of court or unless he has the consent of the lawyer for that person.[30] If one is not represented by counsel, a lawyer representing another may have to deal directly with the unrepresented person; in such an instance, a lawyer should not undertake to give advice to the person who is attempting to represent himself,[31] except that he may advise him to obtain a lawyer.

Duty of the Lawyer to the Adversary System of Justice

EC 7-19.   Our legal system provides for the adjudication of disputes governed by the rules of substantive, evidentiary, and procedural law. An adversary presentation counters the natural human tendency to judge too swiftly in terms of the familiar that which is not yet fully known;[32] the advocate, by his zealous preparation and presentation of facts and law, enables the tribunal to come to the hearing with an open and neutral mind and to render impartial judgments.[33] The duty of a lawyer to his client and his duty to the legal system are the same: to represent his client zealously within the bounds of the law.[34]

EC 7-20.   In order to function properly, our adjudicative process requires an informed, impartial tribunal capable of administering justice promptly and efficiently[35] according to procedures that command public confidence and respect.[36] Not only

---

[30] *See* ABA CANON 9.

[31] *Id.*

[32] *See Professional Responsibility: Report of the Joint Conference,* 44 A.B.A.J. 1159, 1160 (1958).

[33] "Without the participation of someone who can act responsibly for each of the parties, this essential narrowing of the issues [by exchange of written pleadings or stipulations of counsel] becomes impossible. But here again the true significance of partisan advocacy lies deeper, touching once more the integrity of the adjudicative process itself. It is only through the advocate's participation that the hearing may remain in fact what it purports to be in theory: a public trial of the facts and issues. Each advocate comes to the hearing prepared to present his proofs and arguments, knowing at the same time that his arguments may fail to persuade and that his proof may be rejected as inadequate. . . . The deciding tribunal, on the other hand, comes to the hearing uncommitted. It has not represented to the public that any fact can be proved, that any argument is sound, or that any particular way of stating a litigant's case is the most effective expression of its merits." *Professional Responsibility: Report of the Joint Conference,* 44 A.B.A.J. 1159, 1160-61 (1958).

[34] *Cf.* ABA CANONS 15 and 32.

[35] *Cf.* ABA CANON 21.

[36] See *Professional Responsibility: Report of the Joint Conference,* 44 A.B.A.J. 1159, 1216 (1958).

must there be competent, adverse presentation of evidence and issues, but a tribunal must be aided by rules appropriate to an effective and dignified process. The procedures under which tribunals operate in our adversary system have been prescribed largely by legislative enactments, court rules and decisions, and administrative rules. Through the years certain concepts of proper professional conduct have become rules of law applicable to the adversary adjudicative process. Many of these concepts are the bases for standards of professional conduct set forth in the Disciplinary Rules.

EC 7-21. The civil adjudicative process is primarily designed for the settlement of disputes between parties, while the criminal process is designed for the protection of society as a whole. Threatening to use, or using, the criminal process to coerce adjustment of private civil claims or controversies is a subversion of that process;[37] further, the person against whom the criminal process is so misused may be deterred from asserting his legal rights and thus the usefulness of the civil process in settling private disputes is impaired. As in all cases of abuse of judicial process, the improper use of criminal process tends to diminish public confidence in our legal system.

EC 7-22. Respect for judicial rulings is essential to the proper administration of justice; however, a litigant or his lawyer may, in good faith and within the framework of the law, take steps to test the correctness of a ruling of a tribunal.[38]

EC 7-23. The complexity of law often makes it difficult for a tribunal to be fully informed unless the pertinent law is presented by the lawyers in the cause. A tribunal that is fully informed on the applicable law is better able to make a fair and accurate determination of the matter before it. The adversary system contemplates that each lawyer will present and argue the

---

[37] "We are of the opinion that the letter in question was improper, and that in writing and sending it respondent was guilty of unprofessional conduct. This court has heretofore expressed its disapproval of using threats of criminal prosecution as a means of forcing settlement of civil claims. . . .

"Respondent has been guilty of a violation of a principle which condemns any confusion of threats of criminal prosecution with the enforcement of civil claims. For this misconduct he should be severely censured." Matter of Gelman, 230 App. Div. 524, 527, N.Y.S. 416, 419 (1930).

[38] "An attorney has the duty to protect the interests of his client. He has a right to press legitimate argument and to protest an erroneous ruling." Gallagher v. Municipal Court, 31 Cal. 2d 784, 796, 192 P.2d 905, 913 (1948).

"There must be protection, however, in the far more frequent case of the attorney who stands on his rights and combats the order in good faith and without disrespect believing with good cause that it is void, for it is here that the independence of the bar becomes valuable." Note, 39 COLUM. L. REV. 433, 438 (1939).

existing law in the light most favorable to his client.[39] Where a lawyer knows of legal authority in the controlling jurisdiction directly adverse to the position of his client, he should inform the tribunal of its existence unless his adversary has done so; but, having made such disclosure, he may challenge its soundness in whole or in part.[40]

EC 7-24. In order to bring about just and informed decisions, evidentiary and procedural rules have been established by tribunals to permit the inclusion of relevant evidence and argument and the exclusion of all other considerations. The expression by a lawyer of his personal opinion as to the justness of a cause, as to the credibility of a witness, as to the culpability of a civil litigant, or as to the guilt or innocence of an accused is not a proper subject for argument to the trier of fact.[41] It is improper as to factual matters because admissible evidence possessed by a lawyer should be presented only as sworn testimony. It is improper as to all other matters because, were the rule otherwise, the silence of a lawyer on a given occasion could be construed unfavorably to his client. However, a lawyer may argue, on his analysis of the evidence, for any position or conclusion with respect to any of the foregoing matters.

EC 7-25. Rules of evidence and procedure are designed to lead to just decisions and are part of the framework of the law. Thus while a lawyer may take steps in good faith and within the framework of the law to test the validity of rules, he is not justified in consciously violating such rules and he should be diligent in his efforts to guard against his unintentional violation of them.[42] As examples, a lawyer should subscribe to or verify only those pleadings that he believes are in compliance with applicable law and rules; a lawyer should not make any prefatory

---

[39] "Too many do not understand that accomplishment of the layman's abstract ideas of justice is the function of the judge and jury, and that it is the lawyer's sworn duty to portray his client's case in its most favorable light." Rochelle and Payne, *The Struggle for Public Understanding,* 25 TEXAS B.J. 109, 159 (1962).

[40] "We are of the opinion that this Canon requires the lawyer to disclose such decisions [that are adverse to his clients contentions] to the court. He may, of course, after doing so, challenge the soundness of the decisions or present reasons which he believes would warrant the court in not following them in the pending case." *ABA Opinion* 146 (1935).

Cf. ABA Opinion 280 (1949) and Thode, *The Ethical Standard for the Advocate,* 39 TEXAS L. REV. 575, 585-86 (1961).

[41] *See* ABA CANON 15.

"The traditional duty of an advocate is that he honorably uphold the contentions of his client. He should not voluntarily undermine them." Harders v. State of California, 373 F.2d 839, 842 (9th Cir. 1967).

[42] *See* ABA CANON 22.

statement before a tribunal in regard to the purported facts of the case on trial unless he believes that his statement will be supported by admissible evidence; a lawyer should not ask a witness a question solely for the purpose of harassing or embarrassing him; and a lawyer should not by subterfuge put before a jury matters which it cannot properly consider.

EC 7-26. The law and Disciplinary Rules prohibit the use of fraudulent, false, or perjured testimony or evidence.[43] A lawyer who knowingly[44] participates in introduction of such testimony or evidence is subject to discipline. A lawyer should, however, present any admissible evidence his client desires to have presented unless he knows, or from facts within his knowledge should know, that such testimony or evidence is false, fraudulent, or perjured.[45]

EC 7-27. Because it interferes with the proper administration of justice, a lawyer should not suppress evidence that he or his client has a legal obligation to reveal or produce. In like manner, a lawyer should not advise or cause a person to secrete himself or to leave the jurisdiction of a tribunal for the purpose of making him unavailable as a witness therein.[46]

EC 7-28. Witnesses should always testify truthfully[47] and should be free from any financial inducements that might tempt them to do otherwise.[48] A lawyer should not pay or agree to pay a non-expert witness an amount in excess of reimbursement for expenses and financial loss incident to his being a witness; how-

---

[43] Id.; *cf.* ABA CANON 41.

[44] *See generally ABA Opinion* 287 (1953) as to a lawyer's duty when he unknowingly participates in introducing perjured testimony.

[45] "Under any standard of proper ethical conduct an attorney should not sit by silently and permit his client to commit what may have been perjury, and which certainly would mislead the court and the opposing party on a matter vital to the issue under consideration. . . .

. . . .

"Respondent next urges that it was his duty to observe the utmost good faith toward his client, and therefore he could not divulge any confidential information. This duty to the client of course does not extend to the point of authorizing collaboration with him in the commission of fraud." In re Carroll, 244 S.W.2d 474, 474-75 (Ky. 1951).

[46] *See* ABA CANON 5; *cf. ABA Opinion* 131 (1935).

[47] *Cf.* ABA CANON 39.

[48] "The prevalence of perjury is a serious menace to the administration of justice, to prevent which no means have as yet been satisfactorily devised. But there certainly can be no greater incentive to perjury than to allow a party to make payments to its opponents witnesses under any guise or on any excuse, and at least attorneys who are officers of the court to aid it in the administration of justice, must keep themselves clear of any connection which in the slightest degree tends to induce witnesses to testify in favor of their clients." In re Robinson, 151 App. Div. 589, 600, 136 N.Y.S. 548, 556-57 (1912), *aff'd,* 209 N.Y. 354, 103 N.E. 160 (1913).

ever, a lawyer may pay or agree to pay an expert witness a reasonable fee for his services as an expert. But in no event should a lawyer pay or agree to pay a contingent fee to any witness. A lawyer should exercise reasonable diligence to see that his client and lay associates conform to these standards.[49]

EC 7-29. To safeguard the impartiality that is essential to the judicial process, veniremen and jurors should be protected against extraneous influences.[50] When impartiality is present, public confidence in the judicial system is enhanced. There should be no extrajudicial communication with veniremen prior to trial or with jurors during trial by or on behalf of a lawyer connected with the case. Furthermore, a lawyer who is not connected with the case should not communicate with or cause another to communicate with a venireman or a juror about the case. After the trial, communication by a lawyer with jurors is permitted so long as he refrains from asking questions or making comments that tend to harass or embarrass the juror[51] or to influence actions of the juror in future cases. Were a lawyer to be prohibited from communicating after trial with a juror, he could not ascertain if the verdict might be subject to legal challenge, in which event the invalidity of a verdict might go undetected.[52] When an extrajudicial communication by a lawyer with a juror is permitted by law, it should be made considerately and with deference to the personal feelings of the juror.

---

[49] "It will not do for an attorney who seeks to justify himself against charges of this kind to show that he has escaped criminal responsibility under the Penal Law, nor can he blindly shut his eyes to a system which tends to suborn witnesses, to produce perjured testimony, and to suppress the truth. He has an active affirmative duty to protect the administration of justice from perjury and fraud, and that duty is not performed by allowing his subordinates and assistants to attempt to subvert justice and procure results for his clients based upon false testimony and perjured witnesses." *Id.,* 151 App. Div. at 592, 136 N.Y.S. at 551.

[50] *See* ABA CANON 23.

[51] "[I]t is unfair to jurors to permit a disappointed litigant to pick over their private associations in search of something to discredit them and their verdict. And it would be unfair to the public too if jurors should understand that they cannot convict a man of means without risking an inquiry of that kind by paid investigators, with, to boot, the distortions an inquiry of that kind can produce." State v. LaFera, 42 N.J. 97, 107, 199 A.2d 630, 636 (1964).

[52] *ABA Opinion* 319 (1968) points out that "[m]any courts today, and the trend is in this direction, allow the testimony of jurors as to all irregularities in and out of the courtroom except those irregularities whose existence can be determined only by exploring the consciousness of a single particular juror, New Jersey v. Kociolek, 20 N.J. 92, 118 A.2d 812 (1955). Model Code of Evidence Rule 301. Certainly as to states in which the testimony and affidavits of jurors may be received in support of or against a motion for new trial, a lawyer, in his obligation to protect his client, must have the tools for ascertaining whether or not grounds for a new trial exist and it is not unethical for him to talk to and question jurors."

EC 7-30. Vexatious or harassing investigations of veniremen or jurors seriously impair the effectiveness of our jury system. For this reason, a lawyer or anyone on his behalf who conducts an investigation of veniremen or jurors should act with circumspection and restraint.

EC 7-31. Communications with or investigations of members of families of veniremen or jurors by a lawyer or by anyone on his behalf are subject to the restrictions imposed upon the lawyer with respect to his communications with or investigations of veniremen and jurors.

EC 7-32. Because of his duty to aid in preserving the integrity of the jury system, a lawyer who learns of improper conduct by or towards a venireman, a juror, or a member of the family of either should make a prompt report to the court regarding such conduct.

EC 7-33. A goal of our legal system is that each party shall have his case, criminal or civil, adjudicated by an impartial tribunal. The attainment of this goal may be defeated by dissemination of news or comments which tend to influence judge or jury.[53] Such news or comments may prevent prospective jurors

---

[53] *Generally see* ABA Advisory Committee on Fair Trial and Free Press, Standards Relating to Fair Trial and Free Press (1966).

"[T]he trial court might well have proscribed extrajudicial statements by any lawyer, party, witness, or court official which divulged prejudicial matters. . . . See State v. Van Dwyne, 43 N.J. 369, 389, 204 A.2d 841, 852 (1964), in which the court interpreted Canon 20 of the American Bar Association's Canons of Professional Ethics to prohibit such statements. Being advised of the great public interest in the case, the mass coverage of the press, and the potential prejudicial impact of publicity, the court could also have requested the appropriate city and county officials to promulgate a regulation with respect to dissemination of information about the case by their employees. In addition, reporters who wrote or broadcast prejudicial stories, could have been warned as to the impropriety of publishing material not introduced in the proceedings. . . . In this manner, Sheppard's right to a trial free from outside interference would have been given added protection without corresponding curtailment of the news media. Had the judge, the other officers of the court, and the police placed the interest of justice first, the news media would have soon learned to be content with the task of reporting the case as it unfolded in the courtroom—not pieced together from extrajudicial statements." Sheppard v. Maxwell, 384 U.S. 333, 361-62, 16 L. Ed. 2d 600, 619-20, 86 S. Ct. 1507, 1521-22 (1966).

"Court proceedings are held for the solemn purpose of endeavoring to ascertain the truth which is the *sine qua non* of a fair trial. Over the centuries Anglo-American courts have devised careful safeguards by rule and otherwise to protect and facilitate the performance of this high function. As a result, at this time those safeguards do not permit the televising and photographing of a criminal trial, save in two States and there only under restrictions. The federal courts prohibit it by specific rule. This is weighty evidence that our concepts of a fair trial do not tolerate such an indulgence. We have always held that the atmosphere essential to the preservation of a

from being impartial at the outset of the trial[54] and may also
interfere with the obligation of jurors to base their verdict solely
upon the evidence admitted in the trial.[55] The release by a
lawyer of out-of-court statements regarding an anticipated or

---

fair trial—the most fundamental of all freedoms—must be maintained at all
costs." Estes v. State of Texas, 381 U.S. 532, 540, 14 L. Ed. 2d 543, 549, 85
S. Ct. 1628, 1631-32 (1965), *rehearing denied,* 382 U.S. 875, 15 L. Ed. 2d 118,
86 S. Ct. 18 (1965).

[54] "Pretrial can create a major problem for the defendant in a criminal
case. Indeed, it may be more harmful than publicity during the trial for it
may well set the community opinion as to guilt or innocence. . . . The trial
witnesses present at the hearing, as well as the original jury panel, were
undoubtedly made aware of the peculiar public importance of the case by
the press and television coverage being provided, and by the fact that they
themselves were televised live and their pictures rebroadcast on the evening
show." *Id.,* 381 U.S. at 536-37, 14 L. Ed. 2d at 546-47, 85 S. Ct. at 1629-30.

[55] "The undeviating rule of this Court was expressed by Mr. Justice
Holmes over half a century ago in Patterson v. Colorado, 205 U.S. 454, 462
(1907):
The theory of our system is that the conclusions to be reached in a case
will be induced only by evidence and argument in open court, and not by
any outside influence, whether of private talk or public print." Sheppard v.
Maxwell, 384 U.S. 333, 351, 16 L. Ed. 2d 600, 614, 86 S. Ct. 1507, 1516 (1966).
"The trial judge has a large discretion in ruling on the issue of prejudice
resulting from the reading by jurors of news articles concerning the trial.
. . . Generalizations beyond that statement are not profitable, because each
case must turn on its special facts. We have here the exposure of jurors to
information of a character which the trial judge ruled was so prejudicial it
could not be directly offered as evidence. The prejudice to the defendant is
almost certain to be as great when that evidence reaches the jury through
news accounts as when it is a part of the prosecution's evidence. . . . It may
indeed be greater for it is then not tempered by protective procedures."
Marshall v. United States, 360 U.S. 310, 312-13, 3 L. Ed. 2d 1250, 1252, 79
S. Ct. 1171, 1173 (1959).
"The experienced trial lawyer knows that an adverse public opinion is
a tremendous disadvantage to the defense of his client. Although grand jurors
conduct their deliberations in secret, they are selected from the body of the
public. They are likely to know what the general public knows and to reflect
the public attitude. Trials are open to the public, and aroused public opinion
respecting the merits of a legal controversy creates a court room atmosphere
which, without any vocal expression in the presence of the petit jury, makes
itself felt and has its effect upon the action of the petit jury. Our fundamental concepts of justice and our American sense of fair play require that
the petit jury shall be composed of persons with fair and impartial minds
and without preconceived views as to the merits of the controversy, and that
it shall determine the issues presented to it solely upon the evidence adduced
at the trial and according to the law given in the instructions of the trial
judge.
"While we may doubt that the effect of public opinion would sway or
bias the judgment of the trial judge in an equity proceeding, the defendant
should not be called upon to run that risk and the trial court should not
have his work made more difficult by any dissemination of statements to
the public that would be calculated to create a public demand for a particular judgment in a prospective or pending case." *ABA Opinion* 199 (1940).
Cf. Estes v. State of Texas, 381 U.S. 532, 544-45, 144 L. Ed. 2d 543, 551,
85 S. Ct. 1628, 1634 (1965), *rehearing denied,* 381 U.S. 875, 15 L. Ed. 2d 118,
86 S. Ct. 18 (1965).

pending trial may improperly affect the impartiality of the tribunal.[56] For these reasons, standards for permissible and prohibited conduct of a lawyer with respect to trial publicity have been established.

[C18] EC 7-34. The impartiality of a public servant in our legal system may be impaired by the receipt of gifts or loans. A lawyer,[57] therefore, is never justified in making a gift or a loan to a judge, a hearing officer, or an official or employee of a tribunal.[58]

EC 7-35. All litigants and lawyers should have access to tribunals on an equal basis. Generally, in adversary proceedings a lawyer should not communicate with a judge relative to a matter pending before, or which is to be brought before, a tribunal over which he presides in circumstances which might have the effect or give the appearance of granting undue advantage to one party.[59] For example, a lawyer should not communicate with a tribunal by a writing unless a copy thereof is promptly delivered to opposing counsel or to the adverse party if he is not represented by a lawyer. Ordinarily an oral communication by a lawyer with a judge or hearing officer should be made only upon adequate notice to opposing counsel, or, if there is none, to the opposing party. A lawyer should not condone or lend himself to private importunities by another with a judge or hearing officer on behalf of himself or his client.

EC 7-36. Judicial hearings ought to be conducted through dignified and orderly procedures designed to protect the rights of all parties. Although a lawyer has the duty to represent his client zealously, he should not engage in any conduct that offends the dignity and decorum of proceedings.[60] While maintaining

---

[56] *See* ABA CANON 20.

[57] Canon 3 observes that a lawyer "deserves rebuke and denunciation for any device or attempt to gain from a judge special personal consideration or favor."

See ABA CANON 32.

[58] *"Judicial Canon 32* provides:

A judge should not accept any presents or favors from litigants, or from lawyers practicing before him or from others whose interests are likely to be submitted to him for judgment.

The language of this Canon is perhaps broad enough to prohibit campaign contributions by lawyers, practicing before the court upon which the candidate hopes to sit. However, we do not think it was intended to prohibit such contributions when the candidate is obligated, by force of circumstances over which he has no control, to conduct a campaign, the expense of which exceeds that which he should reasonably be expected to personally bear!" *ABA Opinion* 226 (1941).

[59] *See* ABA CANONS 3 and 32.

[60] *Cf.* ABA CANON 18.

his independence, a lawyer should be respectful, courteous, and above-board in his relations with a judge or hearing officer before whom he appears.[61] He should avoid undue solicitude for the comfort or convenience of judge or jury and should avoid any other conduct calculated to gain special consideration.

EC 7-37.   In adversary proceedings, clients are litigants and though ill feeling may exist between clients, such ill feeling should not influence a lawyer in his conduct, attitude, and demeanor towards opposing lawyers.[62] A lawyer should not make unfair or derogatory personal reference to opposing counsel. Haranguing and offensive tactics by lawyers interfere with the orderly administration of justice and have no proper place in our legal system.

EC 7-38.   A lawyer should be courteous to opposing counsel and should accede to reasonable requests regarding court proceedings, settings, continuances, waiver of procedural formalities, and similar matters which do not prejudice the rights of his client.[63] He should follow local customs of courtesy or practice, unless he gives timely notice to opposing counsel of his intention not to do so.[64] A lawyer should be punctual in fulfilling all professional commitments.[65]

EC 7-39.   In the final analysis, proper functioning of the adversary system depends upon cooperation between lawyers and tribunals in utilizing procedures which will preserve the impartiality of tribunals and make their decisional processes prompt and just, without impinging upon the obligation of lawyers to represent their clients zealously within the framework of the law.

Disciplinary Rules

DR 7-101.   Representing a Client Zealously.

(A)   A lawyer shall not intentionally:[66]

(1)   Fail to seek the lawful objectives of his client through reasonably available means[67] permitted by law and the Disciplinary Rules, except as provided by DR 7-101(B). A lawyer does not violate this Disciplinary Rule, however, by acceding to reasonable requests of opposing counsel which do not prejudice

---

[61] *See* ABA CANONS 1 and 3.
[62] *See* ABA CANON 17.
[63] *See* ABA CANON 24.
[64] *See* ABA CANON 25.
[65] *See* ABA CANON 21.
[66] *See* ABA CANON 15.
[67] *See* ABA CANONS 5 and 15; *cf.* ABA CANONS 4 and 32.

the rights of his client, by being punctual in fulfilling all professional commitments, by avoiding offensive tactics, or by treating with courtesy and consideration all persons involved in the legal process.

(2) Fail to carry out a contract of employment entered into with a client for professional services, but he may withdraw as permitted under DR 2-110, DR 5-102, and DR 5-105.

(3) Prejudice or damage his client during the course of the professional relationship,[68] except as required under DR 7-102(B).

(B) In his representation of a client, a lawyer may:

(1) Where permissible, exercise his professional judgment to waive or fail to assert a right or position of his client.

(2) Refuse to aid or participate in conduct that he believes to be unlawful, even though there is some support for an argument that the conduct is legal.

DR 7-102. Representing a Client Within the Bounds of the Law.

(A) In his representation of a client, a lawyer shall not:

(1) File a suit, assert a position, conduct a defense, delay a trial, or take other action on behalf of his client when he knows or when it is obvious that such action would serve merely to harass or maliciously injure another.[69]

(2) Knowingly advance a claim or defense that is unwarranted under existing law, except that he may advance such claim or defense if it can be supported by good faith argument for an extension, modification, or reversal of existing law.

(3) Conceal or knowingly fail to disclose that which he is required by law to reveal.

(4) Knowingly use perjured testimony or false evidence.[70]

(5) Knowingly make a false statement of law or fact.

(6) Participate in the creation or preservation of evidence when he knows or it is obvious that the evidence is false.

(7) Counsel or assist his client in conduct that the lawyer knows to be illegal or fraudulent.

(8) Knowingly engage in other illegal conduct or conduct contrary to a Disciplinary Rule.

(B) A lawyer who receives information clearly establishing that:

---

[68] *Cf.* ABA Canon 24.
[69] *See* ABA Canon 30.
[70] *Cf.* ABA Canons 22 and 29.

[C19] (1)   His client has, in the course of the representation, perpetrated a fraud upon a person or tribunal shall promptly call upon his client to rectify the same, and if his client refuses or is unable to do so, he shall reveal the fraud to the affected person or tribunal.[71]

(2)   A person other than his client has perpetrated a fraud upon a tribunal shall promptly reveal the fraud to the tribunal.[72]

[C20] DR 7-103.   Performing the Duty of Public Prosecutor or Other Government Lawyer.[73]

(A)   A public prosecutor or other government lawyer shall not institute or cause to be instituted criminal charges when he knows or it is obvious that the charges are not supported by probable cause.

(B)   A public prosecutor or other government lawyer in criminal litigation shall make timely disclosure to counsel for the defendant, or to the defendant if he has no counsel, of the existence of evidence, known to the prosecutor or other government lawyer, that tends to negate the guilt of the accused, mitigate the degree of the offense, or reduce the punishment.

DR 7-104.   Communicating With One of Adverse Interest.[74]

(A) During the course of his representation of a client a lawyer shall not:

(1)   Communicate or cause another to communicate on the subject of the representation with a party he knows to be represented by a lawyer in that matter unless he has the prior consent of the lawyer representing such other party[75] or is authorized by law to do so.

---

[71] *See* ABA Canon 41; *cf.* Hinds v. State Bar, 19 Cal. 2d 87, 92-93, 119 P.2d 134, 137 (1941); *but see ABA Opinion* 287 (1953) and Texas Canon 38. *Also see* Code of Professional Responsibility, DR 4-101(C)(2).

[72] *See* Precision Inst. Mfg. Co. v. Automotive M.M. Co., 324 U.S. 806, 89 L. Ed. 1381, 65 S. Ct. 993 (1945).

[73] *Cf.* ABA Canon 5.

[74] *"Rule 12. . . .* A member of the State Bar shall not communicate with a party represented by counsel upon a subject of controversy, in the absence and without the consent of such counsel. This rule shall not apply to communications with a public officer, board, committee or body." Cal. Business and Professions Code § 6076 (West 1962).

[75] *See* ABA Canon 9; *cf. ABA Opinions* 124 (1934), 108 (1934), 95 (1933), and 75 (1932); *also see* In re Schwabe, 242 Or. 169, 174-75, 408 P.2d 922, 924 (1965).

"It is clear from the earlier opinions of this committee that *Canon 9* is to be construed literally and does not allow a communication with an opposing party, without the consent of his counsel, though the purpose merely be to investigate the facts. *Opinions 117, 95, 66." ABA Opinion* 187 (1938).

(2)   Give advice to a person who is not represented by a lawyer, other than the advice to secure counsel,[76] if the interests of such person are or have a reasonable possibility of being in conflict with the interests of his client.[77]

DR 7-105.   Threatening Criminal Prosecution.

(A)   A lawyer shall not present, participate in presenting, or threaten to present criminal charges solely to obtain an advantage in a civil matter.

DR 7-106.   Trial Conduct.

(A)   A lawyer shall not disregard or advise his client to disregard a standing rule of a tribunal or a ruling of a tribunal made in the course of a proceeding, but he may take appropriate steps in good faith to test the validity of such rule or ruling.

(B)   In presenting a matter to a tribunal, a lawyer shall disclose:[78]

(1)   Legal authority in the controlling jurisdiction known to him to be directly adverse to the position of his client and which is not disclosed by opposing counsel.[79]

(2)   Unless privileged or irrelevant, the identities of the clients he represents and of the persons who employed him.[80]

---

[76] Cf. ABA Opinion 102 (1933).

[77] Cf. ABA Canon 9 and ABA Opinion 58 (1931).

[78] Cf. Note, 38 Texas L. Rev. 107, 108-09 (1959).

[79] "In the brief summary in the 1947 edition of the Committee's decisions (p. 17), Opinion 146 was thus summarized: Opinion 146—A lawyer should disclose to the court a decision directly adverse to his client's case that is unknown to his adversary.

. . . .

"We would not confine the Opinion to 'controlling authorities'—i.e., those decisive of the pending case—but, in accordance with the tests hereafter suggested, would apply it to a decision directly adverse to any proposition of law on which the lawyer expressly relies, which would reasonably be considered important by the judge sitting on the case.

. . . .

". . . The test in every case should be: Is the decision which opposing counsel has overlooked one which the court should clearly consider in deciding the case? Would a reasonable judge properly feel that a lawyer who advanced, as the law, a proposition adverse to the undisclosed decision, was lacking in candor and fairness to him? Might the judge consider himself misled by an implied representation that the lawyer knew of no adverse authority?" ABA Opinion 280 (1949).

[80] "The authorities are substantially uniform against any privilege as applied to the fact of retainer or identity of the client. The privilege is limited to confidential communications, and a retainer is not a confidential communication, although it cannot come into existence without some communication between the attorney and the—at that stage prospective—client." United States v. Pape, 144 F.2d 778, 782 (2d Cir. 1944), cert. denied, 323 U.S. 752, 89 L. Ed. 2d 602, 65 S. Ct. 86 (1944).

"To be sure, there may be circumstances under which the identification of a client may amount to the prejudicial disclosure of a confidential com-

(C)   In appearing in his professional capacity before a tribunal, a lawyer shall not:

(1)   State or allude to any matter that he has no reasonable basis to believe is relevant to the case or that will not be supported by admissible evidence.[81]

(2)   Ask any question that he has no reasonable basis to believe is relevant to the case and that is intended to degrade a witness or other person.[82]

(3)   Assert his personal knowledge of the facts in issue, except when testifying as a witness.

(4)   Assert his personal opinion as to the justness of a cause, as to the credibility of a witness, as to the culpability of a civil litigant, or as to the guilt or innocence of an accused;[83] but he may argue, on his analysis of the evidence, for any position or conclusion with respect to the matters stated herein.

(5)   Fail to comply with known local customs of courtesy or practice of the bar or a particular tribunal without giving to opposing counsel timely notice of his intent not to comply.[84]

---

munication, as where the substance of a disclosure has already been revealed but not its source." Colton v. United States, 306 F.2d 633, 637 (2d Cir. 1962).

[81] See ABA Canon 22; cf. ABA Canon 17.

"The rule allowing counsel when addressing the jury the widest latitude in discussing the evidence and presenting the client's theories falls far short of authorizing the statement by counsel of matter not in evidence, or indulging in argument founded on no proof, or demanding verdicts for purposes other than the just settlement of the matters at issue between the litigants, or appealing to prejudice or passion. The rule confining counsel to legitimate argument is not based on etiquette, but on justice. Its violation is not merely an overstepping of the bounds of propriety, but a violation of a party's rights. The jurors must determine the issues upon the evidence. Counsel's address should help them do this, not tend to lead them astray." Cherry Creek Nat. Bank v. Fidelity & Cas. Co., 207 App. Div. 787, 790-91, 202 N.Y.S. 611, 614 (1924).

[82] Cf. ABA Canon 18.

"§ 6068. . . . It is the duty of an attorney:

. . . .

" (f) To abstain from all offensive personality, and to advance no fact prejudicial to the honor or reputation of a party or witness, unless required by the justice of the cause with which he is charged." Cal. Business and Professions Code § 6068 (West 1962).

[83] "The record in the case at bar was silent concerning the qualities and character of the deceased. It is especially improper, in addressing the jury in a murder case, for the prosecuting attorney to make reference to his knowledge of the good qualities of the deceased where there is no evidence in the record bearing upon his character. . . . A prosecutor should never inject into his argument evidence not introduced at the trial." People v. Dukes, 12 Ill. 2d 334, 341, 146 N.E.2d 14, 17-18 (1957).

[84] "A lawyer should not ignore known customs or practice of the Bar or of a particular Court, even when the law permits, without giving timely notice to the opposing counsel." ABA Canon 25.

(6)   Engage in undignified or discourteous conduct which is degrading to a tribunal.

(7)   Intentionally or habitually violate any established rule of procedure or of evidence.

[C21]   DR 7-107.   Trial Publicity.[85]

(A)   A lawyer participating in or associated with the investigation of a criminal matter shall not make or participate in making an extrajudicial statement that a reasonable person would expect to be disseminated by means of public communication and that does more than state without elaboration:

(1)   Information contained in a public record.

(2)   That the investigation is in progress.

(3)   The general scope of the investigation including a description of the offense and, if permitted by law, the identity of the victim.

(4)   A request for assistance in apprehending a suspect or assistance in other matters and the information necessary thereto.

(5)   A warning to the public of any dangers.

(B)   A lawyer or law firm associated with the prosecution or defense of a criminal matter shall not, from the time of the filing

---

[85] The provisions of Sections (A), (B), (C), and (D) of this Disciplinary Rule incorporate the fair trial-free press standards which apply to lawyers as adopted by the ABA House of Delegates, Feb. 19, 1968, upon the recommendation of the Fair Trial and Free Press Advisory Committee of the ABA Special Committee on Minimum Standards for the Administration of Criminal Justice.

Cf. ABA CANON 20; *see generally* ABA ADVISORY COMMITTEE ON FAIR TRIAL AND FREE PRESS. STANDARDS RELATING TO FAIR TRIAL AND FREE PRESS (1966).

"From the cases coming here we note that unfair and prejudicial news comment on pending trials has become increasingly prevalent. Due process requires that the accused receive a trial by an impartial jury free from outside influences. Given the pervasiveness of modern communications and the difficulty of effacing prejudicial publicity from the minds of the jurors, the trial courts must take strong measures to ensure that the balance is never weighed against the accused. And appellate tribunals have the duty to make an independent evaluation of the circumstances. Of course, there is nothing that prescribes the press from reporting events that transpire in the courtroom. But where there is a reasonable likelihood that prejudicial news prior to trial will prevent a fair trial, the judge should continue the case until the threat abates, or transfer it to another county not so permeated with publicity. . . . The courts must take such steps by rule and regulation that will protect their processes from prejudicial outside interferences. Neither prosecutors, counsel for defense, the accused, witnesses, court staff nor enforcement officers coming under the jurisdiction of the court should be permitted to frustrate its function. Collaboration between counsel and the press as to information affecting the fairness of a criminal trial is not only subject to regulation, but is highly censurable and worthy of disciplinary measures." Sheppard v. Maxwell, 834 U.S. 333, 362-63, 16 L. Ed. 2d 600, 620, 86 S. Ct. 1507, 1522 (1966).

of a complaint, information, or indictment, the issuance of an arrest warrant, or arrest until the commencement of the trial or disposition without trial, make or participate in making an extra-judicial statement that a reasonable person would expect to be disseminated by means of public communication and that relates to:

(1) The character, reputation, or prior criminal record (including arrests, indictments, or other charges of crime) of the accused.

(2) The possibility of a plea of guilty to the offense charged or to a lesser offense.

(3) The existence or contents of any confession, admission, or statement given by the accused or his refusal or failure to make a statement.

(4) The performance or results of any examinations or tests or the refusal or failure of the accused to submit to examinations or tests.

(5) The identity, testimony, or credibility of a prospective witness.

(6) Any opinion as to the guilt or innocence of the accused, the evidence, or the merits of the case.

(C) DR 7-107(B) does not preclude a lawyer during such period from announcing:

(1) The name, age, residence, occupation, and family status of the accused.

(2) If the accused has not been apprehended, any information necessary to aid in his apprehension or to warn the public of any dangers he may present.

(3) A request for assistance in obtaining evidence.

(4) The identity of the victim of the crime.

(5) The fact, time, and place of arrest, resistance, pursuit, and use of weapons.

(6) The identity of investigating and arresting officers or agencies and the length of the investigation.

(7) At the time of seizure, a description of the physical evidence seized, other than a confession, admission, or statement.

(8) The nature, substance, or text of the charge.

(9) Quotations from or references to public records of the court in the case.

(10) The scheduling or result of any step in the judicial proceedings.

(11) That the accused denies the charges made against him.

(D)   During the selection of a jury or the trial of a criminal matter, a lawyer or law firm associated with the prosecution or defense of a criminal matter shall not make or participate in making an extrajudicial statement that a reasonable person would expect to be disseminated by means of public communication and that relates to the trial, parties, or issues in the trial or other matters that are reasonably likely to interfere with a fair trial, except that he may quote from or refer without comment to public records of the court in the case.

(E)   After the completion of a trial or disposition without trial of a criminal matter and prior to the imposition of sentence, a lawyer or law firm associated with the prosecution or defense shall not make or participate in making an extrajudicial statement that a reasonable person would expect to be disseminated by public communication and that is reasonably likely to affect the imposition of sentence.

(F)   The foregoing provisions of DR 7-107 also apply to professional disciplinary proceedings and juvenile disciplinary proceedings when pertinent and consistent with other law applicable to such proceedings.

(G)   A lawyer or law firm associated with a civil action shall not during its investigation or litigation make or participate in making an extrajudicial statement, other than a quotation from or reference to public records, that a reasonable person would expect to be disseminated by means of public communication and that relates to:

(1)   Evidence regarding the occurrence or transaction involved.

(2)   The character, credibility, or criminal record of a party, witness, or prospective witness.

(3)   The performance or results of any examinations or tests or the refusal or failure of a party to submit to such.

(4)   His opinion as to the merits of the claims or defenses of a party, except as required by law or administrative rule.

(5)   Any other matter reasonably likely to interfere with a fair trial of the action.

(H)   During the pendency of an administrative proceeding, a lawyer or law firm associated therewith shall not make or participate in making a statement, other than a quotation from or reference to public records, that a reasonable person would expect to be disseminated by means of public communication if it is made outside the official course of the proceeding and relates to:

(1)   Evidence regarding the occurrence or transaction involved.

(2)   The character, credibility, or criminal record of a party, witness, or prospective witness.

(3)   Physical evidence or the performance or results of any examinations or tests or the refusal or failure of a party to submit to such.

(4)   His opinion as to the merits of the claims, defenses, or positions of an interested person.

(5)   Any other matter reasonably likely to interfere with a fair hearing.

(I)   The foregoing provisions of DR 7-107 do not preclude a lawyer from replying to charges of misconduct publicly made against him or from participating in the proceedings of legislative, administrative, or other investigative bodies.

(J)   A lawyer shall exercise reasonable care to prevent his employees and associates from making an extrajudicial statement that he would be prohibited from making under DR 7-107.

DR 7-108.   Communication with or Investigation of Jurors.

(A)   Before the trial of a case a lawyer connected therewith shall not communicate with or cause another to communicate with anyone he knows to be a member of the venire from which the jury will be selected for the trial of the case.

(B)   During the trial of a case:

(1)   A lawyer connected therewith shall not communicate with or cause another to communicate with any member of the jury.[86]

(2)   A lawyer who is not connected therewith shall not communicate with or cause another to communicate with a juror concerning the case.

(C)   DR 7-108(A) and (B) do not prohibit a lawyer from communicating with veniremen or jurors in the course of official proceedings.

(D)   After discharge of the jury from further consideration of a case with which the lawyer was connected, the lawyer shall not ask questions of or make comments to a member of that jury that are calculated merely to harass or embarrass the juror or to influence his actions in future jury service.[87]

(E)   A lawyer shall not conduct or cause, by financial support or otherwise, another to conduct a vexatious or harassing investigation of either a venireman or a juror.

---

[86] *See* ABA CANON 23.

[87] "[I]t would be unethical for a lawyer to harass, entice, induce or exert influence on a juror to obtain his testimony." *ABA Opinion* 319 (1968).

(F)   All restrictions imposed by DR 7-108 upon a lawyer also apply to communications with or investigations of members of a family of a venireman or a juror.

(G)   A lawyer shall reveal promptly to the court improper conduct by a venireman or a juror, or by another toward a venireman or a juror or a member of his family, of which the lawyer has knowledge.

DR 7-109.   Contact with Witnesses.

(A)   A lawyer shall not suppress any evidence that he or his client has a legal obligation to reveal or produce.[88]

(B)   A lawyer shall not advise or cause a person to secrete himself or to leave the jurisdiction of a tribunal for the purpose of making him unavailable as a witness therein.[89]

(C)   A lawyer shall not pay, offer to pay, or acquiesce in the payment of compensation to a witness contingent upon the content of his testimony or the outcome of the case.[90] But a lawyer may advance, guarantee, or acquiesce in the payment of:

(1)   Expenses reasonably incurred by a witness in attending or testifying.

(2)   Reasonable compensation to a witness for his loss of time in attending or testifying.

(3)   A reasonable fee for the professional services of an expert witness.

DR 7-110.   Contact with Officials.[91]

[C22] (A)   A lawyer shall not give or lend any thing of value to a judge, official, or employee of a tribunal.

[C23] (B)   In an adversary proceeding, a lawyer shall not communicate, or cause another to communicate, as to the merits of the cause with a judge or an official before whom the proceeding is pending, except:

(1)   In the course of official proceedings in the cause.

(2)   In writing if he promptly delivers a copy of the writing to opposing counsel or to the adverse party if he is not represented by a lawyer.

---

[88] *See* ABA CANON 5.

[89] *Cf.* ABA CANON 5.

"*Rule 15.* . . . A member of the State Bar shall not advise a person, whose testimony could establish or tend to establish a material fact, to avoid service of process, or secrete himself, or otherwise to make his testimony unavailable." CAL. BUSINESS AND PROFESSIONS CODE § 6076 (West 1962).

[90] *See* In re O'Keefe, 49 Mont. 369, 142 P. 638 (1914).

[91] *Cf.* ABA CANON 3.

(3) Orally upon adequate notice to opposing counsel or to the adverse party if he is not represented by a lawyer.

(4) As otherwise authorized by law.[92]

CANON 8 [C24]—A LAWYER SHOULD ASSIST IN IMPROVING THE LEGAL SYSTEM.

Ethical Considerations

EC 8-1. Changes in human affairs and imperfections in human institutions make necessary constant efforts to maintain and improve our legal system.[1] This system should function in a manner that commands public respect and fosters the use of legal remedies to achieve redress of grievances. By reason of education and experience, lawyers are especially qualified to recognize deficiencies in the legal system and to initiate corrective measures therein. Thus they should participate in proposing and supporting legislation and programs to improve the system,[2] without regard to the general interests or desires of clients or former clients.[3]

---

[92] *"Rule 16. . . .* A member of the State Bar shall not, in the absence of opposing counsel, communicate with or argue to a judge or judicial officer except in open court upon the merits of a contested matter pending before such judge or judicial officer; nor shall he, without furnishing opposing counsel with a copy thereof, address a written communication to a judge or judicial officer concerning the merits of a contested matter pending before such judge or judicial officer. This rule shall not apply to ex parte matters." CAL. BUSINESS AND PROFESSIONS CODE § 6076 (West 1962).

[1] ". . . [Another] task of the great lawyer is to do his part individually and as a member of the organized bar to improve his profession, the courts, and the law. As President Theodore Roosevelt aptly put it, 'Every man owes some of his time to the upbuilding of the profession to which he belongs.' Indeed, this obligation is one of the great things which distinguishes a profession from a business. The soundness and the necessity of President Roosevelt's admonition insofar as it relates to the legal profession cannot be doubted. The advances in natural science and technology are so startling and the velocity of change in business and in social life is so great that the law along with the other social sciences, and even human life itself, is in grave danger of being extinguished by new gods of its own invention if it does not awake from its lethargy. Vanderbilt, *The Five Functions of the Lawyer: Service to Clients and the Public,* 40 A.B.A.J. 31, 31-32 (1954).

[2] *See* ABA CANON 29; *Cf.* Cheatham, *The Lawyer's Role and Surroundings,* 25 ROCKY MT. L. REV. 405, 406-07 (1953).

"The lawyer tempted by repose should recall the heavy costs paid by his profession when needed legal reform has to be accomplished through the initiative of public-spirited laymen. Where change must be thrust from without upon an unwilling Bar, the public's least flattering picture of the lawyer seems confirmed. The lawyer concerned for the standing of his profession will, therefore, interest himself actively in the improvement of the law. In doing so he will not only help to maintain confidence in the Bar, but will have the satisfaction of meeting a responsibility inhering in the nature of his calling." *Professional Responsibility: Report of the Joint Conference,* 44 A.B.A.J. 1159, 1217 (1958).

[3] *See* Stayton, *Cum Honore Officium,* 19 TEX. B.J. 765, 766 (1956); *Professional Responsibility: Report of the Joint Conference,* 44 A.B.A.J.

EC 8-2.   Rules of law are deficient if they are not just, understandable, and responsive to the needs of society. If a lawyer believes that the existence or absence of a rule of law, substantive or procedural, causes or contributes to an unjust result, he should endeavor by lawful means to obtain appropriate changes in the law. He should encourage the simplification of laws and the repeal or amendment of laws that are outmoded.[4] Likewise, legal procedures should be improved whenever experience indicates a change is needed.

EC 8-3.   The fair administration of justice requires the availability of competent lawyers. Members of the public should be educated to recognize the existence of legal problems and the resultant need for legal services, and should be provided methods for intelligent selection of counsel. Those persons unable to pay for legal services should be provided needed services. Clients and lawyers should not be penalized by undue geographical restraints upon representation in legal matters, and the bar should address itself to improvements in licensing, reciprocity, and admission procedures consistent with the needs of modern commerce.

EC 8-4.   Whenever a lawyer seeks legislative or administrative changes, he should identify the capacity in which he appears, whether on behalf of himself, a client, or the public.[5] A lawyer may advocate such changes on behalf of a client even though he does not agree with them. But when a lawyer purports to act on behalf of the public, he should espouse only those changes which he conscientiously believes to be in the public interest.

EC 8-5.   Fraudulent, deceptive, or otherwise illegal conduct by a participant in a proceeding before a tribunal or legislative body is inconsistent with fair administration of justice, and it should never be participated in or condoned by lawyers. Unless constrained by his obligation to preserve the confidences and secrets of his client, a lawyer should reveal to appropriate authorities any knowledge he may have of such improper conduct.

1159, 1162 (1958); and Paul, *The Lawyer as a Tax Adviser*, 25 ROCKY MT. L. REV. 412, 433-34 (1953).

4 "There are few great figures in the history of the Bar who have not concerned themselves with the reform and improvement of the law. The special obligation of the profession with respect to legal reform rests on considerations too obvious to require enumeration. Certainly it is the lawyer who has both the best chance to know when the law is working badly and the special competence to put it in order." *Professional Responsibility: Report of the Joint Conference,* 44 A.B.A.J. 1159, 1217 (1958).

5 "*Rule 14.* . . . A member of the State Bar shall not communicate with, or appear before, a public officer, board, committee or body, in his professional capacity, without first disclosing that he is an attorney representing interests that may be affected by action of such officer, board, committee or body." CAL. BUSINESS AND PROFESSIONS CODE § 6076 (West 1962).

EC 8-6.   Judges and administrative officials having adjudicatory powers ought to be persons of integrity, competence, and suitable temperament. Generally, lawyers are qualified, by personal observation or investigation, to evaluate the qualifications of persons seeking or being considered for such public offices, and for this reason they have a special responsibility to aid in the selection of only those who are qualified.[6] It is the duty of lawyers to endeavor to prevent political considerations from outweighing judicial fitness in the selection of judges. Lawyers should protest earnestly against the appointment or election of those who are unsuited for the bench and should strive to have elected[7] or appointed thereto only those who are willing to forego pursuits, whether of a business, political, or other nature, that may interfere with the free and fair consideration of questions presented for adjudication. Adjudicatory officials, not being wholly free to defend themselves, are entitled to receive the support of the bar against unjust criticism.[8] While a lawyer as a citizen has a right to criticize such officials publicly,[9] he should be certain of the merit of his complaint, use appropriate language, and avoid petty criticisms, for unrestrained and intemperate statements tend to lessen public confidence in our legal system.[10] Criticisms

---

[6] See ABA CANON 2.

"Lawyers are better able than laymen to appraise accurately the qualifications of candidates for judicial office. It is proper that they should make that appraisal known to the voters in a proper and dignified manner. A lawyer may with propriety endorse a candidate for judicial office and seek like endorsement from other lawyers. But the lawyer who endorses a judicial candidate or seeks that endorsement from other lawyers should be actuated by a sincere belief in the superior qualifications of the candidate for judicial service and not by personal or selfish motives; and a lawyer should not use or attempt to use the power or prestige of the judicial office to secure such endorsement. On the other hand, the lawyer whose endorsement is sought, if he believes the candidate lacks the essential qualifications for the office or believes the opposing candidate is better qualified, should have the courage and moral stamina to refuse the request for endorsement." *ABA Opinion* 189 (1938).

[7] "[W]e are of the opinion that, whenever a candidate for judicial office merits the endorsement and support of lawyers, the lawyers may make financial contributions toward the campaign if its cost, when reasonably conducted, exceeds that which the candidate would be expected to bear personally." *ABA Opinion* 226 (1941).

[8] See ABA CANON 1.

[9] "Citizens have a right under our constitutional system to criticize governmental officials and agencies. Courts are not, and should not be, immune to such criticism." Konigsberg v. State Bar of California, 353 U.S. 252, 269 (1957).

[10] "[E]very lawyer, worthy of respect, realizes that public confidence in our courts is the cornerstone of our governmental structure, and will refrain from unjustified attack on the character of the judges, while recognizing the duty to denounce and expose a corrupt or dishonest judge." Kentucky State Bar Ass'n v. Lewis, 282 S.W.2d 321, 326 (Ky. 1955).

motivated by reasons other than a desire to improve the legal system are not justified.

EC 8-7. Since lawyers are a vital part of the legal system, they should be persons of integrity, of professional skill, and of dedication to the improvement of the system. Thus a lawyer should aid in establishing, as well as enforcing, standards of conduct adequate to protect the public by insuring that those who practice law are qualified to do so.

EC 8-8. Lawyers often serve as legislators or as holders of other public offices. This is highly desirable, as lawyers are uniquely qualified to make significant contributions to the improvement of the legal system. A lawyer who is a public officer, whether full or part-time, should not engage in activities in which his personal or professional interests are or foreseeably may be in conflict with his official duties.[11]

"We should be the last to deny that Mr. Meeker has the right to uphold the honor of the profession and to expose without fear or favor corrupt or dishonest conduct in the profession, whether the conduct be that of a judge or not. . . . However, this Canon [29] does not permit one to make charges which are false and untrue and unfounded in fact. When one's fancy leads him to make false charges, attacking the character and integrity of others, he does so at his peril. He should not do so without adequate proof of his charges and he is certainly not authorized to make careless, untruthful and vile charges against his professional brethren." In re Meeker, 76 N.M. 354, 364-65, 414 P.2d 862, 869 (1966), *appeal dismissed,* 385 U.S. 449, 17 L. Ed. 2d 510, 87 S. Ct. 613 (1967).

11 "*Opinions 16, 30, 34, 77, 118* and *134* relate to *Canon 6,* and pass on questions concerning the propriety of the conduct of an attorney who is a public officer, in representing private interests adverse to those of the public body which he represents. The principle applied in those opinions is that an attorney holding public office should avoid all conduct which might lead the layman to conclude that the attorney is utilizing his public position to further his professional success or personal interests." *ABA Opinion* 192 (1939).

"The next question is whether a lawyer-member of a legislative body may appear as counsel or co-counsel at hearings before a zoning board of appeals, or similar tribunal, created by the legislative group of which he is a member. We are of the opinion that he may practice before fact-finding officers, hearing bodies and commissioners, since under our views he may appear as counsel in the courts where his municipality is a party. Decisions made at such hearings are usually subject to administrative review by the courts upon the record there made. It would be inconsistent to say that a lawyer-member of a legislative body could not participate in a hearing at which the record is made, but could appear thereafter when the cause is heard by the courts on administrative review. This is subject to an important exception. He should not appear as counsel where the matter is subject to review by the legislative body of which he is a member. . . . We are of the opinion that where a lawyer does so appear there would be conflict of interests between his duty as an advocate for his client on the one hand and the obligation to his governmental unit on the other." In re Becker, 16 Ill. 2d 488, 494-95, 158 N.E.2d 753, 756-57 (1959).

Cf. ABA Opinions 186 (1938), 136 (1935), 118 (1934), and 77 (1932).

EC 8-9. The advancement of our legal system is of vital importance in maintaining the rule of law and in facilitating orderly changes; therefore, lawyers should encourage, and should aid in making, needed changes and improvements.

Disciplinary Rules

DR 8-101. Action as a Public Official.

(A) A lawyer who holds public office shall not:

(1) Use his public position to obtain, or attempt to obtain, a special advantage in legislative matters for himself or for a client under circumstances where he knows or it is obvious that such action is not in the public interest.

(2) Use his public position to influence, or attempt to influence, a tribunal to act in favor of himself or of a client.

(3) Accept any thing of value from any person when the lawyer knows or it is obvious that the offer is for the purpose of influencing his action as a public official.

DR 8-102. Statements Concerning Judges and Other Adjudicatory Officers.[12]

(A) A lawyer shall not knowingly make false statements of fact concerning the qualifications of a candidate for election or appointment to a judicial office.

(B) A lawyer shall not knowingly make false accusations against a judge or other adjudicatory officer.

[C25]

CANON 9—A LAWYER SHOULD AVOID EVEN THE APPEARANCE OF PROFESSIONAL IMPROPRIETY.

Ethical Considerations

EC 9-1. Continuation of the American concept that we are to be governed by rules of law requires that the people have faith that justice can be obtained through our legal system.[1] A lawyer should promote public confidence in our system and in the legal profession.[2]

---

[12] *Cf.* ABA CANONS 1 and 2.

[1] "Integrity is the very breath of justice. Confidence in our law, our courts, and in the administration of justice is our supreme interest. No practice must be permitted to prevail which invites towards the administration of justice a doubt or distrust of its integrity." Erwin M. Jennings Co. v. DiGenova, 107 Conn. 491, 499, 141 A. 866, 868 (1928).

[2] "A lawyer should never be reluctant or too proud to answer unjustified criticism of his profession, of himself, or of his brother lawyer. He should guard the reputation of his profession and of his brothers as zealously as he

EC 9-2. Public confidence in law and lawyers may be eroded by irresponsible or improper conduct of a lawyer. On occasion, ethical conduct of a lawyer may appear to laymen to be unethical. In order to avoid misunderstandings and hence to maintain confidence, a lawyer should fully and promptly inform his client of material developments in the matters being handled for the client. While a lawyer should guard against otherwise proper conduct that has a tendency to diminish public confidence in the legal system or in the legal profession, his duty to clients or to the public should never be subordinate merely because the full discharge of his obligation may be misunderstood or may tend to subject him or the legal profession to criticism. When explicit ethical guidance does not exist, a lawyer should determine his conduct by acting in a manner that promotes public confidence in the integrity and efficiency of the legal system and the legal profession.[3]

EC 9-3. After a lawyer leaves judicial office or other public employment, he should not accept employment in connection with any matter in which he had substantial responsibility prior to his leaving, since to accept employment would give the appearance of impropriety even if none exists.[4]

EC 9-4. Because the very essence of the legal system is to provide procedures by which matters can be presented in an impartial manner so that they may be decided solely upon the merits, any statement or suggestion by a lawyer that he can or would attempt to circumvent those procedures is detrimental to the legal system and tends to undermine public confidence in it.

EC 9-5. Separation of the funds of a client from those of his lawyer not only serves to protect the client but also avoids even the appearance of impropriety, and therefore commingling of such funds should be avoided.

EC 9-6. Every lawyer owes a solemn duty to uphold the integrity and honor of his profession: to encourage respect for the law and for the courts and the judges thereof; to observe the Code of Professional Responsibility; to act as a member of a learned profession, one dedicated to public service; to cooperate with his brother lawyers in supporting the organized bar through the devoting of his time, efforts, and financial support as his professional standing and ability reasonably permit; to conduct him-

---

guards his own." Rochelle and Payne, *The Struggle for Public Understanding*, 25 TEXAS B.J. 109, 162 (1962).

[3] *See* ABA CANON 29.

[4] *See* ABA CANON 36.

self so as to reflect credit on the legal profession and to inspire the confidence, respect, and trust of his clients and of the public; and to strive to avoid not only professional impropriety but also the appearance of impropriety.[5]

Disciplinary Rules

DR 9-101. Avoiding Even the Appearance of Impropriety.[6]

(A) A lawyer shall not accept private employment in a matter upon the merits of which he has acted in a judicial capacity.[7]

---

[5] "As said in Opinion 49, of the Committee on Professional Ethics and Grievances of the American Bar Association, page 134: 'An attorney should not only avoid impropriety but should avoid the appearance of impropriety.' " State ex rel. Nebraska State Bar Ass'n v. Richards, 165 Neb. 80, 93, 84 N.W.2d 136, 145 (1957).

"It would also be preferable that such contribution [to the campaign of a candidate for judicial office] be made to a campaign committee rather than to the candidate personally. In so doing, possible appearances of impropriety would be reduced to a minimum." *ABA Opinion* 226 (1941).

"The lawyer assumes high duties, and has imposed upon him grave responsibilities. He may be the means of much good or much mischief. Interests of vast magnitude are entrusted to him; confidence is reposed in him; life, liberty, character and property should be protected by him. He should guard, with jealous watchfulness, his own reputation, as well as that of his profession." People ex rel. Cutler v. Ford, 54 Ill. 520, 522 (1870), and also quoted in State Board of Law Examiners v. Sheldon, 43 Wyo. 522, 526, 7 P.2d 226, 227 (1932).

See ABA Opinion 150 (1936).

[6] *Cf.* CODE OF PROFESSIONAL RESPONSIBILITY, EC 5-6.

[7] *See* ABA CANON 36.

"It is the duty of the judge to rule on questions of law and evidence in misdemeanor cases and examinations in felony cases. That duty calls for impartial and uninfluenced judgment, regardless of the effect on those immediately involved or others who may, directly or indirectly, be affected. Discharge of that duty might be greatly interfered with if the judge, in another capacity, were permitted to hold himself out to employment by those who are to be, or who may be, brought to trial in felony cases, even though he did not conduct the examination. His private interests as a lawyer in building up his clientele, his duty as such zealously to espouse the cause of his private clients and to defend against charges of crime brought by law-enforcement agencies of which he is a part, might prevent, or even destroy, that unbiased judicial judgment which is so essential in the administration of justice.

"In our opinion, acceptance of a judgeship with the duties of conducting misdemeanor trials, and examinations in felony cases to determine whether those accused should be bound over for trial in a higher court, ethically bars the judge from acting as attorney for the defendants upon such trial, whether they were examined by him or by some other judge. Such a practice would not only diminish public confidence in the administration of justice in both courts, but would produce serious conflict between the private interests of the judge as a lawyer, and of his clients, and his duties as a judge in adjudicating important phases of criminal processes in other cases. The public and private duties would be incompatible. The prestige of the judicial office would be diverted to private benefit, and the judicial office would be demeaned thereby." *ABA Opinion* 242 (1942).

(B)   A lawyer shall not accept private employment in a matter in which he had substantial responsibility while he was a public employee.[8]

(C)   A lawyer shall not state or imply that he is able to influence improperly or upon irrelevant grounds any tribunal, legislative body,[9] or public official.

DR 9-102.   Preserving Identity of Funds and Property of a Client.[10]

(A)   All funds of clients paid to a lawyer or law firm, other than advances for costs and expenses, shall be deposited in one or more identifiable bank accounts maintained in the state in which the law office is situated and no funds belonging to the lawyer or law firm shall be deposited therein except as follows:

(1)   Funds reasonably sufficient to pay bank charges may be deposited therein.

"A lawyer, who has previously occupied a judicial position or acted in a judicial capacity, should refrain from accepting employment in any matter involving the same facts as were involved in any specific question which he acted upon in a judicial capacity and, for the same reasons, should also refrain from accepting any employment which might reasonably appear to involve the same facts." *ABA Opinion* 49 (1931).

See ABA Opinion 110 (1934).

[8] *See ABA Opinions* 135 (1935) and 134 (1935); *cf.* ABA CANON 36 and *ABA Opinions* 39 (1931) and 26 (1930). *But see ABA Opinion* 37 (1931).

[9] "[A statement by a governmental department or agency with regard to a lawyer resigning from its staff that includes a laudation of his legal ability] carries implications, probably not founded in fact, that the lawyer's acquaintance and previous relations with the personnel of the administrative agencies of the government place him in an advantageous position in practicing before such agencies. So to imply would not only represent what probably is untrue, but would be highly reprehensible." *ABA Opinion* 184 (1938).

[10] *See* ABA CANON 11.

"*Rule 9*. . . . A member of the State Bar shall not commingle the money or other property of a client with his own; and he shall promptly report to the client the receipt by him of all money and other property belonging to such client. Unless the client otherwise directs in writing, he shall promptly deposit his client's funds in a bank or trust company . . . in a bank account separate from his own account and clearly designated as 'Clients' Funds Account' or 'Trust Funds Account' or words of similar import. Unless the client otherwise directs in writing, securities of a client in bearer form shall be kept by the attorney in a safe deposit box at a bank or trust company, . . . which safe deposit box shall be clearly designated as 'Clients' Account' or 'Trust Account' or words of similar import, and be separate from the attorney's own safe deposit box." CAL. BUSINESS AND PROFESSIONS CODE § 6076 (West 1962).

"[C]ommingling is committed when a client's money is intermingled with that of his attorney and its separate identity lost so that it may be used for the attorney's personal expenses or subjected to claims of his creditors. . . . The rule against commingling was adopted to provide against the probability in some cases, the possibility in many cases, and the danger in all cases that such commingling will result in the loss of clients' money." Black v. State Bar, 57 Cal. 2d 219, 225-26, 368 P.2d 118, 122, 18 Cal. Rptr. 518, 522 (1962).

(2)   Funds belonging in part to a client and part presently or potentially to the lawyer or law firm must be deposited therein, but the portion belonging to the lawyer or law firm may be withdrawn when due unless the right of the lawyer or law firm to receive it is disputed by the client, in which event the disputed portion shall not be withdrawn until the dispute is finally resolved.

(B)   A lawyer shall:

(1)   Promptly notify a client of the receipt of his funds, securities, or other properties.

(2)   Identify and label securities and properties of a client promptly upon receipt and place them in a safe deposit box or other place of safekeeping as soon as practicable.

(3)   Maintain complete records of all funds, securities, and other properties of a client coming into the possession of the lawyer and render appropriate accounts to his client regarding them.

(4)   Promptly pay or deliver to the client as requested by a client the funds, securities, or other properties in the possession of the lawyer which the client is entitled to receive.

DEFINITIONS*

As used in the Disciplinary Rules of the Code of Professional Responsibility:

(1)   "Differing interests" include every interest that will adversely affect either the judgment or the loyalty of a lawyer to a client, whether it be a conflicting, inconsistent, diverse, or other interest.

(2)   "Law firm" includes a professional legal corporation.

(3)   "Person" includes a corporation, an association, a trust, a partnership, and any other organization or legal entity.

(4)   "Professional legal corporation" means a corporation, or an association treated as a corporation, authorized by law to practice law for profit.

(5)   "State" includes the District of Columbia, Puerto Rico, and other federal territories and possessions.

(6)   "Tribunal" includes all courts and all other adjudicatory bodies.

[C26] (7)   "A Bar association representative of the general bar" includes a bar association of specialists as referred to in DR 2-105(A)(1) or (4).

---

* "Confidence" and "secret" are defined in DR 4-101(A).

Index

Intermediary, prohibition against use of, 193-95, 198-99

Interview
    with opposing party, 211-12, 222
    with news media, 217-19, 225-28
    with witness, 215-16, 229

Investigation expenses, advancing or guaranteeing payment, 187, 196

J

Judges
    false statements concerning, 234
    improper influences on
        gifts to, 219, 229
        private communication with, 219-20, 229-30
    misconduct toward
        criticisms of, 232
        disobedience of orders, 214-15, 224-25
        false statement regarding, 234
    name in partnership name, use of, 150-51, 165
    retirement from bench, 235, 236
    selection of, 232

Judgment of lawyer. *See* Adverse effect on professional judgment of lawyer.

Jury
    arguments before, 216, 228
    investigation of members, 217, 228-29
    misconduct of, duty to reveal, 217, 229
    questioning members of after their dismissal, 216, 228

K

Knowledge of intended crime, revealing, 183

L

Law firm. *See* Partnership.

Law lists. *See* Advertising, law lists.

Law office. *See* Partnership.

Law school, working with legal aid office or public defender office sponsored by, 167, 168

Lawyer-client privilege. *See* Attorney-client privilege.

Lawyer referral services
    fee for listing, propriety of paying, 166
    listing of type referrals accepted, propriety of, 169
    request for referrals, propriety of, 166
    working with, 152, 156-57, 166-68

Laymen. *See also* Unauthorized practice of law.
    need of legal services, 144, 231
    recognition of legal problems, need to improve, 145, 231
    selection of lawyer, need to facilitate, 149-52, 231

Legal aid offices, working with, 152, 156-57, 166-68

Legal corporation. *See* Professional legal corporation.

Legal directory. *See* Advertising, legal directories.

Legal documents of clients, duty to safeguard, 181

Legal education programs. *See* Continuing legal education programs.

Legal problems, recognition of by laymen, 144-47, 231

Legal system, duty to improve, 230-34

Legislature
    improper influence upon, 237
    representation of client before, 211, 237
    serving as member of, 233

Letterhead. *See* Advertising, letterheads.

Liability to client, 138, 201

Licensing of lawyers
    control of, 177
    modernization of, 177, 231

Liens, attorneys', 187, 196

Limited practice, holding out as having, 152, 169-70

Litigation
    acquiring an interest in, 187, 196
    expenses of, advancing or guaranteeing payment of, 187, 196
    pending, media discussion of, 217-19, 225-28
    responsibility for conduct of, 205-07, 209-10, 219-20, 221
    to harass another, duty to avoid, 159, 172
    to maliciously harm another, duty to avoid, 159, 172

Living expenses of client, advances to client of, 187, 196

Loan to judicial officer, 219, 229

Loyalty to client. *See* Zeal.

Lump-sum settlements, 198

M

Mandatory withdrawal. *See* Employment, withdrawal from, mandatory.

Mediator, lawyer serving as, 192-93

Medical expenses, 187, 196

C. ANNOTATIONS TO THE CODE OF PROFESSIONAL RESPONSIBILITY

C1. DR 1-102 was amended by the District of Columbia Court of Appeals in April, 1972. The effect of the amendment is to restrict the scope of "misconduct" (*i.e.,* cause for disciplinary action) by combining subsections (3) and (6), so that those provisions qualify each other rather than stand alone. As a result of the amendment, subsection (6) is eliminated, and subsection (3) reads as follows: "(3) Engage in illegal conduct involving moral turpitude that adversely reflects on his fitness to practice law."

That amendment had previously been adopted in 1970 by the Bar Association of the District of Columbia, in accordance with a 70 percent affirmative vote of those responding on a mail ballot. The arguments for amendment were stated on the ballot as follows:

> Provision (6) is unusually vague and indefinite. It might permit censure of a lawyer unpopular in the community, or for conduct not related to his activities as a lawyer, or for legal activities in behalf of unpopular causes or clients. The appropriate objective is accomplished by EC 1-5 and by the proposed amendment to provision (3), which ties the conduct to activities as a lawyer. With the changes proposed there is no conduct warranting censure which is not adequately provided for in the Code.

The arguments against amendment were stated on the ballot as follows:

> It is impossible for any written code to provide specifically, in advance, for every form of conduct which should be censured. Therefore, a general "catch-all" provision is necessary in addition to that already provided in provision (5), which relates only to conduct as a lawyer. The more general proscription on conduct adversely reflecting on fitness to practice law is like that usually applied on initial admission to the bar. There is no reason to think it will be abused in application.

Thus, under the amendment, illegal conduct involving moral turpitude does not constitute "misconduct" meriting disciplinary action unless that conduct also adversely reflects on the attorney's fitness to practice law. Note, however, that under subsections (4) and (5) any conduct involving dishonesty, fraud, deceit, or misrepresentation, or that is prejudicial to the administration of

justice, does constitute "misconduct" within the Disciplinary
Rule.

C2. DR 1-103 was amended by the District of Columbia
Court of Appeals on April 1, 1972. The effect of the amendment
is to eliminate the requirement that an attorney voluntarily report
knowledge of another attorney's violation of a disciplinary rule.
As amended, the provision reads: "(A) A lawyer possessing unprivileged knowledge or evidence concerning another lawyer or a
judge shall reveal fully such knowledge or evidence upon proper
request of a tribunal or other authority empowered to investigate
or act upon the conduct of lawyers or judges."

That amendment had previously been adopted in 1970 by the
Bar Association of the District of Columbia, pursuant to a 72
percent affirmative vote of those responding on a mail ballot.
The arguments for amendment were set forth on the ballot as
follows:

> This provision requires every lawyer to become an "in-
> former" on every other lawyer and requires him to volunteer
> knowledge in the absence of a request from a qualified agency
> or body for such information. It is contrary to basic American
> traditions. The remaining provisions of the Code will fully
> protect the public without establishing an "informer" re-
> quirement. In particular, there will remain the following
> provisions: DR 1-103(B), which requires a lawyer to reveal
> such information upon proper request of an authorized tri-
> bunal or authority, and EC 1-4, which states that a lawyer
> should (not must) voluntarily reveal knowledge of Code
> violations.

The arguments against amendment were stated on the ballot as
follows:

> As an officer of the court, a lawyer should reveal un-
> privileged knowledge of Code violations, whether or not
> requested to do so. Otherwise, the public may feel that
> lawyers are trying to "cover up" for each other. The public
> interest in exposure of unethical conduct should be para-
> mount. The Code requires reporting only of actual violations
> of which the lawyer has affirmative knowledge, and not of
> suspicion. The lawyer is not required to spy, or run down
> rumors. The thrust of the recent report of the ABA Special
> Committee on Disciplinary Enforcement, "Problems and
> Recommendations in Disciplinary Enforcement," is for re-
> tention of this provision.

I disagree strongly with the amendment. The so-called "basic American tradition" of condoning misconduct, by not volunteering unprivileged knowledge about it, may or may not be appropriate to the schoolyard, street, or alley, but it is not an acceptable norm for a profession concerned with the administration of justice.

C3. *See,* Text, Chapter 10.

C4. The third sentence of EC 2-18 (and the accompanying footnote), indicating approval of fee schedules and bar association "guidance on the subject of reasonable fees", was deleted by the American Bar Association as of March 1, 1974. The amendment is a welcome one. Fee schedules are a form of price-fixing, which is a monopolistic device that has no place in a Code of Professional Responsibility.

C5. A new provision, EC 2-33, was added by the American Bar Association in February, 1975. The new provision reads as follows:

EC 2-33.   As a part of the legal profession's commitment to the principle that high quality legal services should be available to all, attorneys are encouraged to cooperate with qualified legal assistance organizations providing prepaid legal services. Such participation should at all times be in accordance with the basic tenets of the profession: independence, integrity, competence and devotion to the interests of individual clients. An attorney so participating should make certain that his relationship with a qualified legal assistance organization in no way interferes with his independent, professional representation of the interests of the individual client. An attorney should avoid situations in which officials of the organization who are not lawyers attempt to direct attorneys concerning the manner in which legal services are performed for individual members, and should also avoid situations in which considerations of economy are given undue weight in determining the attorneys employed by an organization or the legal services to be performed for the member or beneficiary rather than competence and quality of service. An attorney interested in maintaining the historic traditions of the profession and preserving the function of a lawyer as a trusted and independent advisor to individual members of society should carefully assess such factors when accepting employment by, or otherwise participating in, a particular qualified legal assistance organization, and while so participating should adhere to the highest professional standards of effort and competence.

C6. DR 2-101(B) was amended by the American Bar Association, in February, 1975, to read as follows:

(B) A lawyer shall not publicize himself, or his partner, or associate, or any other lawyer affiliated with him or his firm, as a lawyer through newspaper or magazine advertisements, radio or television announcements, display advertisements in city or telephone directories or other means of commercial publicity, nor shall he authorize or permit others to do so in his behalf. However, a lawyer recommended by, paid by or whose legal services are furnished by, a qualified legal assistance organization may authorize or permit or assist such organization to use means of dignified commercial publicity, which does not identify any lawyer by name, to describe the availability or nature of its legal services or legal service benefits. This rule does not prohibit limited and dignified identification of a lawyer as a lawyer as well as by name:

(1)-(5)　*　*　*

(6) In communications by a qualified legal assistance organization, along with the biographical information permitted under DR 2-102(A)(6), directed to a member or beneficiary of such organization.

C7. DR 2-103(B), (C) and (D) were amended by the American Bar Association in February, 1975, to read as follows:

(B) A lawyer shall not compensate or give anything of value to a person or organization to recommend or secure his employment by a client, or as a reward for having made a recommendation resulting in his employment by a client, except that he may pay the usual and reasonable fees or dues charged by any of the organizations listed in DR 2-103(D).

(C) A lawyer shall not request a person or organization to recommend or promote the use of his services or those of his partner or associate, or any other lawyer affiliated with him or his firm, as a private practitioner, except that:

(1) He may request referrals from a lawyer referral service operated, sponsored, or approved by a bar association and may pay its fees incident thereto.

(2) He may cooperate with the legal service activities of any of the offices or organizations enumerated in DR 2-103(D)(1) through (4) and may perform legal services for those to whom he was recommended by it to do such work if:

(a) The person to whom the recommendation is made is a member or beneficiary of such office or organization; and

(b) The lawyer remains free to exercise his independent professional judgment on behalf of his client.

(D) A lawyer shall not knowingly assist a person or organization that furnishes or pays for legal services to others to promote the use of his services or those of his partner or associate or any other lawyer affiliated with him or his firm except as permitted in DR 2-101(B). However, this does not prohibit a lawyer or his partner or associate or any other lawyer affiliated with him or his firm from being recommended, employed or paid by, or cooperating with, one of the following offices or organizations that promote the use of his services or those of his partner or associate or any other lawyer affiliated with him or his firm if there is no interference with the exercise of independent professional judgment in behalf of his client:

(1) A legal aid office or public defender office:

(a) Operated or sponsored by a duly accredited law school.

(b) Operated or sponsored by a bona fide nonprofit community organization.

(c) Operated or sponsored by a governmental agency.

(d) Operated, sponsored, or approved by a bar association.

(2) A military legal assistance office.

(3) A lawyer referral service operated, sponsored, or approved by a bar association.

(4) Any bona fide organization that recommends, furnishes or pays for legal services to its members or beneficiaries provided the following conditions are satisfied:

(a) Such organization, including any affiliate, is so organized and operated that no profit is derived by it from the rendition of legal services by lawyers, and that, if the organization is organized for profit, the legal services are not rendered by lawyers employed, directed, supervised or selected by it except in connection with matters where such organization bears ultimate liability of its member or beneficiary.

(b) Neither the lawyer, nor his partner, nor associate, nor any other lawyer affiliated with him or his firm, nor any non-lawyer, shall have initiated or promoted such organization for the primary purpose of providing financial or other benefit to such lawyer, partner, associate or affiliated lawyer.

(c) Such organization is not operated for the purpose of procuring legal work or financial benefit for any lawyer as a private practitioner outside of the legal services program of the organization.

(d) The member or beneficiary to whom the legal services are furnished, and not such organization, is recognized as the client of the lawyer in the matter.

(e) Any member or beneficiary who is entitled to have legal services furnished or paid for by the organization may, if such member or beneficiary so desires, select counsel other than that furnished, selected or approved by the organization for the particular matter involved; and the legal service plan of such organization provides appropriate relief for any member or beneficiary who asserts a claim that representation by counsel furnished, selected or approved would be unethical, improper or inadequate under the circumstances of the matter involved and the plan provides an appropriate procedure for seeking such relief.

(f) The lawyer does not know or have cause to know that such organization is in violation of applicable laws, rules of court and other legal requirements that govern its legal service operations.

(g) Such organization has filed with the appropriate disciplinary authority at least annually a report with respect to its legal service plan, if any, showing its terms, its schedule of benefits, its subscription charges, agreements with counsel, financial results of its legal service activities or, if it has failed to do so, the lawyer does not know or have cause to know of such failure.

C8. DR 2-103(D)(5) was amended by the District of Columbia Court of Appeals on April 1, 1972, to read as follows:

(5) Any other bona fide, non-profit organization which, as an incident to its primary activities, furnishes, pays for, or recommends lawyers to its members or beneficiaries, provided that

(a) Such organization does not derive a financial profit from the rendition of legal services by the lawyer.

(b) The member or beneficiary for whom the legal services are rendered, and not such organization, is recognized as the client of the lawyer in that matter.

That amendment had previously been adopted in 1970 by the Bar Association of the District of Columbia, pursuant to a 69 percent affirmative vote of those responding on a mail ballot. The arguments for amendment were set forth on the ballot as follows:

The Committee recommends adopting an earlier ABA Code approach, discarded in favor of the provision which was finally adopted by the ABA. In its present form, the Code provision might prohibit a lawyer from testing the constitutionality of a law or of administrative action. This seems inconsistent with other provisions of the Code which specifically authorized the presentation of a claim or defense "not warranted under existing law" where "it can be supported by good faith argument for an extension, modification, or reversal of existing law." DR 2-109(A)(2). See also DR 7-102(A)(2) and EC 7-23. The present ABA Code provision might permit censure even if the Court should ultimately sustain a lawyer's constitutional argument.

The arguments against amendment were stated on the ballot as follows:

If group practice is permitted to "run wild," without proper limitations, it could destroy the traditional form of law practice. It might prevent an individual from obtaining legal services attuned to his particular needs. A lawyer's services can be of the most personal character, and no group, however lofty its motives, should be permitted to intervene between the lawyer and his client except under the most rigorous limitations and to the extent constitutionally required at the time the services are rendered. For constitutional requirements at the present time, see *UMWA v. Illinois State Bar Ass'n*, 389 U.S. 217 (1967), *Brotherhood of R.R.T. v. Virginia*, 377 U.S. 1 (1964), and *NAACP v. Button*, 371 U.S. 415 (1963).

C9. DR 2-104(A) was amended by the American Bar Association in February, 1975, to read as follows:

DR 2-104. Suggestion of Need of Legal Services.
    (A) * * *
        (1)-(2) * * *
        (3) A lawyer who is recommended, furnished or paid by a qualified legal assistance organization enumerated in

DR 2-103(D)(1) through (4) may represent a member or beneficiary thereof, to the extent and under the conditions prescribed therein.

C10. *See,* Text, Chapters 1 and 3.

C11. A potential conflict of interest that is not dealt with directly in the Code may arise when a lawyer employed by the government receives incriminating information from a fellow employee, who may be assuming that the lawyer will treat the information as confidential. That problem has been addressed in supplemental ethical considerations (designated FECs) adopted by the National Council of the Federal Bar Association on November 17, 1973. The pertinent provisions are as follows:

FEC 4-1. If, in the conduct of official business of his department or agency, it appears that a fellow employee of the department or agency is revealing or about to reveal information concerning his own illegal or unethical conduct to a federal lawyer acting in his official capacity the lawyer should inform the employee that a federal lawyer is responsible to the department or agency concerned and not the individual employee and, therefore, the information being discussed is not privileged.

FEC 4-2. If a fellow employee volunteers information concerning himself which appears to involve illegal or unethical conduct or is violative of department or agency rules and regulations which would be pertinent to that department's or agency's consideration of disciplinary action, the federal lawyer should inform the individual that the lawyer is responsible to the department or agency concerned and not the individual employee.

FEC 4-3. The federal lawyer has the ethical responsibility to disclose to his supervisor or other appropriate departmental or agency official any unprivileged information of the type discussed above in FEC 4-1 and 2.

FEC 4-4. The federal lawyer who has been duly designated to act as an attorney for a fellow employee who is the subject of disciplinary, loyalty, or other personnel administration proceedings or as defense counsel for court-martial matters or for civil legal assistance to military personnel and their dependents is for those purposes acting as an attorney for a client and communications between them shall be secret and privileged. . . .

C12. DR 5-105(A) was amended by the American Bar Association, effective March 1, 1974, to add the italicized clause:

A lawyer shall decline proffered employment if the exercise of his independent professional judgment in behalf of a client will be or is likely to be adversely affected by the acceptance of the proffered employment, *or if it would be likely to involve him in representing differing interests,* except to the extent permitted under DR 5-105(C).

C13. DR 5-105(B) was amended by the American Bar Association, effective March 1, 1974, to add the italicized clause:

A lawyer shall not continue multiple employment if the exercise of his independent professional judgment in behalf of a client will be or is likely to be adversely affected by his representation of another client, *or if it would be likely to involve him in representing differing interests,* except to the extent permitted under DR 5-105(C).

C14. DR 5-105(D) was amended by the American Bar Association, effective March 1, 1974, to add the italicized phrase:

If a lawyer is required to decline employment or to withdraw from employment under a *Disciplinary Rule, no partner, or associate, or any other lawyer affiliated with him* or his firm, may accept or continue such employment.

C15. *See,* Text, Chapters 1-4, 6.

C16. *See,* C24 *infra.*

C17. *See,* C24 *infra.*

C18. EC 7-34 was amended by the American Bar Association as of March 1, 1974, to add the following clause at the end: ". . . except as permitted by section C(4) of Canon 5 of the Code of Judicial Conduct, but a lawyer may make a contribution to the campaign fund of a candidate for judicial office in conformity with Section B(2) under Canon 7 of the Code of Judicial Conduct."

C19. According to the ABA Standards Relating to the Prosecution Function and the Defense Function, DR 7-102(B)(1) "is construed as not embracing the giving of false testimony in a criminal case". (Supplement, at 18.) *Compare also,* EC 8-5, which indicates more generally that even where the client has engaged in "[f]raudulent, deceptive, or otherwise illegal conduct" in a proceeding, the lawyer may be "constrained by his obligation to preserve the confidences and secrets of his client", from revealing the client's improper conduct to the appropriate authorities.

The District of Columbia Court of Appeals amended DR 7-102(B)(1) on April 1, 1972, so as to eliminate the "and if" clause entirely. That amendment had previously been adopted in 1970 by the Bar Association of the District of Columbia, pursuant to a 74 percent affirmative vote of those responding on a mail ballot. The arguments for amendment were set forth on the ballot as follows:

> The effect of the Code provision can be illustrated by a divorce case. At the husband's deposition, he produces his tax return and testifies that it is complete and accurate. Through confidential communications from his client, the husband's attorney learns that the husband has additional, unreported income. The attorney urges him to correct his false testimony, and he refuses to do so. The proposed DR subjects the attorney to discipline if he does not reveal the unreported income to the wife and her attorney, to the court, and to the IRS. Thus the DR would turn the lawyer into his client's judge and prosecutor instead of his advocate, and make clients fearful of confiding relevant information fully and freely to their attorneys. It would require an abridgment of the long-established confidentiality of the lawyer-client relationship. There is sufficient protection against the lawyer being made a participant in the client's fraud in the permissible withdrawal provisions of DR 2-110(C).

The arguments against amendment were stated on the ballot as follows:

> The lawyer is first and foremost an officer of the court and as such participates in a search for truth. The false tax return and testimony in the illustration are perjurious and are a fraud on the client's wife, the court, and the IRS. A lawyer who knows that his client is committing perjury and fails to reveal it is betraying the law itself, to which he owes his highest allegiance. A confidential communication from a client does not privilege the client to bind the lawyer to become a partner and participant in a fraudulent and illegal course of conduct. By definition, information concerning the perpetration of a fraud "in the course of the representation" is unprivileged and not entitled to confidence. Nor is it sufficient simply to permit the lawyer to withdraw from the case and remain silent. The proposed DR is necessary to put the bar and the public on notice that the lawyer's devotion to integrity precludes participation in a client's "dirty work."

The American Bar Association subsequently took similar action to eliminate the suggestion that an attorney must violate a client's confidences. As of March 1, 1974, the ABA added a third clause to DR 7-102(B)(1), so that the attorney is called upon to reveal the client's fraud "except when the information is protected as a privileged communication".

See generally, Text, Chapter 3.

C20. *See,* C24 *infra.*

C21. These provisions place extremely broad restrictions upon freedom of speech, and do so, moreover, in circumstances in which the right to speak would be most important. They seem, beyond any reasonable doubt, to violate the First Amendment.

Subsections (G) and (H), which relate to trial publicity in connection with civil or administrative proceedings (as distinguished from criminal proceedings), were deleted by the District of Columbia Court of Appeals as of April 1, 1972. In their place, the Court substituted Canon 20 of the Canons of Professional Ethics, which read as follows:

No. 20. Newspaper Discussion of Pending Litigation.

Newspaper publications by a lawyer as to pending or anticipated litigation may interfere with a fair trial in the Courts and otherwise prejudice the due administration of justice. Generally they are to be condemned. If the extreme circumstances of a particular case justify a statement to the public, it is unprofessional to make it anonymously. An ex parte reference to the facts should not go beyond quotation from the records and papers on file in the court; but even in extreme cases it is better to avoid any ex parte statement.

The same amendment had previously been adopted in 1970 by the Bar Association of the District of Columbia, pursuant to a 71 percent affirmative vote of those responding on a mail ballot. The arguments for amendment were set forth on the ballot as follows:

No question is raised about the provisions dealing with publicity in criminal proceedings. However, those dealing with civil and administrative proceedings obviously need more thought. In their present form, they would bar an attorney's participation in preparing a client's press release responding to an FTC or SEC release alleging fraud. They would bar a labor union's attorney from participating in a press conference in which the union denied charges filed with the NLRB. They would prevent a lawyer from aiding a defendant in a libel action in describing the situation as he sees it. They would also bar a professional opinion about pending litigation given expressly for inclusion in a corporation's annual report.

The arguments against amendment were stated on the ballot as follows:

> The objective of a fair trial is as important in civil and administrative proceedings as criminal proceedings. All truth-seeking proceedings shall be tried and decided on evidence adduced in a proper tribunal, free from the extraneous influence of statements and charges made in media of mass communication. If provisions (G) and (H) are too sweeping, necessary exceptions should be proposed instead of deleting the basic provisions. For instance, it would be relatively easy to except a professional opinion given expressly for inclusion in a corporate annual report. The old Canon 20 is too vague to be useful, and should not be perpetuated even on an interim basis.

The extraordinary thing about that action by the Bar—preserving freedom of speech for litigants in civil and administrative proceedings, but not for criminal defendants—is the failure to recognize that the criminal defendant, no less than the defendant in a libel action, is entitled to a lawyer's assistance in publicly "describing the situation as he sees it". Indeed, the criminal defendant, who will have been subjected to privileged defamation in a published indictment, may be far more necessitous of an effective, public rebuttal. Significantly, the administrative proceedings used by way of illustration in the arguments for amendment are those most closely resembling criminal prosecution— that is, charges filed against a union with the NLRB, or charges of fraud by the FTC or SEC.

C22. DR 7-110(A) was amended by the American Bar Association, as of March 1, 1974, to add the following clause at the end: ". . . except as permitted by Section C(4) of Canon 5 of the Code of Judicial Conduct, but a lawyer may make a contribution to the campaign fund of a candidate for judicial office in conformity with Section B(2) under Canon 7 of the Code of Judicial Conduct."

C23. DR 7-110(B) was amended by the American Bar Association, as of March 1, 1974, to add the following phrase at the end of subsection (4): ". . . , or by Section A(4) under Canon 3 of the Code of Judicial Conduct."

C24. Supplemental ethical considerations for government lawyers under Canon 8 were adopted by the National Council of the Federal Bar Association on November 17, 1973. The relevant substantive provisions are as follows:

FEC 8-1.   The general obligation to assist in improving the legal system applies to federal lawyers. In such situations he may have a higher obligation than lawyers generally. Since his duties include responsibility for the application of law to the resolution of problems incident to his employment there is a continuing obligation to seek improvement. This may be accomplished by the application of legal considerations to the day to day decisional process. Moreover it may eventuate that a federal lawyer by reason of his particular tasks may have insight which enhances his ability to initiate reforms, thus giving rise to a special obligation under Canon 8. In all these matters paramount consideration is due the public interest.

FEC 8-2.   The situation of the federal lawyer which may give rise to special considerations, not applicable to lawyers generally, include certain limitations on complete freedom of action in matters relating to Canon 8. For example, a lawyer in the office of the Chief Counsel of the Internal Revenue Service may reasonably be expected to abide, without public criticism, with certain policies or rulings closely allied to his sphere of responsibility even if he disagrees with the position taken by the agency. But even if involved personally in the process of formulating policy or ruling there may be rare occasions when his conscience compels him publicly to attack a decision which is contrary to his professional, ethical or moral judgment. In that event, however, he should be prepared to resign before doing so, and he is not free to abuse professional confidences reposed in him in the process leading to the decision.

FEC 8-3.   The method of discharging the obligations imposed by Canon 8 may vary depending upon the circumstances. The federal lawyer is free to seek reform through the processes of his agency even if the agency has no formal procedure for receiving and acting upon suggestions from lawyers employed by it. Such intra-agency activities may be the only appropriate course for him to follow if he is not prepared to leave the agency's employment. However, there may be situations in which he could appropriately bring intra-agency problems to the attention of other federal officials (such as those in the Office of Management and Budget or the Department of Justice) with responsibility and authority to correct the allegedly improper activities of the employing agency. Furthermore, it may be possible for the lawyer to participate in bar association or other activities designed to improve the legal system within his agency without being involved in a public attack on the agency's practices, so long as the requirement to protect confidences is observed.

Sound policy favors encouraging government officials to invite and consider the views of counsel. This tends to prevent the adoption of illegal policies. Even where there are choices between legal alternatives, the lawyer's viewpoint may be valuable in affecting the choice. Lawyers in federal service accordingly should conduct themselves so as to encourage utilization of their advice within the agencies, retaining at all times an obligation to exercise independent professional judgment, even though their conclusions may not always be warmly embraced. The failure of lawyers to respect official and proper confidences discourages this desirable resort to them.

These provisions are somewhat inconsistent and troublesome. On the one hand, a federal lawyer "may have a higher obligation than lawyers generally" under Canon 8 to assist in improving the legal system. On the other hand, the federal lawyer may be subject to "certain limitations" that are "not applicable to lawyers generally" in fulfilling responsibilities under Canon 8. The overall thrust of those FECs seems to be to discourage the government lawyer from revealing that a government agency is acting in a way that is contrary to the lawyer's professional, ethical or moral judgment. Such a rule is of doubtful merit, at least under what former Vice President Agnew has referred to as the "post-Watergate morality".

Moreover, it is not clear why a lawyer "should be prepared to resign" before stating publicly that a government decision is contrary to the lawyer's professional, ethical or moral judgment (*i.e.*, not just a disagreement on policy). Why should loss of employment be the price of honesty? For example, FEC 4-4 notes that: "In respects not applicable to the private practitioner the federal lawyer is under obligation to the public to assist his department or agency in complying with the Freedom of Information Act, 5 U.S.C. Sec. 552 (1970), and regulations and authoritative decisions thereunder." (*See also,* EC 7-13 and EC 7-14.) If, then, a federal agency were to violate its obligation under the Freedom of Information Act (or any other law or professional responsibility), a lawyer for the agency should be able to publicly advocate obedience to the law without having to resign from government service as a precondition of doing so.

C25. The American Bar Association, as of March 1, 1974, added a new provision, DR 8-103(A), which reads as follows: "A lawyer who is a candidate for judicial office shall comply with the applicable provisions of Canon 7 of the Code of Judicial Conduct."

C26. The American Bar Association, in February, 1975, amended definition (7) and added definition (8), as follows:

(7) "A Bar association" includes a bar association of specialists as referred to in DR 2-105(A)(1) or (4).

(8) "Qualified legal assistance organization" means an office or organization of one of the four types listed in DR 2-103(D)(1)-(4), inclusive, that meets all the requirements thereof.

Selected Listing of Books and
Articles on Legal Ethics

Alschuler, *Courtroom Misconduct by Prosecutors and Trial Judges,* 50 Texas Law Review 629 (1972).

Andrias, *The Criminal Defendant in England,* 172 New York Law Journal, No. 84, p. 1 (1975).

W. W. Boulton, A Guide to Conduct and Etiquette at the Bar of England and Wales (5th ed., Butterworth, 1970).

Bowman, *Standards of Conduct for Prosecution and Defense Personnel: An Attorney's Viewpoint,* 5 American Criminal Law Quarterly 28 (1966).

Braun, *Ethics in Criminal Cases: A Response,* 55 Georgetown Law Journal 1048 (1967).

Bress, *Professional Ethics in Criminal Trials—A View of Defense Counsel's Responsibility,* 64 Michigan Law Review 1469 (1966).

——————, *Standards of Conduct for Prosecution and Defense Function: An Attorney's Viewpoint,* 5 American Criminal Law Quarterly 23 (1966).

Brickman, *Of Arterial Passageways Through the Legal Process: The Right of Universal Access to Courts and Lawyering Services,* 48 New York University Law Review 595 (1973).

Burger, *Standards of Conduct for Prosecution and Defense Personnel: A Judge's Viewpoint,* 5 American Criminal Law Quarterly 11 (1966).

——————, *The Necessity for Civility,* 1 Litigation 8 (1975).

——————, *The Special Skills of Advocacy: Are Specialized Training and Certification of Advocates Essential to Our System of Justice?* 42 Fordham Law Review 227 (1973).

Chernoff & Schaffer, *Defending the Mentally Ill: Ethical Quicksand,* 10 American Criminal Law Review 505 (1972).

Cohen, *Pluralism in the American Legal Profession,* 19 Alabama Law Review 247 (1967).

Comment, *Actions Against Prosecutors Who Suppress or Falsify Evidence,* 47 Texas Law Review 642 (1969).

Comment, *Controlling Lawyers by Bar Associations and Courts,* 5 Harvard Civil Rights/Civil Liberties Law Review 301 (1970).

Connolly, *Civility in the Courtroom,* 1 Litigation 14 (1975).

C. Curtis, It's Your Law (1954).

Dash, *The Emerging Role and Function of the Criminal Defense Lawyer*, 47 NORTH CAROLINA LAW REVIEW 598 (1969).

N. DORSEN & L. FRIEDMAN, DISORDER IN THE COURT: REPORT OF THE ASSOCIATION OF THE BAR OF THE CITY OF NEW YORK SPECIAL COMMITTEE ON COURTROOM CONDUCT (Pantheon 1974).

H. DRINKER, LEGAL ETHICS (Columbia University Press 1953).

Freedman, *Professional Responsibility of the Civil Practitioner: Teaching Legal Ethics in the Contracts Course*, 21 JOURNAL OF LEGAL EDUCATION 569 (1969).

—————, *Professional Responsibility of the Criminal Defense Lawyer: The Three Hardest Questions*, 64 MICHIGAN LAW REVIEW 1469 (1966).

—————, *Professional Responsibility of the Prosecuting Attorney*, 55 GEORGETOWN LAW JOURNAL 1030 (1967).

—————, *Solicitation of Clients*, JURIS DOCTOR (April 1971).

—————, Book Review: Carlin, Lawyer's Ethics, 16 AMERICAN UNIVERSITY LAW REVIEW 177 (1966).

Friedman, *Professional Responsibility in D.C.: A Survey*, RES IPSA LOQUITUR 60 (Fall 1972).

J. GOULDEN, THE SUPER-LAWYERS: THE SMALL AND POWERFUL WORLD OF THE GREAT WASHINGTON LAW FIRMS (Weybright & Talley 1972).

Griffiths, *Ideology in Criminal Procedure or a Third "Model" of the Criminal Process*, 79 YALE LAW JOURNAL 359, 404 (1970).

Jackson, *The Federal Prosecutor*, 24 JOURNAL OF THE AMERICAN JUDICATURE SOCIETY 18 (1940).

Jaworski, *Judicial Intimidation*, 1 LITIGATION 11 (1975).

Kaplan, *Prosecutorial Discretion—A Comment*, 60 NORTHWESTERN UNIVERSITY LAW REVIEW 174 (1965).

Kaufman, *The Lawyers' New Code*, 22 HARVARD LAW SCHOOL BULLETIN 19 (1970).

T. LUND, A GUIDE TO THE PROFESSIONAL CONDUCT OF SOLICITORS (Solicitors' Law Stationery Society, Ltd. 1960)

D. MELLINKOFF, THE CONSCIENCE OF A LAWYER (West 1973).

Noonan, *The Purposes of Advocacy and the Limits of Confidentiality*, 64 MICHIGAN LAW REVIEW 1485 (1966).

Radin, *Maintenance by Champerty*, 24 CALIFORNIA LAW REVIEW 48 (1935).

Riley, *The Challenge to the New Lawyers: Public Interest and Private Clients*, 38 GEORGE WASHINGTON LAW REVIEW 527 (1970).

Schuchman, *Ethics and Legal Ethics: The Propriety of the Canons as a Group Moral Code*, 37 GEORGE WASHINGTON LAW REVIEW 244 (1968).

Starrs, *Professional Responsibility: Three Basic Propositions*, 5 AMERICAN CRIMINAL LAW QUARTERLY 17 (1966).

H. SUBIN, CRIMINAL JUSTICE IN A METROPOLITAN COURT (U.S. Dep't of Justice 1966).

Uviller, *The Virtuous Prosecutor in Quest of an Ethical Standard: Guidance from the ABA*, 71 MICHIGAN LAW REVIEW 1145 (1973).

Weinstein, *On the Teaching of Legal Ethics*, 72 COLUMBIA LAW REVIEW 452 (1972).

————, *Some Ethical and Political Problems of a Government Attorney*, 18 MAINE LAW REVIEW 155 (1966).

Younger, *The Perjury Routine*, 3 CRIMINAL LAW BULLETIN 551 (1967).

M. ZANDER, CASES AND MATERIALS ON THE ENGLISH LEGAL SYSTEM (George Weidenfeld & Nicholson, Ltd. 1973).

————, LAWYERS AND THE PUBLIC INTEREST (George Weidenfeld & Nicholson, Ltd. 1968).

Index